Sacred Tzolk'in

Daily Planner

Ahaw, the Sun God from the Chilam Balam

Laura LaBrie

Dedication

For Max who has been with me through thick and thin and helped me make this daily planner a reality and for the Maya people who continue to so generously share their culture, their homes, and their time with me.

To Walk the Path

Vulture from the Grolier Codex
Represents taking time and having patience

To walk the path is to come into alignment with the energies of creation. Long ago, the Maya devised a powerful calendar that moves in rhythm with the gods. The energies flow like a wave, rising and falling, going through the cycles of life that are common to all of us. This wave touches on rest and action, giving thanks, providing food and shelter, learning, and connecting with the earth, beginning and ending, gathering and finding truth, growth, loss, travel, and illumination. The Sacred Calendar guides us through these courses and shows us when to move and when to be still. It brings us into harmony with the available energies and teaches us to rest on a day when the gods are resting and the build on a day when the lord who builds is at work.

To walk the path is to move with the energies, to give thanks to the gods who rule the days, and to work with them, rather than resist them. It is a beautiful walk, a walk that leads us toward balance. For we must all work, and we must all play. We must all ponder, and we must all sleep.

As you read on, please read slowly and allow each new section time and space for absorption. For as you do, you will find the secret of life coming to you. And that secret is to move in harmony, to live in balance with the ways of the universe, with each other, and with yourself.

I greet you today as the Maya greet each other, "Biix a bel?" . . . How is your path?

Table of Contents

9 Ahaw, 10 Imix, 11 Ik, 12 Ak'bal, 13 K'an.

206 Trecena Chikchan the Feathered Serpent: 1 Chikchan, 2 Kimi, 3 Manik, 4 Lamat, 5 Muluk, 6 Ok, 7 Chuwen, 8 Eb', 9 Ben, 10 Ix, 11 Men, 12 Kib, 13 Kab'an.

227 Trecena Etz'nab the Knife: 1 Etz'nab, 2 Kawak, 3 Ahaw, 4 Imix, 5 Ik, 6 Ak'bal, 7 K'an, 8 Chikchan, 9 Kimi, 10 Manik, 11 Lamat, 12 Muluk, 13 Ok.

248 Trecena Chuwen the Monkey: 1 Chuwen, 2 Eb', 3 Ben, 4 Ix, 5 Men, 6 Kib, 7 Kab'an, 8 Etz'nab, 9 Kawak, 10 Ahaw, 11 Imix, 12 Ik, 13 Ak'bal.

269 Trecena K'an the Seed: 1 K'an, 2 Chikchan, 3 Kimi, 4 Manik, 5 Lamat, 6 Muluk, 7 Ok, 8 Chuwen, 9 Eb', 10 Ben, 11 Ix, 12 Men, 13 Kib.

290 Trecena Kab'an the Earth: 1 Kab'an, 2 Etz'nab, 3 Kawak, 4 Ahaw, 5 Imix, 6 Ik, 7 Ak'bal, 8 K'an, 9 Chikchan, 10 Kimi, 11 Manik, 12 Lamat, 13 Muluk.

311 Trecena Ok the Dog: 1 Ok, 2 Chuwen, 3 Eb', 4 Ben, 5 Ix, 6 Men, 7 Kib, 8 Kab'an, 9 Etz'nab, 10 Kawak, 11 Ahaw, 12 Imix, 13 Ik.

332 Trecena Ak'bal the Night: 1 Ak'bal, 2 K'an, 3 Chikchan, 4 Kimi, 5 Manik, 6 Lamat, 7 Muluk, 8 Ok, 9 Chuwen, 10 Eb', 11 Ben, 12 Ix, 13 Men.

353 Trecena Kib the Owl: 1 Kib, 2 Kab'an, 3 Etz'nab, 4 Kawak, 5 Ahaw 6 Imix, 7 Ik, 8 Ak'bal, 9 K'an, 10 Chikchan, 11 Kimi, 12 Manik, 13 Lamat.

374 Trecena Muluk the Moon: 1 Muluk, 2 Ok, 3 Chuwen, 4 Eb', 5 Ben, 6 Ix, 7 Men, 8 Kib, 9 Kab'an, 10 Etz'nab, 11 Kawak, 12 Ahaw 13 Imix.

395 Trecena Ik the Wind: 1 Ik, 2 Ak'bal, 3 K'an, 4 Chikchan, 5 Kimi, 6 Manik, 7 Lamat, 8 Muluk, 9 Ok, 10 Chuwen, 11 Eb', 12 Ben, 13 Ix.

416 Trecena Men the Eagle: 1 Men, 2 Kib, 3 Kab'an, 4 Etz'nab, 5 Kawak, 6 Ahaw, 7 Imix, 8 Ik, 9 Ak'bal, 10 K'an, 11 Chikchan, 12 Kimi, 13 Manik.

437 Trecena Lamat the Star Flower: 1 Lamat, 2 Muluk, 3 Ok, 4 Chuwen, 5 Eb, 6 Ben, 7 Ix, 8 Men, 9 Kib, 10 Kab'an, 11 Etzn'ab, 12 Kawak, 13 Ahaw

How to Use This Book

Getting Started

The first thing you will want to do is **pick what date** you will be starting on. The Sacred Tzolk'in Daily Planner is set up so you can start at any time. All you need to do is find out what day it is on the Maya calendar. To discover that, just go to my website at www.lauralabrie.com and **click on the TZOLKIN tab**. There you will find a button marked CALENDER CONVERTER. When you click on it, a modern calendar with the normal weeks and months you are used to will appear. In each day's box it tells you what the Maya Tzolk'in day is. For example, today is September 8, 2020. In the box for Sept. 8 it says, *1 Etzn'ab*. Then go to the Table of Contents in the book to find which page 1 Etz'nab is on, turn to it, and write in today's date (Sept 8). That will be the beginning of the planner for you! (Keep in mind that you will be beginning somewhere in the middle of this book and then, when you get to the end, go back to the beginning!) That way, no matter when you choose to start, you still get the full 260 days of the Tzolk'in year!

Planning Ahead

The Sacred Tzolk'in Daily Planner is set up so you can plan ahead in two different ways. You can fill in the monthly calendar pages (on pages 29-37) with the Tzol'kin days simply by going to my website www.lauralabrie.com, clicking on the TZOLK'IN tab and then the button for the CALENDAR CONVERTER. All the information you need is there. Just write/copy it into the book as you chose to do!

The second way you can plan ahead is by using the **Trecena Planner Pages**. A trecena is like a month of 13 days. (There are 20 of them in total). At the beginning of each trecena you will find lots of information explaining what the energy of that 13-day month is about. You will also find space to write in the modern calendar dates next to the Maya days in order to keep everything clear and simple. Take a look at the energy of the days in the trecena to see when the best time would be to plan a party, have a garage sale, or take a day trip!

Suggestions for Activities that Flow with Each Day's Energy

Every day has a short list of things you can do that would be a great fit for that day's energy. Take time to read through them and then see if there are other things you can think of that would also be a good fit for that day. The more you can line up your plans with the energy of each day, the more you will be flowing in the energy river and not struggling against it. Why try to paddle upstream when you can float along and enjoy the ride!?!

Ceremonies

Every day there is a small Day Ceremony you can do. There is also a longer ceremony called "Calling in the 4 Directions" that you can do on days 1 and 8 of each trecena. You can also do this longer ceremony any time you feel a need for extra clarity, cleansing, or help. The directions for these ceremonies are on pages 20-21.

Coloring Pages

Just for fun, this book is filled with coloring pages. All the pictures are black and white reproductions created just for you from actual ancient Maya art. They come from a variety of sources including, ancient codices (books), Maya ruins, stone carvings, and pottery. Each picture has a title telling you what it is and where it is from.

Intentions

Every day has a lot of information. To help you focus and keep things simple and clear, you will find an intention that sums up the energy for that day. This is a short, simple sentence (intention) you can say, post on your fridge, or write on a sticky note and post on your bathroom mirror. That way you can repeat it throughout the day to help keep yourself aligned, in the flow, right in the middle of the energy river, and empowered to work with the energy of each day!

Notes, Reflections & Synchronicities

At the bottom of each daily page you will find space to write down whatever feels important to you. I love to keep track of interesting ways I see the energy unfolding in my life. As you begin to work with the sacred Tzolk'in calendar, you will find your life starting to naturally line up with it. Recording these synchronicities is not only fun and empowering, but will also help you to see how, the longer you "walk the path," the more inline with the energies your life naturally becomes. Remember, it's all about going with the flow!

Thoughts About the Past Trecena

At the end of each 13-day month (trecena) you will find a page where you can do a little journaling about how things are going. This is a great place to keep a record of how your life is beginning to line up with the flow of Universal energy!

Other Fun Things You Will Find

~ Every day has a color associated with it. Try wearing the color.

~ Every day also has energetic power places. It's wonderful to find these places and spend time in them just opening yourself up to the energy and peace of the Universe. These are also great places to do your Day Ceremonies and Calling in the 4 Directions Ceremonies!

~ Every day has an amulet suggested. Try carrying one in your pocket or wearing a small treasure associated with each day. These small reminders carry more power than you know!

~ Have fun and keep in mind that being in the energy is like being in a river. You can go against it and it will feel like trying to paddle upstream, possibly against a strong current on high energy days. Or, you can turn your boat downstream and let the current take you along, easily, effortlessly, and in the flow of the ancient gods and the energy of creation.

Tzolk'in Basics

This section is designed to give you a basic understanding of the sacred Maya Tzolk'in Calendar. The word *Tzolk'in* can be translated in Yucatec Mayan as *Tzol* (to count) *k'in* (sun/day) or to count the suns or to count the day.

There are 3 Maya calendars

1. The Long Count which is called the Universal Cycle and is an astrological calendar. Its lasts about 7885 solar years.
2. The Haab which is the civil calendar and has 365 days like our modern calendar.
3. And the Tzolk'in which is called the Divine Calendar or the Sacred Round and has 260 days.

To get a complete Maya date, you read all three calendars together. This is the job of the Maya day keepers and is very complex. But no worries. **We are going to focus on the Tzolk'in calendar** because it is the one that tells you how to plan your life based on the energy of what each day is good for.

Here are some interesting things about the Sacred Tzolk'in Calendar:

Each day IS a god

Each day is named after that particular god. So, the day and the god are the same thing.

Wak: The energy of nine
From the Chilam Balam

The Tzolk'in is still used today to plan ceremonies and religious occasions. You would get married on a day that is good for getting married and begin your training as a religious leader on a day that is good for that.

But it is MORE than that.

Everything about life is sacred. The Tzolk'in is not just for official ceremonies and religious occasions.

Each day is governed by a god. There are 20 day-gods and they are called *nawales* (Nawal is the singular and sometimes it is spelled Nahual or Nagual) Each nawal is symbolized by a Mayan glyph. (A glyph is picture-word. IN the journal section of this book, each day has its glyph with it). Each nawal also has an animal or force of nature associated with them. The animals and natural forces associated with each day help you to better understand the nature of that day. For example, the day Ok is associated with the dog and so has the attributes of a dog, like protecting, guiding, being faithful and loyal, and also being a bit of a party animal!

The Nawales and Their Colors

Imix: Red Crocodile
Ik: White Wind
Ak'bal: Blue Night
K'an: Yellow Seed
Chikchan: Red Feathered Serpent
Kimi: White World Bringer
Manik: Blue Deer
Lamat: Yellow Star Flower
Muluk: Red Moon
Ok: White Dog
Chuwen: Blue Monkey
Eb': Yellow Path
B'en: Red Corn Stalk
Ix: White Jaguar
Men: Blue Eagle
Kib: Yellow Warrior Owl
Kab'an: Red Earth
Etznab: White Knife
Kawak: Blue Storm
Ahaw: Yellow Sun

Frog from the Grolier Codex

These words are Yucatec Mayan. Keep in mind that there are many Maya tribes and they speak different languages. So, if you are doing some research online, you will find these days with different names in addition to these. No worries! Because I live here on the Yucatan Peninsula, and because the people I talk to and learn from are Yucatec Maya, I am sticking with this language. Sometimes even in this language you can find small differences, so allow space for that. For example: Ahaw will sometimes look like Ajaw. Its ok. It is just because the language and ideas are fluid. I will keep it as simple and straightforward here as I can.

There are 13 sets of these 20 days making a total of 260 days in this calendar. Many believe the 260 days are based on the time it takes for a human baby to develop. Some think it is related to the movement of Venus. Either way, it is not based on the moon like many calendars are, nor is it based on the seasons.

Each Nawal/Day God has a different personality. Ahaw is the god of the sun. Imix is the god of water. (I am simplifying this to keep it easy to understand because some day gods are really gods of more than one thing). So, on Ahaw, you do things that are in alignment with the energy or the sun. What does the sun god Ahaw bring? Illumination, warmth, growth. So, it's a good day to plant, to ask for things to come to light, or to work on a project. Do you see the connections?

What might Imix, the god of water be good for?

Think of the properties of water and what you associate it with. If you read tarot or are into understanding things about the elements, you will know that water is a female element. It is associated with intuition, creativity, and emotion. Water is also cleansing. So, the things that the day Imix are good for are in alignment with that energy. For example: Imix is good for being creative, asking for rain, working with your emotions, and cleansing negative energy.

As you are going through your day, you can pray to the god of the day for help in the area the god is aligned with. Ask Ahaw for sun and ask Imix for rain. On Ahaw you can looking for hidden answers and ask Ahaw to help bring them to light because Ahaw is god of the sun and you are in the energy of that day of the sun. So, it is a profound connection. This is why it is so powerful!

Waterlily Monster on a Vase

How the Tzolk'in Days & Numbers Work Together

The Tzolk'in Calendar has a total of 260 days. It is considered the divine calendar. It is a calendar designed for people to help us work with the energies and live more aligned, productive, and tranquil lives.

There are two basic parts to the calendar:

• The 20 Day Gods or "Nawales"
• The 13 Energies or "Tones"

The cycle is a bit confusing so I will write it out so you can get a better understanding of it. The confusion is because even though there are 20 days, there are only 13 numbers. So, you have to start a new cycle of numbers before you start a new cycle of days. You only get about 2/3 of the way through the 20 days when you have to start with the number 1 again. It is often depicted by a smaller circle inside a larger circle like the picture here. But want to write out the example for you because I think it will help you to also see it in a linear fashion.

1 Imix, 2 Ik, 3 Ak'bal, 4 K'an, 5 Chikchan, 6 Kimi, 7 Manik, 8 Lamat, 9 Muluk, 10 Ok, 11 Chuwen, 12 Eb', 13 Ben, 1 Ix, 2 Men, 3 Kib, 4 Kab'an, 5 Etz'nab, 6 Kawak, 7 Ahaw

Notice how you had to start with a 1 when you got to Ix?

So, when the cycle keeps going it takes 260 days before you get back to 1 Imix and that is a full Tzolk'in year. You end up with 20 "months" called *trecenas* that are 13 days each. Here is the whole thing written out for you. Each trecena is named after the first day in that cycle. I put the name of each trecena in bold to make it easier to think of them as the name of "months."

Altogether, the Tzolk'in 260-day year looks like this:

1 Imix, 2 Ik, 3 Ak'bal, 4 K'an, 5 Chikchan, 6 Kimi, 7 Manik, 8 Lamat, 9 Muluk, 10 Ok, 11 Chuwen, 12 Eb', 13 Ben.
1 Iix, 2 Men, 3 Kib, 4 Kab'an, 5 Etz'nab, 6 Kawak, 7 Ahaw, 8 Imix, 9 Ik, 10 Ak'bal, 11 K'an, 12 Chikchan, 13 Kimi.
1 Manik, 2 Lamat, 3 Muluk, 4 Ok, 5 Chuwen, 6 Eb', 7 Ben, 8 Ix, 9 Men, 10 Kib, 11 Kab'an, 12 Etz'nab, 13 Kawak.
1 Ahaw, 2 Imix, 3 Ik, 4 Ak'bal, 5 K'an, 6 Chikchan, 7 Kimi, 8 Manik, 9 Lamat, 10 Muluk, 11 Ok, 12 Chuwen, 13 Eb'.
1 Ben, 2 Ix, 3 Men, 4 Kib, 5 Kab'an, 6 Etz'nab, 7 Kawak, 8 Ahaw 9 Imix, 10 Ik, 11 Ak'bal, 12 K'an, 13 Chikchan.
1 Kimi, 2 Manik, 3 Lamat, 4 Muluk, 5 Ok, 6 Chuwen, 7 Eb', 8 Ben, 9 Ix, 10 Men, 11 Kib, 12 Kab'an, 13 Etz'nab.
1 Kawak, 2 Ahaw, 3 Imix, 4 Ik, 5 Ak'bal, 6 K'an, 7 Chikchan, 8 Kimi, 9 Manik, 10 Lamat, 11 Muluk, 12 Ok, 13 Chuwen.
1 Eb', 2 Ben, 3 Ix, 4 Men, 5 Kib, 6 Kab'an, 7 Etz'nab, 8 Kawak, 9 Ahaw, 10 Imix, 11 Ik, 12 Ak'bal, 13 K'an.

1 Chikchan, 2 Kimi, 3 Manik, 4 Lamat, 5 Muluk, 6 Ok, 7 Chuwen, 8 Eb', 9 Ben, 10 Ix, 11 Men, 12 Kib, 13 Kab'an.

1 Etz'nab, 2 Kawak, 3 Ahaw, 4 Imix, 5 Ik, 6 Ak'bal, 7 K'an, 8 Chikchan, 9 Kimi, 10 Manik, 11 Lamat, 12 Muluk, 13 Ok.

1 Chuwen, 2 Eb', 3 Ben, 4 Ix, 5 Men, 6 Kib, 7 Kab'an, 8 Etz'nab, 9 Kawak, 10 Ahaw, 11 Imix, 12 Ik, 13 Ak'bal.

1 K'an, 2 Chikchan, 3 Kimi, 4 Manik, 5 Lamat, 6 Muluk, 7 Ok, 8 Chuwen, 9 Eb', 10 Ben, 11 Ix, 12 Men, 13 Kib.

1 Kab'an, 2 Etz'nab, 3 Kawak, 4 Ahaw, 5 Imix, 6 Ik, 7 Ak'bal, 8 K'an, 9 Chikchan, 10 Kimi, 11 Manik, 12 Lamat, 13 Muluk.

1 Ok, 2 Chuwen, 3 Eb', 4 Ben, 5 Ix, 6 Men, 7 Kib, 8 Kab'an, 9 Etz'nab, 10 Kawak, 11 Ahaw, 12 Imix, 13 Ik.

1 Ak'bal, 2 K'an, 3 Chikchan, 4 Kimi, 5 Manik, 6 Lamat, 7 Muluk, 8 Ok, 9 Chuwen, 10 Eb', 11 Ben, 12 Ix, 13 Men.

1 Kib, 2 Kab'an, 3 Etz'nab, 4 Kawak, 5 Ahaw 6 Imix, 7 Ik, 8 Ak'bal, 9 K'an, 10 Chikchan, 11 Kimi, 12 Manik, 13 Lamat.

1 Muluk, 2 Ok, 3 Chuwen, 4 Eb', 5 Ben, 6 Ix, 7 Men, 8 Kib, 9 Kab'an, 10 Etz'nab, 11 Kawak, 12 Ahaw 13 Imix.

1 Ik, 2 Ak'bal, 3 K'an, 4 Chikchan, 5 Kimi, 6 Manik, 7 Lamat, 8 Muluk, 9 Ok, 10 Chuwen, 11 Eb', 12 Ben, 13 Ix.

1 Men, 2 Kib, 3 Kab'an, 4 Etz'nab, 5 Kawak, 6 Ahaw, 7 Imix, 8 Ik, 9 Ak'bal, 10 K'an, 11 Chikchan, 12 Kimi, 13 Manik.

1 Lamat, 2 Muluk, 3 Ok, 4 Chuwen, 5 Eb', 6 Ben, 7 Ix, 8 Men, 9 Kib, 10 Kab'an, 11 Etz'nab, 12 Kawak, 13 Ahaw.

Waterlily god. Painted Vase.

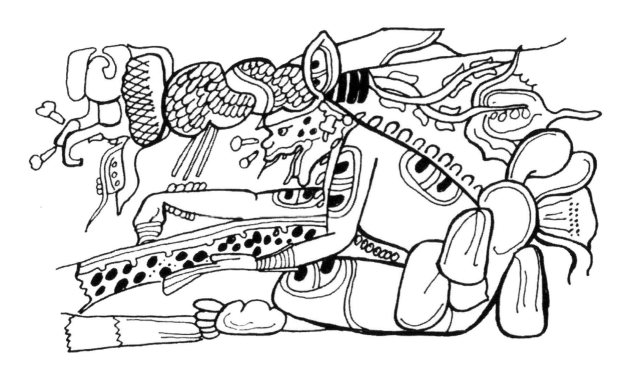

Calendar round from the Chilam Balam

The Magical Energy Wave

The thirteen energies (also known as *tones* like musical sounds) are like a magical wave, staring at rest and building to a peak, then breaking like a wave of the ocean with frothy surf that crashes on the shore. The number one is still. It is the potential of all things. Two is rising and polarizing, like the mountains of earth coming out of the sea in the beginning of all things. Three is taking the action of creating. Four is forming, taking shape and stabilizing. Five is becoming empowered. Six through eight are strong and stable. They are the days when many rituals and ceremonies are done. They are considered powerful and yet stable enough to work with. Six is when your energy is flowing. Seven offers you the gift of aligning with your mystical powers, and eight is when things are in harmony. Nine is strong energy. It is the divine power of the female and that of expanding. Ten is the crest of the wave. It is the point where it begins to break, and white water is seen, and the rush begins. It is the point of manifestation where you pull from the other world and bring it into this one. Eleven is when you must simply stand back and let go because the energy is too powerful to work with. Twelve is universalizing, it is when you begin to understand, you look at what you have created and understand what it has become. And thirteen...well thirteen is the cosmic wild card! Thirteen is chaos. It is the power of the white water rushing up on shore, a massive wave that has pounded the earth and in whose waters you cannot stand. It is a day for the unexpected and for the working of magic (if you can handle it!)

To sum up, here are the 13 stages of the magical energy wave:

1. Quiet, Attracting
2. Stirring, Polarizing
3. Lifting, Acting
4. Taking form, Stabilizing
5. Observing, Empowering
6. Flowing, Organizing
7. Inspiring, Reflecting
8. Harmonizing, Balancing
9. Pulsating, Expanding, Divine Feminine
10. Producing, Manifesting
11. Releasing, Dissolving
12. Crystalizing, Universalizing
13. Transcending, Cosmic Wild Card

Turtle from the Chilam Balam

Each energy (tone) has a purpose. They build on each other, revealing your direction in life and helping you navigate the eddies and currents of daily living. Move in harmony with the wave. When the energy is taking form, allow it. Do not expect to be producing when the energy is crystalizing. Take time to understand because that is what "crystalizing" is all about.

The energies combine with the day gods (nawales). For example, Ahaw (the sun) can be at a tone of 4 and that means the sun energy is taking form and stabilizing. Or, it can be at a 10 and that means it is at its peak, manifesting all the lovely things the sun can bring into your life. OR...it could be at a 13, wild and transcending. *This is when magic happens!* The wild card is at play, and the unexpected is right around the corner!

Glyphs from the Chilam Balam

The four directions and their day god counter parts
Maya cross in the center
From the Chilam Balam

The 4 Sacred Cardinal Directions

The four cardinal directions; north, south, east, and west, along with a fifth point, the center, hold a very important place in Maya belief and are an integral part of the sacred calendar. The directions are thought of as winds and when you refer to the east wind, you are referring to the wind that blows from the east. When you talk about them, you always start with east and go in a counterclockwise circle. East is the most important direction because it is where the sun rises. You can think of the directions as following the path of the sun. That means north is up, over your head, where the sun is at its highest point, west is where the sun sets, and south is down, beneath your feet, when the sun is in the middle of the night.

Each direction is represented by a specific color and the colors are very important. They are used during ceremonies, rituals, and are considered to help you channel the powers of the directions. East is red like the color of the sky at sunrise. North is white. West is blue or black like the night sky. And south is yellow like the corn at harvest or the leaves in the fall.

Every direction also has an element that goes with it. East is fire. North is air. West is water, and south is earth.

The most important part, however, is that each direction, like each day, has an energy that goes with it. They are forces you can pray to and ask for help. You can think of them as gods, or benevolent beings if you like. It is best to use the Mayan names when you talk to them because the names carry power. Here are the 4 cardinal directions with their Mayan names, their colors, their elements, and their energies/winds:

Lak'in is the wind that blows from the east. Its color is *red* and its element is fire. Its energy is about *beginnings, unity and the future*. The activity that goes with it is *creating*.

Xaman is the wind that blows from the north. Its color is *white* and its element is air. Its energy is about *transparency, clarity, wisdom and truth*. The activity that is associate with it is *reducing or minimizing*.

Chik'in is the wind that blows from the *west*. Its color is *blue/black* and its element is water. Its energy is about *duality, change, and the past or endings*. The activity associated with it is *adjusting*.

Nohol is the wind that blows from the *south*. Its color is *yellow* and its element is earth. Its energy is about *abundance, increasing and harvest*. The activity that goes with Nohol is *gaining*.

Each of the calendar days is intrinsically tied to a direction. 20 days and 4 directions mean that there are 5 days that go with each direction.

The days that go with Lak'in (east) are Imix the crocodile, Chikchan the feathered serpent, Muluk the moon, Ben the corn, and Kaban the earth.

The days that go with Xaman (north) are Ik the wind, Kimi the Lord of Death, Ok the dog, Ix the jaguar, and Etz'nab the knife.

The days that go with Chik'in (west) are Ak'bal the night, Manic the deer, Chuen the monkey, Men the eagle, and Cauac the storm.

The days that go with Nohol (south) are K'an the seed, Lamat the star flower, Eb the path, Cib the warrior owl, and Ahau the sun.

Yaxche is the fifth point. It is the center, is represented by the beautiful world tree and is blue-green in color. It doesn't go with a day, but it so very important because life is about being centered. If all the winds are in balance, if the energies that blow from the 4 directions are in balance, then you will be centered.

The Day Ceremony

As you begin your journey of *walking the path*, you can consider making *Day Ceremonies* a part of your routine. They are simple and only take a few minutes but are considered powerful and very helpful as you align with the energies of each day.

To do the rituals you will need candles, preferably in four colors, red, white, black, and yellow. If you don't have candles in all these colors, you can gather treasures in the corresponding colors and place them near the candle you are burning each day. Also the Maya often substitute similar colors like purple or blue for black. It is more about your intention than following a strict rule.

Here are the directions for a basic Day Ceremony:

1. First see what color candle you need for the day (to make it easy, every day in this journal tells you which color it is). If you are using all white candles, find a small treasure in the color of the day.

2. Face the direction of the day (again, to make it easy, every day in this journal tells you what its direction is) while holding your candle (and treasure if you have one) in front of you.

3. Light the candle

4. Ask the energy of the day to come and work with you. Use the Mayan name because it is more powerful that way. You could say something like, "Lak'in, energy from the east, I welcome you here today and ask you to bring the power of new beginnings and unity."

5. If you have anything on your heart that you need help with specifically, this is a good time to ask for help. There are also suggestions of things to ask for or give thanks for on many of the days in this journal. Look for them under the heading, *Rituals* on each day.

6. When you finish, simply say. "Thank you." Saying thank you is very important.

7. If you like, place your candle and any treasures in the day's color in a special place and let it burn for a while to remind you of the energy of the day.

Ceremony: Calling in The 4 Directions

The Ceremony of the 4 Directions is a more elaborate version of the day ceremony. A good time to do this is on the first day of each trecena (These days are highlighted in your journal) and on the 8th days of the trecena. You can also do it any time you feel a need for cleansing, help, or an extra boost in your day.

To do this ceremony, you will need one candle in each of the 5 colors, red, white, black(or blue or purple), yellow, and blue-green (or green). You can also use white candles along with small treasures in all these colors. It is appropriate to also use flowers or treasures in addition to your colored candles. It just depends on how elaborate you want to make it. For example, try placing something red that reminds you fire or the sunrise next to your red candle, something white that reminds you of air or transparency next to your white candle, something blue or black that reminds you of water or night next to your blue or black candle, and something yellow that reminds you of earth or harvest next to your yellow candle.

Here are the directions for the Calling in the 4 Directions Ceremony:

1. Place the four candles and their treasures on the ground at the four cardinal directions. Place the red candle to the east, the white candle to the north, the black candle to the west, and the yellow candle to the south. The Maya make this very beautiful, so feel free to use fresh flowers if you like, beautiful stones, even offerings of cacao beans and corn can be included.

2. Place the blue-green candle in the center. The center is where the underworld, called Xibalba, the physical world, and the overworld all connect.

3. Light the candles and stand in the center next to the blue-green candle.

4. Then you will start with the east/red/Lak'in and follow the same routine as you did with the Day ceremony, expect that you will do all 4 directions Begin by facing the east and ask the energy of Lak'in to work with you. Lak'in is new beginnings and unity. When you are finished, say, Thank you." Then turn to your left and face north and ask the energy of Xaman to work with you. Xaman is clarity and truth. Remember to say thank you when you are done. Then turn left again and face west. Ask the energy of Chik'in, who brings duality and change, to work with you and again give thanks. The turn left again and face south. Ask the energy of Nohol, the bringer of harvest and abundance, to work with you and say, "Thank you," when you finish.

Look for days with this symbol to for the best days to do this ceremony:

Call in the 4 Directions

A Summary of the Days & Some Mythology

Imix: The Crocodile

Imix is a day of turbulent, stirring waters, of birth, and new beginnings. Imix is the nawal (god) of the sea and is linked to the creation of the earth. It is a day of raw creative power! Imix is the reptilian body of the earth and the waterlily monster. It is a day of nurturing because the crocodile and the waterlily both live in the still waters of the mangroves where the baby fish are born, nurtured, and protected. In the Popul Vuh, the crocodile's back is the surface of the planet surrounded by a primordial sea. The waters are turbulent because, in the creation story, when Heart of Sky and The Plumed Serpent called the mountains to come forth from the sea, the emerging continents were rocked by the still swirling seas. The glyph contains a waterlily. Its element is Fire.

Ik: The Wind

Ik is the breath of life, both physical and spiritual. It is your voice, creativity and change. The Great Plumed Serpent, also known as Kukulkan, is the god of wind. He made his home in Chichen Itza. He gave the magic mushrooms to the people. Ik is also a day of heavy showers, and the hurricane. The glyph has a T in the center of it that represents the tree of life that connects the underworld, the physical world, and the overworld. T is the Maya symbol for wind. Its element is air.

Ak'bal: The Night

Ak'bal is the night house, the underworld, and the realm of the eternal jaguar sun (the night sun). It is the darkness before the dawn. It is a day of good luck, especially in love! It is a generally, a tranquil and happy day ♡ The hero twins in the Popul Vuh had to spend the night in the "night house." Caves (of which there are many in the Yucatan) are places of twilight and darkness and are considered portals to the otherworld, Xibalba! The glyph for Ak'bal contains the eyes and lower jaw of the jaguar. The mouth of the jaguar is considered a portal to the underworld. It also contains with a pyramid or possibly a cave entrance in the center. Its element is water.

K'an: The Seed

K'an is a day of gathering, collecting, harvest, and abundance. An abundant harvest is indicated here. The meaning is also linked to the net that is traditionally used to gather the corn and can represent tangling or untangling. The books of Chilam Balam say this day is the day of the Lord of Corn (seeds). Also, the Popul Vuh tells us the story of Blood Woman who, in order to prove she was pregnant with the hero twins, had to bring a net filled with corn to her mother in law. The glyph is often yellow and, in some versions, shows a representation of the Corn god. Its element is earth.

Chikchan: The Feathered Serpent

Chikchan (also written Chicchan) is the sky serpent, the cosmological snake, also known as Kukulkan. He is the Framer and shaper of the Universe. This is an extremely powerful sign. It is the fire at the base of the spine, the Kundalini. It is associated with sexual magic and the rain gods. In the Popul Vuh, the Great Plumed (feathered) Serpent and Heart of Sky created the Universe. The mouth of the snake is a portal that links this world with the Otherworld. Some of the glyphs for Chikchan have four dots which represent the four celestial sky serpents and others depict the head of a snake. Its element is fire.

Kimi: The World Bringer

Kimi is the god of death, the lords of the underworld. Sometimes Kimi (also written Cimi) is called The World Bringer. It is all about transformation and change. This usually applies to things like a job, relationship, living location, or some other part of your life that is in flux. Energies end and others begin. Change is an integral part of life and, if we harness it correctly, it can keep moving us toward becoming more enlightened beings. In the Popul Vuh, the final set of hero twines (there were two sets) defeated the Lords of Death in Xibalba (the underworld). They saved the planet from an ultimate death and ended human sacrifice! Also, a kernel of corn is sometimes called a "little skull" by the Maya and is a symbol of life. And, a very interesting mystery is the crystal skulls that have been found in the Maya-lands and seem to be objects of power without a known origin! The glyph shows a closed eye of the face of death. It element is air.

Manik: The Deer

Balance, support, and the game of life. Manik (also written Manic) is the deer and the Lord of the hunt. It is a day to get into the game of life. You can think of hunting in our modern world as doing any activities that involve the pursuit of sustenance and strength. That makes Manik a good day for business. Manik is also a very important day to focus on balance. Without balance, support cannot function properly. Think of the four legs of a table. If all the legs are different heights (unbalanced) how good is the table? The deer is strength, balance and support. It is the 4 corners of the earth and one of the 4 means of support that hold up the sky. Deer is also connected to heaven because the sacred mushrooms grow in its droppings! The glyph shows the hunter's hand as it's grasping the spear. Its element is water.

Lamat: The Star Flower

Today is all about abundance and growing! It is the four seasons and also symbolizes all of life, humans, plants, and animals. Lamat is the color gold, the sugar cane and the three colors of the sun. It symbolizes the four seasons and growth among humans, plants and animals. It is the star, Venus, who is fertility and the flower of abundance. Sometimes Lamat is associated with a happy drunk rabbit! The glyph shows four corn seeds in the four colors of the sacred directions (red, white, black and yellow). They also represent the four seasons and the four pillars of the world. Its element is earth.

Muluk: The Moon

A day to make payments, give offerings, and ask for dark things to come to light, Muluk (also written Muluc) is related to the moon cycle of the woman who gave birth to the hero twins in the Popul Vu. It is a day to use intuition and connect with the things of the spirit. The glyph represents the moon and is connected to the moon goddess. The circle in the middle may represent a drop of menstrual blood that women "pay" for giving birth. Its element is fire.

Ok: The Dog

The one who guides the night sun through the underworld. Ok (also written Oc) is the dog who guarded the corn field and helped Blood Woman gather the corn to prove to the gods that she was pregnant with the last set of hero twins (Popul Vuh). He is the nawal (god) of spiritual and material justice and on this day one can ask to judge both the good and the bad and be free from remorse. The glyph sometimes shows an entire dogs head and sometimes only shows the ear. Its element is air.

Chuwen: The Monkey

Cheuwen (also written Chuen) is the great craftsman, the patron of the arts, and the thread of time and the development of humans and animals that symbolizes destiny and maintains the continuity the past, the present, and the future. Monkey is all about being creative and having fun! It is a highly positive day that is full of energy that is friendly and happy! The hero twins, Batz and Chuen, were called 1 Monkey and 1 Artisan in the Popul Vuh. They created music, painting, literature, and weaving and so they are associated with the arts. The glyph shows the mouth of a howler monkey. Its element is water.

Eb: The Path

Travel and destiny...your path in life and force of Eb (also written Eib). This day can also be about following the path of the sacred calendar. It is a day when the ancestors are ready to listen. The books of Chilam Balam tell how a ladder was created on 2 Eb to facilitate travel from heaven to earth. The steps on the pyramids remind us of this ladder. The glyph shows dots representing a path or road. Some versions include a tooth signaling to watch for dangers along the way. Its element is earth.

Ben: The Corn Stalk

Ben is the rod of virtues of divine power! It is represented by the corn stalk and is associated with both harvest and success! The energy of corn is not only growing but surging upward like corn stalks shoot up after a heavy rain. It is a very meaningful day and associated with triumph! ALSO, the staff (or corn stalk) symbolizes the spine and the internal fire which moves upward and activates the secret powers. (I love this stuff!) One of the earliest stories in the Popul Vuh tells of how Sovereign Plumed Serpent and Heart of Sky made man out of corn. They used four colors of corn, red, white, black/blue and yellow. These four colors represent the four races of humanity and the four cardinal directions. The glyph shows cornstalks rising from the earth. Some versions show the god of corn. Its element is fire.

Ix: The Jaguar

Ix (pronounced *Ish* and also written Hiix) is feminine energy and all things related to the earth, strength, and vitality. Ix is the Heart of Mountain. Her domain is the darkness. The Chilam Balam books say Jaguar was the day the earth was created, and her mouth is a portal to the Otherworld. She is the energy of Mother earth in all her creative glory. Jaguar is one of the most important totem animals and was one of the first 5 animals created by the gods. The Maya say Ix carries the nighttime sun through the underworld. Ix is also associated with the goddess Ixchel. Its element is air.

Men: The Eagle

Flying high, ambition and vision. This is a day of good fortune, a day of freedom and of spiritual advancement! An eagle served as messenger between Heart of Earth and Heart of Sky, symbolizing the connection between god and man. The main role of the shaman kings was to climb the world tree to communicate with the gods and ancestors in other dimensions and bring back information to help their people. The word "men" means "shaman" in Yucatec Mayan. Its element is water.

Kib: The Warrior Owl

Kib (also written Cib) is about taking it easy, relaxation, patience, and timing. It is the balance of the warrior who waits for perfect timing to inflict his blow. It is the illusion of the material world and the night birds. Sometimes Kib is depicted as a bee, a candle, or a vulture. It is a day for making up for mistakes. People born on this day often become spiritual guides. Its element is earth.

Kaban: The Earth

Kaban (also written Caban) is all about thoughts, logic, ideas, and science. It is movement and the earthquake: A day of formidable power and wisdom and a day to shake the foundations. In the Popul Vuh, the Heart of Sky and the Sovereign Plumed Serpent commenced the creation of this world by saying, "Earth." Its element is fire.

Etz'nab: The Knife

Etzn'ab (also written Ecnab) is the obsidian sacrificial blade. It is a day to cut to the core of things. It is about sacrifice and cutting. It is about cutting away things that no longer serve you. The two-sided blade is also the surgeon's knife that brings healing. In the books of Chilam Balam, the obsidian blade is both for blood-letting and healing, especially healing fever. Its element is air.

Kawak: The Storm

Kawak (also written Cauac) is the power of the storm. It is the celestial dragon serpent and the Chaacs who are the gods of thunder and rain. Kawak is the nawal (god) of women and strength. It is the lightening flash of inspiration, the warmth and safety of the home, and the cleansing and purification of the rain. Hurricane is linked to Kawak and was one of the creator gods. He is the god who created the flood to wipe out the wooden people. Its element is water.

Ahaw: The Sun

Ahaw (also written Ajaw or Ahau) brings illumination and growth. He is the most powerful and positive nawal, radiating energy in all things. He is light, lighting both the day and the night (the moon is a reflection of the sun) He also brings enlightenment and vision! Ahaw is the Father of Lights, the Creator, The supreme god of the world. Its element is earth.

The World Tree: Shield art

Glyphs from the Grolier Codex

The Sacred Tzolk'in Daily Planner

Here the planner begins. On each day you will find information about the energy of the day along with lots of goodies to help you do rituals and ceremonies, gather amulets, and focus on colors and elements associated with the day. The object is to incorporate that which speaks to you. There is no need to do everything suggested (of course you CAN if you want to!) Do not underestimate the power of doing something small that is in alignment with the energy of the day. Simply burning a colored candle or carrying a small trinket in your pocket will increase the power of your personal connection with the energies and gods who rule each day. There is an intention included with each day that combines the energy of the day-god with the energy of the wave-number in a simple sentence. Feel free to repeat this sentence throughout the day to help keep you focused and centered on the energy of the day and help yourself align with it! Of course, this is a journal and the fun really begins when you start writing down what you do each day. Very quickly you will start noticing synchronicities and signs. Documenting your walk on this path will help you to see the connections that are happening all around you. It is a very exciting process!

Note: Each day you can do a simple day ceremony. Rather than write out the directions for this every day, you will find the basic directions under the heading "The Day Ceremony" in the introduction. You will also find the directions for the more complicated Calling in the 4 Directions Ceremony in the same section. In the journal section you will find suggestions about when to do these ceremonies.

The Tzolk'in Calendar here in Yucatan starts on 1 Imix, and so that is where we will begin.

Enjoy!

Sunday	Monday	Tuesday	Wednesday	Thursday	Friday	Saturday

Sunday	Monday	Tuesday	Wednesday	Thursday	Friday	Saturday

Sacred Tzolk'in Daily Journal

Sunday	Monday	Tuesday	Wednesday	Thursday	Friday	Saturday

	Sunday	Monday	Tuesday	Wednesday	Thursday	Friday	Saturday

Sacred Tzolk'in Daily Journal

Sunday	Monday	Tuesday	Wednesday	Thursday	Friday	Saturday

Sunday	Monday	Tuesday	Wednesday	Thursday	Friday	Saturday

Sunday	Monday	Tuesday	Wednesday	Thursday	Friday	Saturday

Sunday	Monday	Tuesday	Wednesday	Thursday	Friday	Saturday

Sacred Tzolk'in Daily Journal

Sunday	Monday	Tuesday	Wednesday	Thursday	Friday	Saturday

What to Expect During Imix

Focus: What do you want to birth during the next 13 days?

Expect the next 13 days to have the
Crocodile. This is a time of powerfully
appears in the Popul Vuh creation story.
sea with his back creating the land.
Plumed Serpent called the mountains to
you can imagine that crocodile swished
erupted and mountains churned the
the sky. So, we find crocodile central to
earth. We find him in several other
the starry Milky Way stretching across
with his mouth at the entrance to
Maya underworld. And he is the Maya
its roots in Xibalba and its branches
heavens.

undercurrent of Imix, the
creative energy! The crocodile
He is swimming in a primordial
Then, when Heart of Sky and The
come forth from the sea,
his great tail as volcanoes
waters and rose into
the creation of
places too. He is
the night sky
Xibalaba, the
Tree of Life with
in the

There is another place we find the crocodile. He
mangroves where the water lilies bloom, his
hiding in the shallows where the water is still
fish and take refuge from preadtors as the
until they are big enough to make the journey
sea.

lives in the
great bulk
and baby
grow
out to

And so together, we find Imix, the crocodile,
unfathomable creation and the nourishing
tiniest of sea creatures. He is the nawal
sea and of all water. Powerful new
beginnings and the energy to nurture them
associated with this day-god. So, if you have
something new you would like to start, this is
wonderful trecena to do it! Remember, the
Imix will be with you for the next 13 days,
the different energies of each day. How do
plan to harness the creative power of
Imix this trecena?

is the strength of
place of the
(god) of the

are

a

energy of
forming a net for
you

Crocodilian World Tree from Stela 25 in Izapa

Waterlily God
Copan, Honduras, building facade

Imix The Red Crocodile

Trecena Planner

Crocodile from Codex Nuttall

1 Imix the Red Crocodile - Day/Date:

_____

_____

_____

_____

_____

_____

_____

2 Ik the White Wind – Day/Date:

_____

_____

_____

_____

_____

_____

_____

3 Ak'bal the Blue Night – Day/Date:

_____

_____

_____

_____

_____

_____

_____

4 K'an the Yellow Seed – Day/Date:

_____

_____

_____

_____

_____

_____

_____

5 Chikchan the Red Serpent – Day/Date:

_____

_____

_____

_____

_____

_____

_____

6 Kimi the White World Bringer – Day/Date:

_____

_____

_____

_____

_____

_____

_____

7 Manik the Blue Deer – Day/Date:

_____

_____

_____

_____

_____

_____

_____

8 Lamat the Yellow Star Flower - Day/Date:

_____

_____

_____

_____

_____

_____

_____

9 Muluk the Red Moon - Day/Date:

_____

_____

_____

_____

_____

_____

_____

10 Ok the White Dog - Day/Date:

_____

_____

_____

_____

_____

_____

_____

_____

11 Chuwen the Blue Monkey - Day/Date:

_____

_____

_____

_____

_____

_____

_____

12 Eb' the Yellow Path - Day/Date:

_____

_____

_____

_____

_____

_____

_____

13 Ben the Red Corn Stalk - Day/Date:

_____

_____

_____

_____

_____

_____

_____

Waterlily Diety

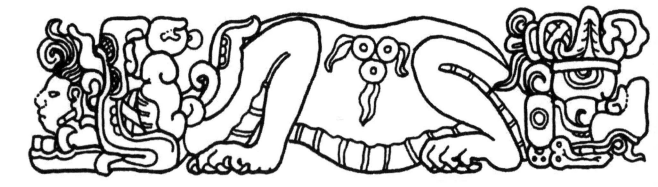

1 Imix: Red Crocodile - Date:

Imix is a day of turbulent, stirring waters, of birth, new beginnings, and nurturing. It is a day of raw creative power! Imagine the back of the crocodile at rest in a primordial sea. When Heart of Sky and The Great Plumed Serpent spoke the earth into existence, the mountains rose from the waters causing swirling waters and great turbulence. This is Imix. This is birth. Because the crocodile lives in the mangroves, water lilies are associated with this day.

The Magical Wave number 1 carries the energy of attraction

Intention: I am attracting wonderful energy for new beginnings.

Call in the 4 Directions

🦋 Today is a good day to:

- Start the day with grounding exercises and/or meditation
- Make sweeping changes and lay new foundations
- Stay aware of the tendency to take wild and unpredictable actions and avoid crazy behavior
- Be creative
- Develop your powers of intuition
- Receive messages from beyond
- Cleanse yourself from negative energy

Color & Direction: Lak'in, the Red East
Ritual: The wind is blowing from the east today, so the Day Ceremony is Lak'in, the East. Lak'in brings new beginnings, unity, and creation. (Look in the introduction under *Day Ceremony* for the directions on how to do this ceremony) During your Day Ceremony, you can ask for guidance as you align with this powerful energy of creation!
Power Places: Lakes, lagoons, and other in-land bodies of water
Amulet: Crocodile, lotus blossom, crystals and images associated with the sea.
Element: Fire

Notes, Reflections, and Synchronicities:

_____

_____

_____

_____

_____

_____

_____

_____

2 Ik: White Wind ~ Date:

The breath of life and creativity. It is also a day of air, heavy showers, and hurricanes. The wind can carry news, bring change, and inspire creativity. It is a day to use your voice and is good for communication and letting your "voice" be heard.

The Magical Wave Energy of 2 is about duality and polarization. It is stabilizing like two opposite things on an old-fashioned scale, balancing each other out.

Intention: I am letting my voice be heard with balance.

🦋 Today is a good day to:

- Use your voice, let your voice be heard.
- This is the best day for writing!
- Do something creative
- Cure respiratory illness
- Work on spiritual growth
- Go on a picnic or hike
- Do some gardening

Color & Direction: Xaman, the White North
Ritual: Burn pine or copal incense. This is the sacred day of stone alters. You can place stones around your altar or in a special place at home. Then perform the day ceremony for Xaman the North. Xaman brings transparency, clarity, and truth. During the day ceremony, you can ask for protection for friends and family and ask for protection against the rage of overly strong human emotions.
Energetic Power Places: Canyons, mountains, valleys, forests, and stone alters
Amulet: Hang wind chimes, a tree or branch, the beautiful quetzal bird
Element: Air

Notes, Reflections, and Synchronicities:

_____

_____

_____

_____

_____

_____

_____

3 Ak'bal: Blue Night - Date:

Ak'bal is the night house, the underworld, and the realm of the eternal jaguar sun (the night sun). It is the darkness before the dawn. It is a day of good luck, especially in love! Ak'bal, the night, is generally, this is a tranquil and happy day.

The Magical Wave Energy of 3 is about activating. It is creative action.

Intention: I am creatively activating the energy of bringing things out of the darkness and into the light.

Today's energy is good for:

- Declaring your love: This is a lucky day for love!
- Looking within to find answers.
- Seeking anything: jobs, lovers, friends, answers, knowledge
- Discovering the underlying causes of problems
- Face personal challenges with intuition rather than strength
- Ask for light to reach all things
- Acknowledge feelings from the heart
- Getting a fresh start or new beginning

Color & Direction: Chik'in, the Blue West
Ritual: Make a fire at dusk or dawn and ask for renewal. The Day Ceremony for today is Chik'in the West. Chik'in brings the energies or cooperation, duality, adjusting, and change. During your Day Ceremony, you can ask the energy of Chik'in to help you find the answers you are looking for.
Energetic Power Places: Caves, pyramids, mountains, and valleys especially at dusk and dawn.
Amulet/Totem: Jaguar, pyramid, the color black
Element: Water

Notes, Reflections, and Synchronicities:

_____

_____

_____

_____

_____

_____

_____

4 K'an: Yellow Seed - Date:

A day of gathering, collecting, harvest, and abundance. An abundant harvest is indicated here. The meaning is also linked to the net that is traditionally used to gather the corn and can represent tangling or untangling.

Magical Wave Energy today is 4. This is the energy of things taking shape and coming into form. It is also the energy of stability and balance.

Intention: Abundance is taking form and becoming stable in my life today.

🦋 Today is good for:

- Paying off debts
- Collecting things (even collecting your thoughts)
- Reaping the rewards of your work
- Piecing things together
- Forming a group of people to work or gather together
- Do something associated with the interNET
- Witchy stuff (casting spells like one might cast a net)
- Disentangling things

Color & Direction: Nohol, the Yellow South
Element: Earth
Ritual: The Day Ceremony is Nohol, the south. Place seeds or yellow flowers around your candle. Nohol brings the energy of harvest, increase, and abundance! As you burn your candle, let it send prayers to the Heart of Sky and ask to be freed (untangled) from anything that prevents you from receiving the harvest you have worked for.
Energetic Power Places: The sea, farmer's fields, gardens
Amulet: Seeded jewelry or accessories, dream catcher (net).
Element: Earth

Notes, Reflections, and Synchronicities:

_____

_____

_____

_____

_____

_____

_____

_____

5 Chikchan: Red Feathered Serpent – Date:

The sky serpent, the cosmological snake, also known as Kukulkan. Chikchan is Framer and shaper of the Universe. This is an extremely powerful sign. It is the fire at the base of the spine, the Kundalini. It is associated with sexual magic and the rain gods. Key elements for this day are truth and justice.

The Magical Wave energy today is a 5. The energy of 5 is all about empowerment. Its gift is the power to look at your creation and take delight in it.

Intention: I am empowered by truth and justice.

Today is a good day to:

- Pursue or deliver truth and knowledge
- Deliver and receive justice
- Find or bring balance
- Pursue inner peace
- Enjoy great sex
- Take fast and direction action
- Beware of fast and direct action
- Stay on guard against anger in both yourself and others

Color & Direction: Lak'in, the Red East
Ritual: The Day Ceremony is Lak'in: unity, beginnings, and creation. This is a powerful day. It is a day to go to the mountains and commune with them. Light a fire and speak directly to the earth and ask for protection. You can also ask for justice, truth, peace, and balance.
Power Places: Mountains, volcanoes, pyramids, starry night
Amulet: Jade, snake, or pyramid—especially the one at Chichen Itza (where the temple of Kukulkan is). An especially powerful totem for today is a jade pyramid.
Element: Fire

Notes, Reflections, and Synchronicities:

_____

_____

_____

_____

_____

_____

_____

_____

6 Kimi: White Death ~ Date:

The god of death and the lords of the underworld, Kimi is all about transformation and change. This usually applies to things like a job, relationship, living location, or a part of your life that is in flux. Energies end and others begin. Change is an integral part of life and, if we harness it correctly, can keep moving us toward becoming more enlightened beings.

The Magical Wave is a 6 today. Six in the energy of being in the flow. Envision yourself letting go of the security of holding onto the bank of a river and allow the water to take you where it will.

Intention: I am in the flow of transformation.

Today is a good day to:

- A great day to make or think about changes
- End relationships (business, friendships, or romantic)
- Work towards tranquility among friends and colleagues, both living and dead
- Both give and ask for forgiveness
- Remember the dead
- Do up-keep on and take care of equipment
- A tranquil day to be patient and conservative in your energy

Color & Direction: Xaman, the White North
Ritual: The Day Ceremony today is for Xaman, the North who brings Transparency, clarity and truth. During your day ceremony you can give thanks to the ancestors who continue to give you guidance and ask for peace, love, money, health, and forgiveness.
Energetic Power Places: Pyramids, sacred sites, ceremonial sites, the fireplace, temples
Amulet: Skull, butterfly (transformation), corn seed, skeleton
Element: Air

Notes, Reflections, and Synchronicities:

_____

_____

_____

_____

_____

_____

_____

_____

7 Manik: Blue Deer – Date:

Balance, support, and the game of life. Manik is a very important day to focus on balance. Without balance, support cannot function properly. Think of the four legs of a table. If all the legs are different heights (unbalanced) how good is the table? Manik is the deer and the Lord of the hunt. It is a day to get into the game of life. You can think of hunting in our modern world as doing any activities that involve the pursuit of sustenance and strength. That makes Manik a good day for business. It is also a good day for long range travel. (Deer travel vast distances.)

The Magical Wave energy is a 7 today. This is the energy of channeling. Its gift is the practical application of your mystical powers.

Intention: I am channeling the power to find balance.

Today is good for:

- Teamwork & meetings
- Business pursuits, getting out "in the field" and talking to customers
- Long range travel
- Staying alert for traps in business and the game of life
- An excellent day for diviners

Color & Direction: Chik'in, the Blue West
Ritual: The Day Ceremony is for Chik'in, the West. Chik'in brings you duality, cooperation, and change. As you perform your Day Ceremony, consider asking Chik'in to bless your finances and business.
Energetic Power Places are forests, and fields (places where you might find deer)
Amulet: Anything to do with the deer, anything with the number 4 or four parts to it.
Element: Water

Notes, Reflections, and Synchronicities:

_____

_____

_____

_____

_____

_____

_____

_____

8 Lamat: Yellow Star Flower - Date:

Today is all about abundance and growing! It's a wonderful day to plant something, be it friendships, project ideas, or actual flowers. Lamat is also about fertility and is represented by the planet (star) Venus and the color gold.

The Magical Wave energy today is at an 8. This is the energy of harmony. With integrity its gift is the power to come into harmony with all the parts of your true self.

Intention: I am in harmony with growing things.

Call in the 4 Directions

🦋 Today is good for:

- Planting new things: flowers, friendships, projects
- Honoring past works
- Tending to your crops (in our modern times, that also means tending to business or whatever it is that sustains you)
- Star gazing (Lamat is also associated with Venus)
- Thinking about the Universe
- Feeding the world
- Fertility

Color: Yellow
Direction: Today the wind is blowing from the south. It brings harvest, abundance, and endings.
Ritual: The Day Ceremony today is Nohol, the South. Try placing some wildflowers, especially yellow ones, or seeds around your candle today.
Energetic Power Places today are forests, places where wildflowers grow, rivers and lakes
Amulet: Flowers (especially yellow ones), stars, or Venus
Element: Earth

Notes, Reflections, and Synchronicities:

_____

_____

_____

_____

_____

_____

_____

9 Muluk: Red Moon – Date:

A day to make payments, give offerings, and ask for dark things to come to light. Muluk is also about emotions and using your intuition. This is a day of cycles, rhythms and water since water is intrinsically connected to the moon.

The Magical Wave energy of 9 rules this day. Bolon is the Mayan name for 9 and it is the divine feminine and is all about expanding.

Intention: I am expanding in my ability to harness my intuition.

Today is good for:

- Paying off debts (financial, relational, societal, spiritual)
- Asking people to pay you back for their debts to you
- Working to end suffering
- Giving offerings to the earth
- Asking for rain
- Asking for dark things to come to light
- Pay attention to your dreams
- Use your intuition

Color & Direction: Lak'in the Red East
Ritual: The day ceremony for today is Lak'in the East. You can also cleanse your candles and other alter items under the moon today.
Energetic Power Places today are the beach, big rocks, oceans, rivers, and lakes
Amulets: Shark or whale or other large aquatic creature, jade, the moon
Element: Fire

Notes, Reflections, and Synchronicities:

_____

_____

_____

_____

_____

_____

_____

_____

_____

_____

10 Ok: White Dog ~ Date:

The one who guides the night sun through the underworld. Ok is about guidance and protection. Your guides are with you today in a powerful way to guide you through the underworld. This is also a day about justice and truth. On the lighter side, Ok is the most sexually charged day of the nawales.

The Magical Wave energy that want to work with you today is 10, which is Lajun in Mayan. Lajun is the power of manifesting. It is the peak of the wave.

Intention: I am manifesting guidance, justice, and truth.

🦋 Today is good for:

- Asking for guidance
- Giving guidance
- Short distance travel (like around your town)
- Being alert for dangers/update home security
- Having great sex
- Looking for hidden truth

Color & Direction: Xaman, the White North.
Element: Air
Ritual: The Day Ceremony for today is for Xaman, the North. Consider asking the energy of Xaman to guide you today. Xaman brings transparency, clarity and truth.
Energetic Power Places today are mountains and beaches. If you don't live near these places, try a watching a video with beautiful scenery to add a little nature energy to your day.
Amulets: Anything related to dogs
Element: Air

Notes, Reflections, and Synchronicities:

_____

_____

_____

_____

_____

_____

_____

_____

11 Chuwen: Blue Monkey – Date:

The great craftsman, patron of the arts, the thread of that symbolizes destiny and maintains the continuity the past, the present, and the future. Monkey is all about being creative and having fun! It is a highly positive day that is full of energy that is friendly and happy!

The Magical Wave energy of 11 is here to work with you today. Buluk in Many, the energy of 11 is about letting go. It is a very high number and is the point where the energy wave crashes onto the shore, becoming uncontrollable.

Intention: I am letting go and having fun!

🦋 Today is good for:

- Partying and celebrating
- Dancing, singing, writing, painting
- Getting married
- Studying the sacred calendar
- Taking time to look for patterns in life
- Starting projects
- Watch for synchronicities today!

Color & Direction: Chik'in the Blue/Black West
Ritual: This is a great day for burning incense, especially copal or frankincense. The Day Ceremony for today is Chik'in, the West.
Element: Water
Energetic Power Places where the energy is strong today are lakes and forests.
Amulet: Try wearing something woven today, especially a cloth wrist band or bracelet or something made from woven threads. Something that reminds you of monkeys.
Element: Water

Notes, Reflections, and Synchronicities:

_____

_____

_____

_____

_____

_____

_____

12 Eb: Yellow Path – Date:

Travel and destiny...your path in life. This day can also be about following the path of the sacred calendar. It is a day when the ancestors are ready to listen.

The Magical Wave energy today is Lajka'a, the number 12. It is about understanding.

Intention: I understand my path. (note, even if you don't understand your path, this is an appropriate intention to set for today. The power of this day will help bring you into alignment so that you DO understand your path)

🦋 **Today is good for:**

- Travel or making plans to travel
- Spending time considering your path in life
- Making changes in your path in life
- Starting a new business or making a business plan
- Asking for good luck in both spiritual and material pursuits
- Being careful of dangers along the way

Color & Direction: Nohol, the Yellow South
Ritual: The Day Ceremony for today is Nohol, the south. Nohol bring abundance, increase and harvest!
Energetic Power Places: Mountains and Woods and paths, especially ancient ones.
Amulets: Good amulets for today are pyramid, ladder, tooth (there is a tooth in the glyph to remind you to be careful of dangers along the road), compass or globe. Anything else that you associate with travel or your path in life.
Element: Earth

Notes, Reflections, and Synchronicities:

_____

_____

_____

_____

_____

_____

_____

_____

13 Ben: Red Corn Stalk – Date:

Ben is the rod of virtues of divine power! It is the corn stalk and is associated with harvest and success! The energy is both growing & surging upward like corn stalks after a heavy rain. It is a very meaningful day, associated with triumph! ALSO, the staff (stalk) symbolizes the spine and the internal fire which moves upward and activates the secret powers

The Magical Wave is the energy of Ooxlajun, the number 13. It is the cosmic wild card! It is unpredictable and can lead to magic!

Intention: I am prepared for secret powers magic!

🦋 Today is a good day to:

- Plant a seed or start a project
- Spend time with family or friends
- Follow your intuition and listen to your dreams
- Ask the ancestors for help in teaching and caretaking
- Study and investigate things
- Ask for rain and growth

Color & Direction: Lak'in the Red East
Ritual: The day ceremony for today is Lak'in the East. Consider requesting help from the ancestors in caring for your home and family or ask for help in starting a new business or project or help with your finances.
Amulet: Carry with you or wear small seeds (especially corn seeds), a small stone (used for grinding corn) ... hahaha....you will like the next one....whisky, bourbon, or rum. . .also sugar, and yellow clothes or jewelry.
Energetic Power Places: fields, meadows, forests, beaches
Element: Fire

Notes, Reflections, and Synchronicities:

_____

_____

_____

_____

_____

_____

_____

_____

Thoughts About this Past Trecena

_____

_____

_____

_____

_____

_____

_____

_____

_____

_____

_____

_____

_____

_____

_____

_____

_____

_____

_____

_____

_____

_____

_____

_____

_____

_____

_____

_____

_____

What to Expect as Ix Comes to Play

Focus: How do you want to increase in vitality over the next 13 days?

Ix is the jaguar who guides the night sun through the underworld. She is feminine energy, fertile and powerful. Some say jaguar was the day the earth was created and certainly, Jaguar was one of the creator gods. Because of her abilities to hunt at night, she is considered a bringer of light and is linked to Ak'bal. the night. Ix, the jaguar is the sign of shamans, healers, and spiritual guides.

Jaguar, Codex Nuttall

you
with

spirit.
powerfully to
a keeper and
the earth. So, this
offerings to the
in nature, and work on
healing powers. You might
learning about medicinal plants
this activity ties together all

During the next trecena, Ix, the lady jaguar, will be with you, working to support you and lending her creative energy filled strength, power, and the healing mysteries of the Because jaguar is connected so the creation of the earth, she is guardian of all things related to trecena is a good time to give earth, work on your home, spend time growing in both your intuition and even consider spending some time and using them in teas and cooking as things Ix.

As you enter this trecena,
want to work on over
supported by the
at learning about
start your
Ix...wonderful
about the earth
cast vision for it
great vision. On 3 Kib
patient with yourself
something new because
patience and relaxing. On
because Kaban is the

ask yourself what projects you might
the next 13 days that can be
energy of Ix. As an example, Lets look
medicinal plants. One 1 Ix, you can
project since it is Ix 1 Ix...double
energy for beginning something
and healing! On 2 Men, you can
since Men is the eagle who has
you could remember to be
as you are learning
Kib the Owl is about timing,

4 Kaban you could plant or harvest your herbs Earth day. On 5 Etz'nab you could make choices about which plants you want to really focus on and which you would let go, because Etzn'ab is the knife and is a good day for pruning. Do you see the pattern? How can you make it work for you? What will you choose to focus on during the trecena of Ix, the Jaguar?

Waterlily Jaguar, Codex Style Vase
A YUi, shapeshifting creature

Ix the White Jaguar
Trecena Planner

Jaguar, Codex Style Vase

1 Ix the White Jaguar - Day/Date:

_____

_____

_____

_____

_____

_____

_____

2 Men the Blue Eagle – Day/Date:

_____

_____

_____

_____

_____

_____

_____

3 Kib the Yellow Owl – Day/Date:

_____

_____

_____

_____

_____

_____

_____

4 Kab'an the Red Earth – Day/Date:

_____

_____

_____

_____

_____

_____

_____

5 Etz'nab the White Knife – Day/Date:

_____

_____

_____

_____

_____

_____

_____

6 Kawak the Blue Storm – Day/Date:

_____
_____
_____
_____
_____
_____
_____

7 Ahaw the Yellow Sun – Day/Date:

_____
_____
_____
_____
_____
_____
_____

8 Imix the Red Crocodile - Day/Date:

_____
_____
_____
_____
_____
_____
_____

9 Ik the White Wind - Day/Date:

_____
_____
_____
_____
_____
_____
_____

10 Ak'bal the Blue Night - Day/Date:

_____
_____
_____
_____
_____
_____
_____

11 K'an the Yellow Seed - Day/Date:

_____
_____
_____
_____
_____
_____
_____

12 Chikchan the Red Serpent - Day/Date:

_____

_____

_____

_____

_____

_____

_____

13 Kimi the White World Bringer - Day/Date:

_____

_____

_____

_____

_____

_____

_____

Jaguar, Codex Style Vase
A Yui, shapeshifting creature

1 Ix: White Jaguar – Date:

Ix (pronounced *Ish*) is feminine energy and all things related to the earth, strength, and vitality. Think of the qualities of a jaguar. They are stealthy, strong, and hunt at night. This energy is powerful and wise and is related to the goddess Ixchel.

The Magical Wave energy of Jun rules this day. It is the unifying power of 1. It brings the power of creation and new beginnings. Its gift is the power of attracting.

Intention: I am attracting all the powerful, feminine energy of the jaguar.

Today is a good day to:

Call in the 4 Directions

- Meditate on the Earth as our home and live in harmony.
- Use magic powers
- Take care of your home, especially by getting rid of things that no longer serve you.
- Use feminine energy
- Get pregnant
- Hunt for things such as knowledge, truth, wisdom
- Any ecological projects

Color & Direction: Xaman, the White North.
Ritual: The Day Ceremony is for Xaman, the North. Xaman brings transparency, clarity and truth. After asking this energy to work with you today, give thanks to the ancestors for all things related to the earth. Consider placing some treasures from the earth around your candle today.
Energetic Power Places: Ceremonial places (especially the pyramids), forests, and mountains (high places)
Amulet: Jaguar, pyramid, or something with a jaguar or spotted design.
Element: Air

Notes, Reflections, and Synchronicities:

_____

_____

_____

_____

_____

_____

_____

_____

2 Men: Blue Eagle – Date:

Men the eagle is all about flying high, ambition, and vision. This is a day of good fortune, a day of freedom and of spiritual advancement! It is also about financial advancement. Men is the day of business, merchants, and money. So, this is also the day to dream big and reach for the sky in regard to your business ideas and dreams.

The Magical Wave energy of Ka'a is the duality of the number 2. It is polarizing and yet stabilizing. Think of two opposite things coming into balance.

Intention: I am finding balance even as I fly high.

🦋 This is a good day to:

- Communicate with Heart of Sky, the creator god
- Ask for money for buying things
- Consider the big picture
- Focus on goals and consider how to best meet them
- Pursue goals that have already been set
- Spiritual elevation
- Work on self-improvement

Color & Direction: Chik'in, the Blue West
Ritual: The Day Ceremony is Chik'in the West. Chik'in brings cooperation, duality and change. This is a very important day for a sacrificial ritual to give thanks for money. The required offering is CHOCOLATE! Simply thank the gods and your ancestors for providing material goods and money, offer them some chocolate. When you finish, then eat it!
Energetic Power Places: Mountains, lakes, misty places, upland forests
Amulet: Bird feathers, dream catchers, anything with a bird, eagle, or quetzal on it
Element: Water

Notes, Reflections, and Synchronicities:

_____

_____

_____

_____

_____

_____

_____

_____

3 Kib: Yellow Owl – Date:

Kib, the warrior owl, is all about taking it easy, relaxation, patience, and timing. The warrior is careful in his timing. He is patient, not rushed. Like the warrior, today is about choosing your timing carefully. This day is also about the illusion of the material world. The night birds Today is a very spiritual day, indeed!

The Magical Wave energy is a level 3 today and is called Oox in Mayan. It is about taking creative action.

Intention: I am taking creative action to go with the flow.

🦋 This is a good day to:

- Go with the flow
- Relax
- Commune with the ancestors
- Wash your clothes, especially your good clothes
- Be a spiritual guide
- Ask for forgiveness for ignoring moral teachings
- This is a very special day to spend time preventing mistakes
- Kib is not a good day to start a new project because the energy is low.

Color & Direction: Nohol, the Yellow South
Ritual: The day ceremony is for Nohol which brings increase, abundance, and harvest. Consider taking time to commune with your ancestors during your Day Ceremony today.
Energetic Power Places: Mountains, volcanoes, tropical forests, lakes
Amulet: The earth, any rocks or crystals
Element: Earth

Notes, Reflections, and Synchronicities:

_____

_____

_____

_____

_____

_____

_____

_____

4 Kaban: Red Earth ~ Date:

Kaban, the earth is the energy of thoughts, logic, ideas and science. It is movement and sweeping change. Kaban is the earthquake: A day of formidable power and wisdom, a day of shaking the foundations and sudden revelations

The Magical Wave energy of Kan is the number 4 and is all about stability and taking form.

Intention: Ideas are taking form within me.

Today is good for:

- Thinking creativity
- Working with others
- Scientific investigation
- Being connected to the earth
- Coming into agreement with the creator
- Movement, travel
- Travel on the spiritual plane
- Shaking things up/sudden revelation/revelations that shake your foundations

Color & Direction: Lak'in, the Red East
Ritual: The Day Ceremony is for Lak'in. Lak'in bring the energy of beginnings, creation, and unity. As you ask Lak'in to work with you today, consider adding some rocks or crystals to your altar space.
Energetic Power Places: Mountains, volcanoes, tropical forests, lakes
Amulet: The earth, any rocks or crystals
Element: Fire

Notes, Reflections, and Synchronicities:

_____

_____

_____

_____

_____

_____

_____

_____

5 Etz'nab: White Knife ~ Date:

The obsidian sacrificial blade. A day to cut to the core of things. This is a day to reduce, clean out, and cleanse. Its energy is also about healing because the knife can both cut and heal. The obsidian blade is shined to the point of reflection and so the energy of the mirror also comes into play today.

The Magical Wave energy of Jo'o the number 5 rules this day. It is all about empowering.

Intention: I am empowered to remove things from my life that do not serve me.

🦋 Today is a good day to:

- Clean out your closet
- Do some editing (writing, song writing)
- Sort things out
- End an unproductive relationship
- Have a sale
- Let go of the past
- Diagnose and cure illness (physical, mental, and spiritual)
- Make predictions about the future

NOTE: Today is not a good day for travel or to start something new.

Color & Direction: Xaman, the White North.
Ritual: The Day Ceremony is for Xaman, the North. Xaman brings transparency, clarity and truth. Today is a good day to make up for things you neglected to do or should not have done and to receive forgiveness. You can also ask for protection from disease and accidents. No other ceremonies are performed on a knife day.
Energetic Power Places: Pyramids, cliffs, waterfalls, lightning storms
Amulet: Obsidian stone, jade, a knife, a pyramid (the glyph has a pyramid on it) or a mirror
Element: Air

Notes, Reflections, and Synchronicities:

_____

_____

_____

_____

_____

_____

_____

_____

6 Kawak: Blue Storm – Date:

Storm is the Nawal of women and strength. It is the lightening flash of inspiration, the warmth and safety of the home, and the cleansing and purification of the rain. Imagine what it feels like to run inside as a storm approaches. That is the energy of Kawak. The rage of the wind and the comfort of home and the care of the woman who wraps loved ones in her arms.

The Magical Wave energy is a 6. In Mayan it is known as Wak and it is all about getting in the flow. Imagine a rushing river. Let go of the bank, your comfort zone, and get into the flow.

Intention: I am flowing with strength and inspiration.

🦋 Today is a good day to:

- Tend to your family and home
- Do volunteer work
- Use your authority
- Ask for the actions of your enemies to turn against them
- Be prepared for trouble
- Heal mental illness
- Receive flashes of inspiration

Color & Direction: Chik'in, the Blue West
Ritual: The Day Ceremony is Chik'in the West. Chik'in brings cooperation, duality and change. As you ask the energy of Chik'in to work with you today, you can also give thanks for the women in your life.
Energetic Power Places: Pine and cypress forests
Amulet: Storm cloud, lightening, Mayan goddess, or pyramid
Element: Water

Notes, Reflections, and Synchronicities:

_____

_____

_____

_____

_____

_____

_____

_____

7 Ahaw: Yellow Sun ~ Date:

Illumination and growth. The most powerful and positive nawal, radiating energy in all things. Its light not only lights up the day and the night (the moon is a reflection of the sun) but it also brings enlightenment and vision!

The Magical Wave energy of Uk, the number 7, is the power to channel. It is the practical application of your mystical powers (how exciting!)

Intention: I am channeling illumination

🦋 Today is a good day to:

- Contact the dead
- Be brave against things that scare you
- Ask for illumination
- Build a house
- Start or continue projects
- Have a party
- Reflect on the positive things in life
- Place flowers on the graves of loved ones
- Seek spiritual illumination

Color & Direction: Nohol, the Yellow South
Ritual: The day ceremony is for Nohol which brings increase, abundance, and harvest. Consider doing this at sunrise or sunset today.
Energetic Power Places: Sunrise and sunset, find a beautiful view, especially on the beach or in a field of flowers
Amulet: Anything that shows the sun or flowers (especially yellow)
Element: Earth

Notes, Reflections, and Synchronicities:

_____

_____

_____

_____

_____

_____

_____

8 Imix: Red Crocodile – Date:

Imix is a day of turbulent, stirring waters, of birth, new beginnings, and nurturing. It is a day of raw creative power! Because the crocodile lives in the mangroves, water lilies and nurturing are also associated with this day.

The Magical Wave number 8 carries the energy of harmony. It is strong and viable. This is a good day for rituals and ceremonies!

Intention: I am in harmony with new beginnings.

Call in the 4 Directions

🦋 Today is a good day to:

- Ask for water/rain
- Start the day with grounding exercises and/or meditation
- Make sweeping changes and lay new foundations
- Stay aware of the tendency to take wild, unpredictable actions
- Be creative
- Develop your powers of intuition
- Receive messages from beyond
- Cleanse yourself from negative energy
- Ask for the calming of mental issues, spiritual problems, & climate change

Color & Direction: Lak'in, the Red East
Ritual: The wind is blowing from the east today, so the Day Ceremony for is Lak'in. Lak'in brings new beginnings, unity, and creation. (Look in the introduction under *Day Ceremony* for the directions on how to do this ceremony) During your Day Ceremony, you can ask for guidance as you align with this powerful energy of creation!
Power Places: Lakes, lagoons, and other in-land bodies of water
Amulet: Crocodile, lotus blossom, crystals and images associated with the sea.
Element: Fire

Notes, Reflections, and Synchronicities:

_____

_____

_____

_____

_____

_____

_____

_____

9 Ik: White Wind – Date:

The breath of life and creativity. It is also a day of air, heavy showers, and hurricanes. The wind can carry news, bring change, and inspire creativity. It is a day to use your voice and is good for communication and letting your "voice" be heard.

The Magical Wave Energy of 9 is the divine feminine and is expanding.

Intention: I am expanding into the energy of letting my voice be heard.

Today is a good day to:

- Use your voice, let your voice be heard.
- This is the best day for writing!
- Do something creative
- Cure respiratory illness
- Work on spiritual growth
- Go on a picnic or hike
- Do some gardening

Color & Direction: Xaman, the White North
Ritual: Burn pine or copal incense. This is the sacred day of stone alters. You can place stones around your altar or in a special place at home. Then perform the day ceremony for Xaman the North. Xaman brings transparency, clarity, and truth. During the day ceremony, you can ask for protection for friends and family and ask for protection against the rage of overly strong human emotions.
Energetic Power Places: Canyons, mountains, valleys, forests, and stone alters
Amulet: Hang wind chimes, a tree or branch, the beautiful quetzal bird
Element: Air

Notes, Reflections, and Synchronicities:

_____

_____

_____

_____

_____

_____

_____

_____

10 Ak'bal: Blue Night – Date:

Ak'bal is the night house, the underworld, and the realm of the eternal jaguar sun (the night sun). It is the darkness before the dawn. It is a day of good luck, especially in love! Ak'bal, the night, is generally, this is a tranquil and happy day.

The Magical Wave Energy of 10 is about manifesting! It is the crest of the wave.

Intention: I am manifesting the energy of bringing things out of the darkness into the light.

🦋 Today's energy is good for:

- Declaring your love: This is a lucky day for love!
- Looking within to find answers.
- Seeking anything: jobs, lovers, friends, answers, knowledge
- Discovering the underlying causes of problems
- Face personal challenges with intuition rather than strength
- Ask for light to reach all things
- Acknowledge feelings from the heart
- Getting a fresh start or new beginning

Color & Direction: Chik'in, the Blue West
Ritual: Make a fire at dusk or dawn and ask for renewal. The Day Ceremony for today is Chik'in the West. Chik'in brings the energies or cooperation, duality, adjusting, and change. During your Day Ceremony, you can ask the energy of Chik'in to help you find the answers you are looking for.
Energetic Power Places: Caves, pyramids, mountains, and valleys especially at dusk and dawn.
Amulet/Totem: Jaguar, pyramid, the color black
Element: Water

Notes, Reflections, and Synchronicities:

_____

_____

_____

_____

_____

_____

_____

_____

11 K'an: Yellow Seed – Date:

A day of gathering, collecting, harvest, and abundance. An abundant harvest is indicated here. The meaning is also linked to the net that is traditionally used to gather the corn and can represent tangling or untangling.

Magical Wave Energy today is 11. This is the energy of letting go. The wave is breaking, and you can no longer control it. So, stand back let is run!

Intention: I am letting go and allowing abundance to come to me.

Today is good for:

- Paying off debts
- Collecting things (even collecting your thoughts)
- Reaping the rewards of your work
- Piecing things together
- Forming a group of people to work or gather together
- Do something associated with the interNET
- Witchy stuff (casting spells like one might cast a net)
- Disentangling things

Color & Direction: Nohol, the Yellow South
Element: Earth
Ritual: The Day Ceremony is Nohol, the south. Place seeds or yellow flowers around your candle. Nohol brings the energy of harvest, increase, and abundance! As you burn your candle, let it send prayers to the Heart of Sky and ask to be freed (untangled) from anything that prevents you from receiving the harvest you have worked for.
Energetic Power Places: The sea, farmer's fields, gardens
Amulet: Seeded jewelry or accessories, dream catcher (net).
Element: Earth

Notes, Reflections, and Synchronicities:

_____

_____

_____

_____

_____

_____

_____

_____

12 Chikchan: Red Feathered Serpent – Date:

The sky serpent, the cosmological snake, also known as Kukulkan. Chikchan is Framer and shaper of the Universe. This is an extremely powerful sign. It is the fire at the base of the spine, the Kundalini. It is associated with sexual magic and the rain gods. Key elements for this day are truth and justice.

The Magical Wave energy today is a 12. The energy of understanding. It is standing back and observing what you have created. It is too strong to control.

Intention: I understand how truth and justice work in my life.

🦋 Today is a good day to:

- Pursue or deliver truth and knowledge
- Deliver and receive justice
- Find or bring balance
- Pursue inner peace
- Enjoy great sex
- Take fast and direction action
- Beware of fast and direct action
- Stay on guard against anger in both yourself and others

Color & Direction: Lak'in, the Red East
Ritual: The Day Ceremony is Lak'in: unity, beginnings, and creation. This is a powerful day. It is a day to go to the mountains and commune with them. Light a fire and speak directly to the earth and ask for protection. You can also ask for justice, truth, peace, and balance.
Power Places: Mountains, volcanoes, pyramids, starry night
Amulet: Jade, snake, or pyramid—especially the one at Chichen Itza (where the temple of Kukulkan is). An especially powerful totem for today is a jade pyramid.
Element: Fire

Notes, Reflections, and Synchronicities:

_____

_____

_____

_____

_____

_____

_____

_____

13 Kimi: White World Bringer – Date:

The god of death and the lords of the underworld. Kimi is all about transformation and change. This usually applies to things like a job, relationship, living location, or some other part of your life that is in flux. Energies end and others begin. Change is an integral part of life and, if we harness it correctly, can keep moving us toward becoming more enlightened beings.

The Magical Wave is a 13 today. Thirteen is the cosmic wild card! It is a day of chaos where everything has been thrown into the air and anything can happen! If you are strong enough, it is a day to control the very elements of creation!

Intention: I am excited to see what will transform in my life.

Today is a good day to:

- A great day to make or think about changes
- End relationships (business, friendships, or romantic)
- Work towards tranquility among friends and colleagues, both living and dead
- Both give and ask for forgiveness
- Remember the dead
- Do up-keep on and take care of equipment
- A tranquil day to be patient and conservative in your energy

Color & Direction: Xaman, the White North
Ritual: The Day Ceremony today is for Xaman, the North who brings Transparency, clarity and truth. During your day ceremony you can give thanks to the ancestors who continue to give you guidance and ask for peace, love, money, health, and forgiveness.
Energetic Power Places: Pyramids, sacred sites, ceremonial sites, the fireplace, temples
Amulet: Skull, butterfly (transformation), corn seed, skeleton
Element: Air

Notes, Reflections, and Synchronicities:

_____

_____

_____

_____

_____

_____

_____

_____

Thoughts About this Past Trecena

What Manik Brings

Manik from The Chilam Balam

Focus: What do you want to bring into balance during the next 13 days?

Manik is the most balanced of all the Nawales. So, you can expect this trecena to being balance into your life. Manik is the deer. The deer is strong, intuitive, and swift. He is master of the jungle and the field, going where he wishes and staying alert to his surroundings. But the most important attribute of the deer in this context, is his beautiful balance. Think of his four legs, long and strong. Four is a very important number to the Maya (4 directions, 4 winds, 4 energies, 4 faces, 4 colors) and the four legs of the deer epitomize the energy of 4. Imagine the 4 legs of a table. They support the table-top, but in order for the top to be useful, the legs but be in balance. Our lives are the same way. We may have support in life, but that support needs to find balance. In fact, when everything is in perfect balance, then we find ourselves feeling centered and whole. That is what this trecena is all about. So, as you move through the 13 days of Deer, keep in mind that all of their different energies will be working in balance with one another and with you.

Deer, Codex Nuttall

As you make your daily plans over the next trecena, ask yourself how you can find balance each day. For example: Imix falls on day 8 (a day of double balance 4x2). Imix is about creation and birth. Ask yourself this, "How can creation bring balance into life?" Or, you can phrase it this way, "How can I find my balance in creation?" Do this on each day during the 13 days of Manik and by the end of this trecena you will be feeling the impact of balance and finding yourself feeling more stable and centered.

Deer with Woman Riding: Codex Style Vase

Manik the Blue Deer

Trecena Planner

Manik from the Nuttall Codex

1 Manik the Blue Deer - Day/Date:

_____

_____

_____

_____

_____

_____

_____

2 Lamat the Yellow Seed – Day/Date:

_____

_____

_____

_____

_____

_____

_____

3 Kib the Yellow Owl – Day/Date:

_____

_____

_____

_____

_____

_____

_____

4 Kab'an the Red Earth – Day/Date:

_____

_____

_____

_____

_____

_____

_____

5 Etz'nab the White Knife – Day/Date:

_____

_____

_____

_____

_____

_____

_____

6 Kawak the Blue Storm – Day/Date:

_____

_____

_____

_____

_____

_____

_____

7 Ahaw the Yellow Sun – Day/Date:

_____

_____

_____

_____

_____

_____

_____

8 Imix the Red Crocodile - Day/Date:

_____

_____

_____

_____

_____

_____

_____

9 Ik the White Wind - Day/Date:

_____
_____
_____
_____
_____
_____
_____

10 Ak'bal the Blue Night - Day/Date:

_____
_____
_____
_____
_____
_____
_____

11 K'an the Yellow Seed - Day/Date:

_____
_____
_____
_____
_____
_____

12 Chikchan the Red Serpent - Day/Date:

_____
_____
_____
_____
_____
_____
_____

13 Kimi the White World Bringer - Day/Date:

_____
_____
_____
_____
_____
_____

Glyphs from the Grolier Codex

1 Manik: Blue Deer – Date:

Balance, support, and the game of life. Manik is a very important day to focus on balance. Without balance, support cannot function properly. Think of the four legs of a table. If all the legs are different heights (unbalanced) how good is the table? Manik is the deer and the Lord of the hunt. It is a day to get into the game of life. You can think of hunting in our modern world as doing any activities that involve the pursuit of sustenance and strength. That makes Manik a good day for business. It is also a good day for long range travel. (Deer travel vast distances.)

The Magical Wave energy is a 1 today. This is a strong energy because it is doubled. Today is Manik, Manik! The energy of 1 is all about attracting!

Intention: I am attracting balance.

Call in the 4 Directions

🦋 Today is good for:

- Teamwork & meetings
- Business pursuits, getting out "in the field" and talking to customers
- Long range travel
- Staying alert for traps in business and the game of life
- An excellent day for diviners

Color & Direction: Chik'in, the Blue West
Ritual: The Day Ceremony is for Chik'in, the West. Chik'in brings you duality, cooperation, and change. As you perform your Day Ceremony, consider asking Chik'in to bless your finances and business.
Energetic Power Places are forests, and fields (places where you might find deer)
Amulet: Anything to do with the deer, anything with the number 4 or four parts to it.
Element: Water

Notes, Reflections, and Synchronicities:

_____
_____
_____
_____
_____
_____
_____

2 Lamat: Yellow Star Flower – Date:

Today is all about abundance and growing! It's a wonderful day to plant something, be it friendships, project ideas, or actual flowers. Lamat is also about fertility and is represented by the planet (star) Venus and the color gold.

The Magical Wave energy today is at a 2. This is the energy of polarity. Think of two opposite things balancing perfectly on a scale. It is about finding balance.

Intention: I have everything I need for things to grow in my life in a balanced way.

🦋 Today is good for:

- Planting new things: flowers, friendships, projects
- Honoring past works
- Tending to your crops (in our modern times, that also means tending to business or whatever it is that sustains you)
- Star gazing (Lamat is also associated with Venus)
- Thinking about the Universe
- Feeding the world
- Fertility

Color: Yellow
Direction: Today the wind is blowing from the south. It brings harvest, abundance, and endings.
Ritual: The Day Ceremony today is Nohol, the South. Try placing some wildflowers, especially yellow ones, or seeds around your candle today.
Energetic Power Places today are forests, places where wildflowers grow, rivers and lakes
Amulet: Flowers (especially yellow ones), stars, or Venus
Element: Earth

Notes, Reflections, and Synchronicities:

_____

_____

_____

_____

_____

_____

_____

_____

3 Muluk: Red Moon – Date:

A day to make payments, give offerings, and ask for dark things to come to light. Muluk is also about emotions and using your intuition. This is a day of cycles, rhythms and water since water is intrinsically connected to the moon.

The Magical Wave energy of 3 rules this day. Three is the power of taking creative action. It is rising and taking form.

Intention: I am taking creative action to harness my intuition.

🦋 Today is good for:

- Paying off debts (financial, relational, societal, spiritual)
- Asking people to pay you back for their debts to you
- Working to end suffering
- Giving offerings to the earth
- Asking for rain
- Asking for dark things to come to light
- Pay attention to your dreams
- Use your intuition

Color & Direction: Lak'in the Red East
Ritual: The day ceremony for today is Lak'in the East. You can also cleanse your candles and other alter items under the moon today.
Energetic Power Places today are the beach, big rocks, oceans, rivers, and lakes
Amulets: Shark or whale or other large aquatic creature, jade, the moon
Element: Fire

Notes, Reflections, and Synchronicities:

_____

_____

_____

_____

_____

_____

_____

_____

_____

4 Ok: White Dog ~ Date:

The one who guides the night sun through the underworld. Ok is about guidance and protection. Your guides are with you today in a powerful way to guide you through the underworld. This is also a day about justice and truth. On the lighter side, Ok is the most sexually charged day of the Nawales.

The Magical Wave energy that want to work with you today is 4. The energy of four is all about balance. It is the 4 directions, the 4 colors, and the 4 winds.

Intention: I am receiving guidance to find balance in my life.

🦋 Today is good for:

- Asking for guidance
- Giving guidance
- Short distance travel (like around your town)
- Being alert for dangers/update home security
- Having great sex
- Looking for hidden truth

Color & Direction: Xaman, the White North.
Element: Air
Ritual: The Day Ceremony for today is for Xaman, the North. Consider asking the energy of Xaman to guide you today. Xaman brings transparency, clarity and truth.
Energetic Power Places today are mountains and beaches. If you don't live near these places, try a watching a video with beautiful scenery to add a little nature energy to your day.
Amulets: Anything related to dogs
Element: Air

Notes, Reflections, and Synchronicities:

_____

_____

_____

_____

_____

_____

_____

5 Chuwen: Blue Monkey – Date:

The great craftsman, patron of the arts, the thread of that symbolizes destiny and maintains the continuity the past, the present, and the future. Monkey is all about being creative and having fun! It is a highly positive day that is full of energy that is friendly and happy!

The Magical Wave energy of 5 is here to work with you today. Five is empowerment! It is a rising energy, growing stronger and easy to handle.

Intention: I am empowered to be creative and have fun!

🦋 Today is good for:

- Partying and celebrating
- Dancing, singing, writing, painting
- Getting married
- Studying the sacred calendar
- Taking time to look for patterns in life
- Starting projects
- Watch for synchronicities today!

Color & Direction: Chik'in the Blue/Black West
Ritual: This is a great day for burning incense, especially copal or frankincense. The Day Ceremony for today is Chik'in, the West.
Element: Water
Energetic Power Places where the energy is strong today are lakes and forests.
Amulet: Try wearing something woven today, especially a cloth wrist band or bracelet or something made from woven threads. Something that reminds you of monkeys.
Element: Water

Notes, Reflections, and Synchronicities:

_____

_____

_____

_____

_____

_____

_____

6 Eb: Yellow Path – Date:

Travel and destiny...your path in life. This day can also be about following the path of the sacred calendar. It is a day when the ancestors are ready to listen.

The Magical Wave energy today is the number 6. Let go of the bank and get into the river. Six is about letting go of control and going with the flow!

Intention: I am in the flow with my destiny.

🦋 Today is good for:

- Travel or making plans to travel
- Spending time considering your path in life
- Making changes in your path in life
- Starting a new business or making a business plan
- Asking for good luck in both spiritual and material pursuits
- Being careful of dangers along the way

Color & Direction: Nohol, the Yellow South
Ritual: The Day Ceremony for today is Nohol, the south. Nohol bring abundance, increase and harvest!
Energetic Power Places: Mountains and Woods and paths, especially ancient ones.
Amulets: Good amulets for today are pyramid, ladder, tooth (there is a tooth in the glyph to remind you to be careful of dangers along the road), compass or globe. Anything else that you associate with travel or your path in life.
Element: Earth

Notes, Reflections, and Synchronicities:

_____
_____
_____
_____
_____
_____
_____
_____

7 Ben: Red Corn Stalk – Date:

Ben is the rod of virtues of divine power! It is the corn stalk and is associated with harvest and success! The energy is both growing & surging upward like corn stalks after a heavy rain. It is a very meaningful day, associated with triumph! ALSO, the staff (stalk) symbolizes the spine and the internal fire which moves upward and activates the secret powers. (I love this stuff!)

The Magical Wave energy of the number 7 is all about channeling. It is the practical application of your magical powers!

Intention: I am channeling the secret powers magic!

🦋 Today is a good day to:

- Plant a seed or start a project
- Spend time with family or friends
- Follow your intuition and listen to your dreams
- Ask the ancestors for help in teaching and caretaking
- Study and investigate things
- Ask for rain and growth

Color & Direction: Lak'in the Red East
Ritual: The day ceremony for today is Lak'in the East. Consider requesting help from the ancestors in caring for your home and family or ask for help in starting a new business or project or help with your finances.
Amulet: Carry with you or wear small seeds (especially corn seeds), a small stone (used for grinding corn) ... hahaha....you will like the next one....whisky, bourbon, or rum. . .also sugar, and yellow clothes or jewelry.
Energetic Power Places: fields, meadows, forests, beaches
Element: Fire

Notes, Reflections, and Synchronicities:

_____

_____

_____

_____

_____

_____

_____

_____

8 Ix: White Jaguar ~ Date:

Ix (pronounced *Ish*) is feminine energy and all things related to the earth, strength, and vitality. Think of the qualities of a jaguar. They are stealthy, strong, and hunt at night. This energy is powerful and wise and is related to the goddess Ixchel.

The Magical Wave energy of 8 rules this day. Its gift is harmonizing! It is a powerful and useful energy and is a day to do ceremonies and rituals.

Intention: I am harmonizing with the powerful, feminine energy of the jaguar.

🦋 **Today is a good day to:**

Call in the 4 Directions

- Meditate on the Earth as our home and live in harmony.
- Use magic powers
- Take care of your home, especially by getting rid of things that no longer serve you.
- Use feminine energy
- Get pregnant
- Hunt for things such as knowledge, truth, wisdom
- Any ecological projects

Color & Direction: Xaman, the White North.
Ritual: The Day Ceremony is for Xaman, the North. Xaman brings transparency, clarity and truth. After asking this energy to work with you today, give thanks to the ancestors for all things related to the earth. Consider placing some treasures from the earth around your candle today.
Energetic Power Places: Ceremonial places (especially the pyramids), forests, and mountains (high places)
Amulet: Jaguar, pyramid, or something with a jaguar or spotted design.
Element: Air

Notes, Reflections, and Synchronicities:

_____

_____

_____

_____

_____

_____

_____

_____

9 Men: Blue Eagle – Date:

Men the eagle is all about flying high, ambition, and vision. This is a day of good fortune, a day of freedom and of spiritual advancement! It is also about financial advancement. Men is the day of business, merchants, and money. So, this is also the day to dream big and reach for the sky in regard to your business ideas and dreams.

The **Magical Wave** energy of Bolon is the divine feminine. It is a very strong energy and is all about expansion and mastery!

Intention: I am mastering the art of flying high!

This is a good day to:

- Communicate with Heart of Sky, the creator god
- Ask for money for buying things
- Consider the big picture
- Focus on goals and consider how to best meet them
- Pursue goals that have already been set
- Spiritual elevation
- Work on self-improvement

Color & Direction: Chik'in, the Blue West
Ritual: The Day Ceremony is Chik'in the West. Chik'in brings cooperation, duality, and change. This is a very important day for a sacrificial ritual to give thanks for money. The required offering is CHOCOLATE! Simply thank the gods and your ancestors for providing material goods and money, offer them some chocolate. When you finish, then eat it!
Energetic Power Places: Mountains, lakes, misty places, upland forests
Amulet: Bird feathers, dream catchers, anything with a bird, eagle, or quetzal on it
Element: Water

Notes, Reflections, and Synchronicities:

_____

_____

_____

_____

_____

_____

_____

_____

10 Kib: Yellow Owl – Date:

Kib, the warrior owl, is all about taking it easy, relaxation, patience, and timing. The warrior is careful in his timing. He is patient, not rushed. Like the warrior, today is about choosing your timing carefully. This day is also about the illusion of the material world. The night birds Today is a very spiritual day, indeed!

The Magical Wave energy is a level 10 today and is called Lajun in Mayan. Ten is the crest of the energy wave. It is the energy of manifestation!

Intention: I am manifesting patience and perfect timing.

This is a good day to:

- Go with the flow
- Relax
- Commune with the ancestors
- Wash your clothes, especially your good clothes
- Be a spiritual guide
- Ask for forgiveness for ignoring moral teachings
- This is a very special day to spend time preventing mistakes
- Kib is not a good day to start a new project because the energy is low.

Color & Direction: Nohol, the Yellow South
Ritual: The day ceremony is for Nohol which brings increase, abundance, and harvest. Consider taking time to commune with your ancestors during your Day Ceremony today.
Energetic Power Places: Mountains, volcanoes, tropical forests, lakes
Amulet: The earth, any rocks or crystals
Element: Earth

Notes, Reflections, and Synchronicities:

_____

_____

_____

_____

_____

_____

_____

_____

11 Kaban: Red Earth – Date:

Kaban, the earth is the energy of thoughts, logic, ideas, and science. It is movement and sweeping change. Kaban is the earthquake: A day of formidable power and wisdom, a day of shaking the foundations and sudden revelations

The Magical Wave energy of 11 is the energy of letting go. The wave has crested, and you can no longer control it. So now stand back and watch!

Intention: I am excitedly letting go and receiving revelation!

Today is good for:

- Thinking creativity
- Working with others
- Scientific investigation
- Being connected to the earth
- Coming into agreement with the creator
- Movement, travel
- Travel on the spiritual plane
- Shaking things up/sudden revelation/revelations that shake your foundations

Color & Direction: Lak'in, the Red East
Ritual: The Day Ceremony is for Lak'in. Lak'in bring the energy of beginnings, creation, and unity. As you ask Lak'in to work with you today, consider adding some rocks or crystals to your altar space.
Energetic Power Places: Mountains, volcanoes, tropical forests, lakes
Amulet: The earth, any rocks or crystals
Element: Fire

Notes, Reflections, and Synchronicities:

_____

_____

_____

_____

_____

_____

_____

_____

12 Etz'nab: White Knife – Date:

The obsidian sacrificial blade. A day to cut to the core of things. This is a day to reduce, clean out, and cleanse. Its energy is also about healing because the knife can both cut and heal. The obsidian blade is shined to the point of reflection and so the energy of the mirror also comes into play today.

The Magical Wave energy of 12 is the energy of understanding.

Intention: I understand how to cleanse my life!

🦋 Today is a good day to:

- Clean out your closet
- Do some editing (writing, song writing)
- Sort things out
- End an unproductive relationship
- Have a sale
- Let go of the past
- Diagnose and cure illness (physical, mental, and spiritual)
- Make predictions about the future

NOTE: Today is not a good day for travel or to start something new.

Color & Direction: Xaman, the White North.
Ritual: The Day Ceremony is for Xaman, the North. Xaman brings transparency, clarity, and truth. Today is a good day to make up for things you neglected to do or should not have done and to receive forgiveness. You can also ask for protection from disease and accidents. No other ceremonies are performed on a knife day.
Energetic Power Places: Pyramids, cliffs, waterfalls, lightning storms
Amulet: Obsidian stone, jade, a knife, a pyramid (the glyph has a pyramid on it) or a mirror
Element: Air

Notes, Reflections, and Synchronicities:

_____

_____

_____

_____

_____

_____

_____

_____

13 Kawak: Blue Storm – Date:

Storm is the Nawal of women and strength. It is the lightening flash of inspiration, the warmth and safety of the home, and the cleansing and purification of the rain. Imagine what it feels like to run inside as a storm approaches. That is the energy of Kawak. The rage of the wind and the comfort of home and the care of the woman who wraps loved ones in her arms.

The Magical Wave energy of 13, Ooxlajun, is ascension! It is the cosmic wild card, and anything can come into play today. This is a day for magic!

Intention: I am in sync with strength and inspiration and allowing it to flow through me.

Today is a good day to:

- Tend to your family and home
- Do volunteer work
- Use your authority
- Ask for the actions of your enemies to turn against them
- Be prepared for trouble
- Heal mental illness
- Receive flashes of inspiration

Color & Direction: Chik'in, the Blue West
Ritual: The Day Ceremony is Chik'in the West. Chik'in brings cooperation, duality and change. As you ask the energy of Chik'in to work with you today, you can also give thanks for the women in your life.
Energetic Power Places: Pine and cypress forests
Amulet: Storm cloud, lightening, Mayan goddess, or pyramid
Element: Water

Notes, Reflections, and Synchronicities:

_____

_____

_____

_____

_____

_____

_____

Thoughts About this Past Trecena

What to Expect During Ahaw

Ahaw from the Chilam Balam

Focus: What would like to illuminate over the next 13 days?

Ahaw is the creator. Some think of Ahaw as the Father/Mother god and of all the other gods as part of the being of Ahaw, or expressions of Ahaw. This means that Ahaw is the most powerful of all the Nawales or day-gods. And what are the attributes of Ahaw, the Sun? All the things you associate with the sun! Brightness, bringing things to light, happiness, wholeness, also illumination as in learning! Ahaw is the god of writing and books and learning! So, remember during this next trecena that the power of illumination is with you! This is a wonderful time to dig into a book and learn something new. It is also a great time to write and share from the riches of what's inside you! You are a reflection of Ahaw, the Sun! Share your light and the light you channel through you!

As you move through the 13 days of Ahaw, consider how the energy of the Sun can impact the energy of each day. For example: The 13th day of this trecena is Eb, the Path. Eb is about travel and about your path in life. So how can the energy of Ahaw impact the day Eb'? Well, it might be a great day to learn something new to help you on your path in life. It might also be a good day to learn about places you would like to travel to!

So, as you go through the trecena Ahaw, keep in mind that you are in the energy of the Sun! Allow illumination to permeate everything you do and see if by the end of the trecena you are noticing things feeling brighter, sunnier, and more illuminated!

Ahaw from the Chilam Balam

Hunahpu, The Sun God
Codex Style vase from Naranjo

Ahaw the Yellow Sun

Trecena Planner

Ahaw from the Grolier Codex

1 Ahaw the Yellow Sun - Day/Date:

_____
_____
_____
_____
_____
_____
_____

2 Imix the Red Crocodile – Day/Date:

_____
_____
_____
_____
_____
_____
_____

3 Ik the White Wind – Day/Date:

_____

_____

_____

_____

_____

_____

_____

4 Ak'bal the Blue Night – Day/Date:

_____

_____

_____

_____

_____

_____

_____

5 K'an the Yellow Seed – Day/Date:

_____

_____

_____

_____

_____

_____

_____

6 Chikchan the Red Serpent – Day/Date:

_____

_____

_____

_____

_____

_____

_____

7 Kimi the White World Bringer – Day/Date:

_____

_____

_____

_____

_____

_____

_____

8 Manik the Blue Deer - Day/Date:

_____

_____

_____

_____

_____

_____

9 Lamat the Yellow Star Flower - Day/Date:

_____

_____

_____

_____

_____

_____

_____

10 Muluk the Red Moon - Day/Date:

_____

_____

_____

_____

_____

_____

_____

11 Ok the White Dog - Day/Date:

_____

_____

_____

_____

_____

_____

_____

12 Chuwen the Blue Monkey - Day/Date:

_____

_____

_____

_____

_____

_____

_____

13 Eb' the Yellow Path - Day/Date:

_____

_____

_____

_____

_____

_____

_____

Glyphs from the Grolier Codex

1 Ahaw: Yellow Sun – Date:

Illumination and growth. The most powerful and positive nawal, radiating energy in all things. Its light not only lights up the day and the night (the moon is a reflection of the sun) but it also brings enlightenment and vision!

The Magical Wave energy of Jun, the number 1, is the power to attract!

Intention: I am attracting powerful and positive illumination

🦋 Today is a good day to:

Call in the 4 Directions

- Contact the dead
- Be brave against things that scare you
- Ask for illumination
- Build a house
- Start or continue projects
- Have a party
- Reflect on the positive things in life
- Place flowers on the graves of loved ones
- Seek spiritual illumination

Color & Direction: Nohol, the Yellow South
Ritual: The day ceremony is for Nohol which brings increase, abundance, and harvest. Consider doing this at sunrise or sunset today.
Energetic Power Places: Sunrise and sunset, find a beautiful view, especially on the beach or in a field of flowers
Amulet: Anything that shows the sun or flowers (especially yellow)
Element: Earth

Notes, Reflections, and Synchronicities:

_____

_____

_____

_____

_____

_____

_____

_____

2 Imix: Red Crocodile – Date:

Imix is a day of turbulent, stirring waters, of birth, new beginnings, and nurturing. It is a day of raw creative power. Because the crocodile lives in the mangroves, water lilies are associated with this day.

The Magical Wave number 2, Ka'a, is the power of opposing forces bringing balance. It is a quiet energy. A good time to make plans.

Intention: Opposing forces are working together bringing new, balanced beginnings in my life.

🦋 Today is a good day to:

- Ask for water/rain
- Start the day with grounding exercises and/or meditation
- Make sweeping changes and lay new foundations
- Stay aware of the tendency to take wild and unpredictable actions.
- Be creative
- Develop your powers of intuition
- Receive messages from beyond
- Cleanse yourself from negative energy
- Ask for the calming of mental issues, spiritual problems, climate change

Color & Direction: Lak'in, the Red East
Ritual: The wind is blowing from the east today, so the Day Ceremony for is Lak'in. Lak'in brings new beginnings, unity, and creation. During your Day Ceremony, you can ask for guidance as you align with this powerful energy of creation!
Power Places: Lakes, lagoons, and other in-land bodies of water
Amulet: Crocodile, lotus blossom, crystals and images associated with the sea.
Element: Fire

Notes, Reflections, and Synchronicities:

_____

_____

_____

_____

_____

_____

_____

_____

3 Ik: White Wind – Date:

The breath of life and creativity. It is also a day of air, heavy showers, and hurricanes. The wind can carry news, bring change, and inspire creativity. It is a day to use your voice and is good for communication and letting your "voice" be heard.

The Magical Wave Energy of 3, Oox, is about taking creative action. It is a lifting, rising energy.

Intention: I am taking creative action to express my authentic voice.

🦋 Today is a good day to:

- Use your voice, let your voice be heard.
- This is the best day for writing!
- Do something creative
- Cure respiratory illness
- Work on spiritual growth
- Go on a picnic or hike
- Do some gardening

Color & Direction: Xaman, the White North
Ritual: Burn pine or copal incense. This is the sacred day of stone alters. You can place stones around your altar or in a special place at home. Then perform the day ceremony for Xaman the North. Xaman brings transparency, clarity, and truth. During the day ceremony, you can ask for protection for friends and family and ask for protection against the rage of overly strong human emotions.
Energetic Power Places: Canyons, mountains, valleys, forests, and stone alters
Amulet: Hang wind chimes, a tree or branch, the beautiful quetzal bird
Element: Air

Notes, Reflections, and Synchronicities:

_____

_____

_____

_____

_____

_____

_____

_____

4 Ak'bal: Blue Night – Date:

Ak'bal is the night house, the underworld, and the realm of the eternal jaguar sun (the night sun). It is the darkness before the dawn. It is a day of good luck, especially in love! Ak'bal, the night, is generally, this is a tranquil and happy day.

The Magical Wave Energy of 4, Kan, is all about balance and stability.

Intention: I am finding stability as things come into the light.

🦋 Today's energy is good for:

- Declaring your love: This is a lucky day for love!
- Looking within to find answers.
- Seeking anything: jobs, lovers, friends, answers, knowledge
- Discovering the underlying causes of problems
- Face personal challenges with intuition rather than strength
- Ask for light to reach all things
- Acknowledge feelings from the heart
- Getting a fresh start or new beginning

Color & Direction: Chik'in, the Blue West
Ritual: Make a fire at dusk or dawn and ask for renewal. The Day Ceremony for today is Chik'in the West. Chik'in brings the energies or cooperation, duality, adjusting, and change. During your Day Ceremony, you can ask the energy of Chik'in to help you find the answers you are looking for.
Energetic Power Places: Caves, pyramids, mountains, and valleys especially at dusk and dawn.
Amulet/Totem: Jaguar, pyramid, the color black
Element: Water

Notes, Reflections, and Synchronicities:

_____

_____

_____

_____

_____

_____

_____

_____

5 K'an: Yellow Seed – Date:

A day of gathering, collecting, harvest, and abundance. An abundant harvest is indicated here. The meaning is also linked to the net that is traditionally used to gather the corn and can represent tangling or untangling.

Magical Wave Energy today is 5, Jo'o. This is the energy of empowerment. It is building and becoming stable.

Intention: I am empowered to bring in an abundant harvest!

🦋 Today is good for:

- Paying off debts
- Collecting things (even collecting your thoughts)
- Reaping the rewards of your work
- Piecing things together
- Do something associated with the interNET
- Witchy stuff (casting spells like one might cast a net)
- Disentangling things

Color & Direction: Nohol, the Yellow South
Element: Earth
Ritual: The Day Ceremony is Nohol, the south. Place seeds or yellow flowers around your candle. Nohol brings the energy of harvest, increase, and abundance! As you burn your candle, let it send prayers to the Heart of Sky and ask to be freed (untangled) from anything that prevents you from receiving the harvest you have worked for.
Energetic Power Places: The sea, farmer's fields, gardens
Amulet: Seeded jewelry or accessories, dream catcher (net).
Element: Earth

Notes, Reflections, and Synchronicities:

_____

_____

_____

_____

_____

_____

_____

_____

6 Chikchan: Red Feathered Serpent – Date:

The sky serpent, the cosmological snake, also known as Kukulkan. Chikchan is Framer and shaper of the Universe. This is an extremely powerful sign. It is the fire at the base of the spine, the Kundalini. It is associated with sexual magic and the rain gods. Key elements for this day: truth & justice.

The Magical Wave energy today is 6, or Wak in Yucatec Mayan. It is the energy of being in the flow. Let go of the riverbank and let the water take you where it will. You can trust it!

Intention: I am trusting the flow of truth, peace, and justice in my life.

Today is a good day to:

- Pursue or deliver truth and knowledge
- Deliver and receive justice
- Find or bring balance
- Pursue inner peace
- Enjoy great sex
- Take fast and direction action
- Beware of fast and direct action
- Stay on guard against anger in both yourself and others

Color & Direction: Lak'in, the Red East
Ritual: The Day Ceremony is Lak'in: unity, beginnings, and creation. This is a powerful day. It is a day to go to the mountains and commune with them. Light a fire and speak directly to the earth and ask for protection. You can also ask for justice, truth, peace, and balance.
Power Places: Mountains, volcanoes, pyramids, starry night
Amulet: Jade, snake, or pyramid—especially the one at Chichen Itza (where the temple of Kukulkan is). An especially powerful totem for today is a jade pyramid.
Element: Fire

Notes, Reflections, and Synchronicities:

_____

_____

_____

_____

_____

_____

_____

_____

7 Kimi: White World Bringer - Date:

The god of death and the lords of the underworld. Kimi is all about transformation and change. This usually applies to things like a job, relationship, living location, or some other part of your life that is in flux. Energies end and others begin. Change is an integral part of life and, if we harness it correctly, can keep moving us toward becoming more enlightened beings.

The Magical Wave is a 7, Uk in Mayan, today. Uk is the practical application of your mystical powers! It is the balanced and strong energy to channel!

Intention: I am channeling positive transformation.

🦋 Today is a good day to:

- A great day to make or think about changes
- End relationships (business, friendships, or romantic)
- Work towards tranquility among friends and colleagues, both living and dead
- Both give and ask for forgiveness
- Remember the dead
- Do up-keep on and take care of equipment
- A tranquil day to be patient and conservative in your energy

Color & Direction: Xaman, the White North
Ritual: The Day Ceremony today is for Xaman, the North who brings Transparency, clarity and truth. During your day ceremony you can give thanks to the ancestors who continue to give you guidance and ask for peace, love, money, health, and forgiveness.
Energetic Power Places: Pyramids, sacred sites, ceremonial sites, the fireplace, temples
Amulet: Skull, butterfly (transformation), corn seed, skeleton
Element: Air

Notes, Reflections, and Synchronicities:

_____

_____

_____

_____

_____

_____

_____

_____

8 Manik: Blue Deer ~ Date:

Balance, support, and the game of life. Manik is a very important day to focus on balance. Without balance, support cannot function properly. Think of the four legs of a table. If all the legs are different heights (unbalanced) how good is the table? Manik is the deer and the Lord of the hunt. It is a day to get into the game of life. You can think of hunting in our modern world as doing any activities that involve the pursuit of sustenance and strength. That makes Manik a good day for business. It is also a good day for long range travel. (Deer travel vast distances.)

The Magical Wave energy is 8, Waxak, today. Waxak is the most balanced energy and today is good for doing rituals and ceremonies. The energy of 8 brings harmony!

Intention: I am moving in harmony with the game of life!

Today is good for:

- Teamwork & meetings
- Business pursuits, getting out "in the field" and talking to customers
- Long range travel
- Staying alert for traps in business and the game of life
- An excellent day for diviners

Call in the 4 Directions

Color & Direction: Chik'in, the Blue West
Ritual: The Day Ceremony is for Chik'in, the West. Chik'in brings you duality, cooperation, and change. As you perform your Day Ceremony, consider asking Chik'in to bless your finances and business.
Energetic Power Places are forests, and fields (places where you might find deer)
Amulet: Anything to do with the deer, anything with the number 4 or four parts to it.
Element: Water

Notes, Reflections, and Synchronicities:

_____

_____

_____

_____

_____

_____

_____

_____

9 Lamat: Yellow Star Flower – Date:

Today is all about abundance and growing! It's a wonderful day to plant something, be it friendships, project ideas, or actual flowers. Lamat is also about fertility and is represented by the planet (star) Venus and the color gold.

The Magical Wave energy today is 9, Bolon in Mayan. Bolon is the divine feminine. It is the power to set intentions without limits! Think expansion and mastery!

Intention: I am planting and growing things with mastery!

Today is good for:

- Planting new things: flowers, friendships, projects
- Honoring past works
- Tending to your crops (in our modern times, that also means tending to business or whatever it is that sustains you)
- Star gazing (Lamat is also associated with Venus)
- Thinking about the Universe
- Feeding the world
- Fertility

Color: Yellow
Direction: Today the wind is blowing from the south. It brings harvest, abundance, and endings.
Ritual: The Day Ceremony today is Nohol, the South. Try placing some wildflowers, especially yellow ones, or seeds around your candle today.
Energetic Power Places today are forests, places where wildflowers grow, rivers and lakes
Amulet: Flowers (especially yellow ones), stars, or Venus
Element: Earth

Notes, Reflections, and Synchronicities:

_____

_____

_____

_____

_____

_____

_____

10 Muluk: Red Moon – Date:

A day to make payments, give offerings, and ask for dark things to come to light. Muluk is also about emotions and using your intuition. This is a day of cycles, rhythms and water since water is intrinsically connected to the moon.

The Magical Wave energy of 10, Lajun in Mayan, rules this day. Lajun is the power to manifest! It is the crest of the wave, the highest point before it becomes to strong to control as it rushes up onto shore.

Intention: I am manifesting great intuition today!

🦋 Today is good for:

- Paying off debts (financial, relational, societal, spiritual)
- Asking people to pay you back for their debts to you
- Working to end suffering
- Giving offerings to the earth
- Asking for rain
- Asking for dark things to come to light
- Pay attention to your dreams
- Use your intuition

Color & Direction: Lak'in the Red East
Ritual: The day ceremony for today is Lak'in the East. You can also cleanse your candles and other alter items under the moon today.
Energetic Power Places today are the beach, big rocks, oceans, rivers, and lakes
Amulets: Shark or whale or other large aquatic creature, jade, the moon
Element: Fire

Notes, Reflections, and Synchronicities:

_____

_____

_____

_____

_____

_____

_____

_____

_____

11 Ok: White Dog – Date:

The one who guides the night sun through the underworld. Ok is about guidance and protection. Your guides are with you today in a powerful way to guide you through the underworld. This is also a day about justice and truth. On the lighter side, Ok is the most sexually charged day of the Nawales.

The Magical Wave energy that wants to work with you today is 11, Buluk in Mayan. Buluk is the time to let go! The wave has crested and broken. The energy is too strong to control!

Intention: I am letting go so guidance can come.

🦋 Today is good for:

- Asking for guidance
- Giving guidance
- Short distance travel (like around your town)
- Being alert for dangers/update home security
- Having great sex
- Looking for hidden truth

Color & Direction: Xaman, the White North.
Element: Air
Ritual: The Day Ceremony for today is for Xaman, the North. Consider asking the energy of Xaman to guide you today. Xaman brings transparency, clarity, and truth.
Energetic Power Places today are mountains and beaches. If you don't live near these places, try a watching a video with beautiful scenery to add a little nature energy to your day.
Amulets: Anything related to dogs
Element: Air

Notes, Reflections, and Synchronicities:

_____

_____

_____

_____

_____

_____

_____

_____

12 Chuwen: Blue Monkey – Date:

The great craftsman, patron of the arts, the thread of that symbolizes destiny and maintains the continuity the past, the present, and the future. Monkey is all about being creative and having fun! It is a highly positive day that is full of energy that is friendly and happy!

The Magical Wave energy of Lajka'a, the number 12, is here to work with you today. Lajka'a is about understanding. The energy has run off on its own and its time to understand what it has become!

Intention: I know how to party!

🦋 Today is good for:

- Partying and celebrating
- Dancing, singing, writing, painting
- Getting married
- Studying the sacred calendar
- Taking time to look for patterns in life
- Starting projects
- Watch for synchronicities today!

Color & Direction: Chik'in the Blue/Black West
Ritual: This is a great day for burning incense, especially copal or frankincense. The Day Ceremony for today is Chik'in, the West.
Element: Water
Energetic Power Places where the energy is strong today are lakes and forests.
Amulet: Try wearing something woven today, especially a cloth wrist band or bracelet or something made from woven threads. Something that reminds you of monkeys.
Element: Water

Notes, Reflections, and Synchronicities:

_____
_____
_____
_____
_____
_____
_____
_____

13 Eb: Yellow Path – Date:

Travel and destiny...your path in life. It's a wonderful day for travel or to consider what you like or don't like about your path in life and how to change it. This day can also be about following the path of the sacred calendar. It is a day when the ancestors are ready to listen.

The Magical Wave energy today is Ooxlajun, the number 13. It is transcendence! The cosmic wild card. It is a day for magic if you are strong enough to control this wild energy!

Intention: I am discovering transcendence as I walk my path!

🦋 Today is good for:

- Travel or making plans to travel
- Spending time considering your path in life
- Making changes in your path in life
- Starting a new business or making a business plan
- Asking for good luck in both spiritual and material pursuits
- Being careful of dangers along the way

Color & Direction: Nohol, the Yellow South
Ritual: The Day Ceremony for today is Nohol, the south. Nohol bring abundance, increase, and harvest!
Energetic Power Places: Mountains and Woods and paths, especially ancient ones.
Amulets: Good amulets for today are pyramid, ladder, tooth (there is a tooth in the glyph to remind you to be careful of dangers along the road), compass or globe. Anything else that you associate with travel or your path in life.
Element: Earth

Notes, Reflections, and Synchronicities:

_____

_____

_____

_____

_____

_____

_____

_____

_____

Thoughts About this Past Trecena

_____

_____

_____

_____

_____

_____

_____

_____

_____

_____

_____

_____

_____

_____

_____

_____

_____

_____

_____

_____

_____

_____

_____

_____

_____

_____

_____

_____

_____

_____

_____

_____

What to Expect During the Trecena Ben

Focus: What would you like to bring tremendous growth to during the next 13 days?

Ben is the corn plant, shooting up after the rain. It is not the seed of the corn, but rather the stalk. It is the tall green shoot rising out of the earth with vigor, strength, and power. The stalk symbolizes the ceremonial staff or rod of power used by the Maya spiritual leader. It is the rod of divinity and the fire of the kundalini rising up the spine!

Wow! That is a lot of strength and power and you can expect it to be with you for the next 13 days, underlying the energy of every day. This is a time of tremendous growth, abundance, and harvest. It is a good time to start new projects, plant seeds, cultivate friendships, and focus on personal growth.

As you move through this trecena, consider how each day's energy comes into play in the light of the Corn Stalk. For example: Etz'nab is the day of the knife. It's a good day for pruning. So, you could do some editing if your project involves writing or you could do some pruning of your project involves gardening, or you could let go of a belief that does not serve you if you are focusing on personal growth. Take some time today to look over the days of this coming trecena to get an overview of the energies and make some plans on fun ways to work with them!

Young Maize God found on A structure in Copan

122

Hunaphu,
the Maize
god, plate

Ben the Red Corn Stalk

Trecena Planner

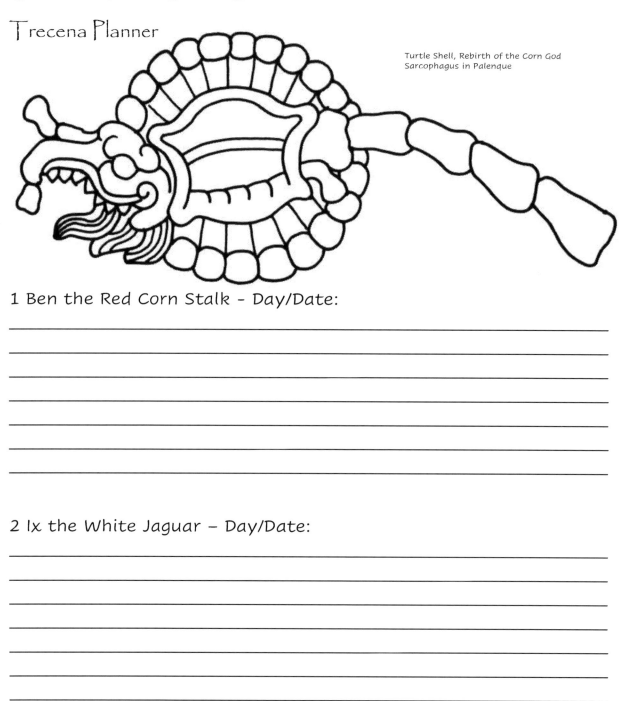

Turtle Shell, Rebirth of the Corn God
Sarcophagus in Palenque

1 Ben the Red Corn Stalk - Day/Date:

_____

_____

_____

_____

_____

_____

_____

2 Ix the White Jaguar – Day/Date:

_____

_____

_____

_____

_____

_____

_____

3 Men the Blue Eagle – Day/Date:

_____

_____

_____

_____

_____

_____

_____

_____

4 Kib the Yellow Owl – Day/Date:

_____

_____

_____

_____

_____

_____

_____

5 Kaban the Red Earth – Day/Date:

_____

_____

_____

_____

_____

_____

_____

6 Etz'nab the White Knife – Day/Date:

_____

_____

_____

_____

_____

_____

_____

7 Kawak the Blue Storm – Day/Date:

_____

_____

_____

_____

_____

_____

_____

8 Ahaw the Yellow Sun - Day/Date:

_____

_____

_____

_____

_____

_____

_____

9 Imix the Red Crocodile - Day/Date:

_____

_____

_____

_____

_____

_____

_____

10 Ik the White Wind - Day/Date:

_____

_____

_____

_____

_____

_____

_____

11 Ak'bal the Blue Night - Day/Date:

_____

_____

_____

_____

_____

_____

12 K'an the Yellow Seed - Day/Date:

_____

_____

_____

_____

_____

_____

_____

13 Chikchan the Red Serpent - Day/Date:

_____

_____

_____

_____

_____

_____

_____

Personified flower pulling a
Corn stalk into his shell.
Tablet in Palenque

1 Ben: Red Corn Stalk – Date:

Ben is the rod of virtues of divine power! It is the corn stalk and is associated with harvest and success! The energy is both growing & surging upward like corn stalks after a heavy rain. It is a very meaningful day, associated with triumph! ALSO, the staff (stalk) symbolizes the spine and the internal fire which moves upward and activates the secret powers. (I love this stuff!)

The Magical Wave is the energy of Jun, the number 1. It is strong because it is the first day of the trecena and brings the power of attracting.

Intention: I am attracting harvest and success!

Call in the 4 Directions

🦋 Today is a good day to:

- Plant a seed or start a project
- Spend time with family or friends
- Follow your intuition and listen to your dreams
- Ask the ancestors for help in teaching and caretaking
- Study and investigate things
- Ask for rain and growth

Color & Direction: Lak'in the Red East
Ritual: The day ceremony for today is Lak'in the East. Consider requesting help from the ancestors in caring for your home and family or ask for help in starting a new business or project or help with your finances.
Amulet: Carry with you or wear small seeds (especially corn seeds), a small stone (used for grinding corn) ... hahaha....you will like the next one....whisky, bourbon, or rum. . .also sugar, and yellow clothes or jewelry.
Energetic Power Places: fields, meadows, forests, beaches
Element: Fire

Notes, Reflections, and Synchronicities:

_____

_____

_____

_____

_____

_____

_____

_____

2 Ix: White Jaguar ~ Date:

Ix (pronounced *Ish*) is feminine energy and all things related to the earth, strength, and vitality. Think of the qualities of a jaguar. They are stealthy, strong, and hunt at night. This energy is powerful and wise and is related to the goddess Ixchel.

The Magical Wave energy of Ka'a, the number 2, rules this day. It is quiet and its gift is the power of polarizing. This is two opposites in perfect balance. We need both rain and sun.

Intention: I am finding balance as I walk in harmony with the Earth.

Today is a good day to:

- Meditate on the Earth as our home and how to live in harmony with Her.
- Use magic powers
- Take care of your home, especially by getting rid of things that no longer serve you.
- Use feminine energy
- Get pregnant
- Hunt for things such as knowledge, truth, wisdom
- Any ecological projects

Color & Direction: Xaman, the White North.
Ritual: The Day Ceremony is for Xaman, the North. Xaman brings transparency, clarity, and truth. After asking this energy to work with you today, give thanks to the ancestors for all things related to the earth. Consider placing some treasures from the earth around your candle today.
Energetic Power Places: Ceremonial places (especially the pyramids), forests, and mountains (high places)
Amulet: Jaguar, pyramid, or something with a jaguar or spotted design.
Element: Air

Notes, Reflections, and Synchronicities:

_____

_____

_____

_____

_____

_____

_____

_____

3 Men: Blue Eagle – Date:

Men the eagle is all about flying high, ambition, and vision. This is a day of good fortune, a day of freedom and of spiritual advancement! It is also about financial advancement. Men is the day of business, merchants, and money. So, this is also the day to dream big and reach for the sky in regard to your business ideas and dreams.

The Magical Wave energy of Oox is the action of the number 3. Its gift is the power of creative energy to benefit all. It is a quiet, rising energy.

Intention: I am taking creative energy in business and projects to benefit myself and others.

This is a good day to:

- Communicate with Heart of Sky, the creator god
- Ask for money for buying things
- Consider the big picture
- Focus on goals and consider how to best meet them
- Pursue goals that have already been set
- Spiritual elevation
- Work on self-improvement

Color & Direction: Chik'in, the Blue West
Ritual: The Day Ceremony is Chik'in the West. Chik'in brings cooperation, duality, and change. This is a very important day for a sacrificial ritual to give thanks for money. The required offering is CHOCOLATE! Simply thank the gods and your ancestors for providing material goods and money, offer them some chocolate. When you finish, then eat it!
Energetic Power Places: Mountains, lakes, misty places, upland forests
Amulet: Bird feathers, dream catchers, anything with a bird, eagle, or quetzal on it
Element: Water

Notes, Reflections, and Synchronicities:

_____

_____

_____

_____

_____

_____

_____

_____

4 Kib: Yellow Owl – Date:

Kib, the warrior owl, is all about taking it easy, relaxation, patience, and timing. The warrior is careful in his timing. He is patient, not rushed. Like the warrior, today is about choosing your timing carefully. This day is also about the illusion of the material world. The night birds Today is a very spiritual day, indeed!

The Magical Wave energy is a level 4 today and is called Kan in Mayan. It is the power of energy taking form and stabilizing. It finds perfect balance in support.

Intention: The ability to relax and go with the flow is taking form in my life today.

🦋 This is a good day to:

- Go with the flow
- Relax
- Commune with the ancestors
- Wash your clothes, especially your good clothes
- Be a spiritual guide
- Ask for forgiveness for ignoring moral teachings
- This is a very special day to spend time preventing mistakes
- Kib is not a good day to start a new project because the energy is low.

Color & Direction: Nohol, the Yellow South
Ritual: The day ceremony is for Nohol which brings increase, abundance, and harvest. Consider taking time to commune with your ancestors during your Day Ceremony today.
Energetic Power Places: Mountains, volcanoes, tropical forests, lakes
Amulet: The earth, any rocks or crystals
Element: Earth

Notes, Reflections, and Synchronicities:

_____

_____

_____

_____

_____

_____

_____

_____

5 Kaban: Red Earth – Date:

Kaban, the earth is the energy of thoughts, logic, ideas, and science. It is movement and sweeping change. Kaban is the earthquake: A day of formidable power and wisdom, a day of shaking the foundations and sudden revelations

The Magical Wave energy of Jo'o is the number 5 and is all about empowerment!

Intention: I am empowered by wisdom.

🦋 Today is good for:

- Thinking creativity
- Working with others
- Scientific investigation
- Being connected to the earth
- Coming into agreement with the creator
- Movement, travel
- Travel on the spiritual plane
- Shaking things up/sudden revelation/revelations that shake your foundations

Color & Direction: Lak'in, the Red East
Ritual: The Day Ceremony is for Lak'in. Lak'in bring the energy of beginnings, creation, and unity. As you ask Lak'in to work with you today, consider adding some rocks or crystals to your altar space.
Energetic Power Places: Mountains, volcanoes, tropical forests, lakes
Amulet: The earth, any rocks or crystals
Element: Fire

Notes, Reflections, and Synchronicities:

_____
_____
_____
_____
_____
_____
_____
_____

6 Etz'nab: White Knife – Date:

The obsidian sacrificial blade. A day to cut to the core of things. This is a day to reduce, clean out, and cleanse. Its energy is also about healing because the knife can both cut and heal. The obsidian blade is shined to the point of reflection and so the energy of the mirror also comes into play today.

The Magical Wave energy of Wak, the number 6, rules this day. It is all about going with the flow. Let go of the riverbank and let the energy take you where it wants to!

Intention: I am in the flow of removing things from my life that do not serve me.

🦋 Today is a good day to:

- Clean out your closet
- Do some editing (writing, song writing)
- Sort things out
- End an unproductive relationship
- Have a sale
- Let go of the past
- Diagnose and cure illness (physical, mental, and spiritual)
- Make predictions about the future

NOTE: Today is not a good day for travel or to start something new.

Color & Direction: Xaman, the White North.
Ritual: The Day Ceremony is for Xaman, the North. Xaman brings transparency, clarity, and truth. Today is a good day to make up for things you neglected to do or should not have done and to receive forgiveness. You can also ask for protection from disease and accidents. No other ceremonies are performed on a knife day.
Energetic Power Places: Pyramids, cliffs, waterfalls, lightning storms
Amulet: Obsidian stone, jade, a knife, a pyramid (the glyph has a pyramid on it) or a mirror
Element: Air

Notes, Reflections, and Synchronicities:

_____

_____

_____

_____

_____

_____

_____

_____

7 Kawak: Blue Storm – Date:

Storm is the Nawal of women and strength. It is the lightening flash of inspiration, the warmth and safety of the home, and the cleansing and purification of the rain. Imagine what it feels like to run inside as a storm approaches. That is the energy of Kawak. The rage of the wind and the comfort of home and the care of the woman who wraps loved ones in her arms.

The Magical Wave energy is a 7, Uk, and it is all about attunement and mystical alignment. Its gift is the power of the practical application of your mystical powers!

Intention: I am in mystical alignment with strength and inspiration.

Today is a good day to:

- Tend to your family and home
- Do volunteer work
- Use your authority
- Ask for the actions of your enemies to turn against them
- Be prepared for trouble
- Heal mental illness
- Receive flashes of inspiration

Color & Direction: Chik'in, the Blue West
Ritual: The Day Ceremony is Chik'in the West. Chik'in brings cooperation, duality and change. As you ask the energy of Chik'in to work with you today, you can also give thanks for the women in your life.
Energetic Power Places: Pine and cypress forests
Amulet: Storm cloud, lightening, Mayan goddess, or pyramid
Element: Water

Notes, Reflections, and Synchronicities:

_____

_____

_____

_____

_____

_____

_____

_____

8 Ahaw: Yellow Sun ~ Date:

Illumination and growth. The most powerful and positive nawal, radiating energy in all things. Its light not only lights up the day and the night (the moon is a reflection of the sun) but it also brings enlightenment and vision!

The Magical Wave energy of Wak, the number 8, is the power of harmonizing. It is demonstrating balance and integrity and its gift is the ability to harmonize with all parts of your authentic self!

Intention: I am channeling illumination

🦋 Today is a good day to:

Call in the 4 Directions

- Contact the dead
- Be brave against things that scare you
- Ask for illumination
- Build a house
- Start or continue projects
- Have a party
- Reflect on the positive things in life
- Place flowers on the graves of loved ones
- Seek spiritual illumination

Color & Direction: Nohol, the Yellow South
Ritual: The day ceremony is for Nohol which brings increase, abundance, and harvest. Consider doing this at sunrise or sunset today.
Energetic Power Places: Sunrise and sunset, find a beautiful view, especially on the beach or in a field of flowers
Amulet: Anything that shows the sun or flowers (especially yellow)
Element: Earth

Notes, Reflections, and Synchronicities:

_____

_____

_____

_____

_____

_____

_____

_____

9 Imix: Red Crocodile – Date:

Imix is a day of turbulent, stirring waters, of birth, new beginnings, and nurturing. It is a day of raw creative power. Because the crocodile lives in the mangroves, water lilies are associated with this day.

The Magical Wave number 9, or Bolon in Mayan, is the divine feminine. Its gift is the power of mastery and expansion.

Intention: I am expanding into and mastering the energy for new beginnings.

🦋 Today is a good day to:

- Ask for water/rain
- Start the day with grounding exercises and/or meditation
- Make sweeping changes and lay new foundations
- Stay aware of the tendency to take wild and unpredictable actions.
- Be creative
- Develop your powers of intuition
- Receive messages from beyond
- Cleanse yourself from negative energy
- Ask for the calming of mental issues, spiritual problems, climate change

Color & Direction: Lak'in, the Red East
Ritual: The wind is blowing from the east today, so the Day Ceremony for is Lak'in. Lak'in brings new beginnings, unity, and creation. During your Day Ceremony, you can ask for guidance as you align with this powerful energy of creation!
Power Places: Lakes, lagoons, and other in-land bodies of water
Amulet: Crocodile, lotus blossom, crystals and images associated with the sea.
Element: Fire

Notes, Reflections, and Synchronicities:

_____

_____

_____

_____

_____

_____

_____

_____

10 Ik: White Wind – Date:

The breath of life and creativity. It is also a day of air, heavy showers, and hurricanes. The wind can carry news, bring change, and inspire creativity. It is a day to use your voice and is good for communication and letting your "voice" be heard.

The Magical Wave Energy of 10, Lajun, is that of manifesting! This is point where the wave is at its peak, cresting, breaking. This is perfect, motivation, and power

Intention: I am manifesting the power of life and creativity!

Today is a good day to:

- Use your voice, let your voice be heard.
- This is the best day for writing!
- Do something creative
- Cure respiratory illness
- Work on spiritual growth
- Go on a picnic or hike
- Do some gardening

Color & Direction: Xaman, the White North
Ritual: Burn pine or copal incense. This is the sacred day of stone alters. You can place stones around your altar or in a special place at home. Then perform the day ceremony for Xaman the North. Xaman brings transparency, clarity, and truth. During the day ceremony, you can ask for protection for friends and family and ask for protection against the rage of overly strong human emotions.
Energetic Power Places: Canyons, mountains, valleys, forests, and stone alters
Amulet: Hang wind chimes, a tree or branch, the beautiful quetzal bird
Element: Air

Notes, Reflections, and Synchronicities:

_____

_____

_____

_____

_____

_____

_____

# 11 Ak'bal: Blue Night – Date:

Ak'bal is the night house, the underworld, and the realm of the eternal jaguar sun (the night sun). It is the darkness before the dawn. It is a day of good luck, especially in love! Ak'bal, the night, is generally, this is a tranquil and happy day.

The Magical Wave Energy of 11, Buluk, is the gift of letting go.

Intention: I am letting go so revelation can come to me.

🦋 Today's energy is good for:

- Declaring your love: This is a lucky day for love!
- Looking within to find answers.
- Seeking anything: jobs, lovers, friends, answers, knowledge
- Discovering the underlying causes of problems
- Face personal challenges with intuition rather than strength
- Ask for light to reach all things
- Acknowledge feelings from the heart
- Getting a fresh start or new beginning

Color & Direction: Chik'in, the Blue West
Ritual: Make a fire at dusk or dawn and ask for renewal. The Day Ceremony for today is Chik'in the West. Chik'in brings the energies or cooperation, duality, adjusting, and change. During your Day Ceremony, you can ask the energy of Chik'in to help you find the answers you are looking for.
Energetic Power Places: Caves, pyramids, mountains, and valleys especially at dusk and dawn.
Amulet/Totem: Jaguar, pyramid, the color black
Element: Water

Notes, Reflections, and Synchronicities:

_____

_____

_____

_____

_____

_____

_____

_____

12 K'an: Yellow Seed ~ Date:

A day of gathering, collecting, harvest, and abundance. An abundant harvest is indicated here. The meaning is also linked to the net that is traditionally used to gather the corn and can represent tangling or untangling.

Magical Wave Energy is Lajka'a, the number 12. It is the crystalizing energy of universalizing. It's a time to stand back and understand what is and what has become.

Intention: I understand what I need to know about harvesting and collecting.

🦋 Today is good for:

- Paying off debts
- Collecting things (even collecting your thoughts)
- Reaping the rewards of your work
- Piecing things together
- Do something associated with the interNET
- Witchy stuff (casting spells like one might cast a net)
- Disentangling things

Color & Direction: Nohol, the Yellow South
Element: Earth
Ritual: The Day Ceremony is Nohol, the south. Place seeds or yellow flowers around your candle. Nohol brings the energy of harvest, increase, and abundance! As you burn your candle, let it send prayers to the Heart of Sky and ask to be freed (untangled) from anything that prevents you from receiving the harvest you have worked for.
Energetic Power Places: The sea, farmer's fields, gardens
Amulet: Seeded jewelry or accessories, dream catcher (net).
Element: Earth

Notes, Reflections, and Synchronicities:

_____

_____

_____

_____

_____

_____

_____

_____

13 Chikchan: Red Feathered Serpent – Date:

The sky serpent, the cosmological snake, also known as Kukulkan. Chikchan is Framer and Shaper of the Universe. This is an extremely powerful sign. It is the fire at the base of the spine, the Kundalini. It is associated with sexual magic and the rain gods. Key elements for this day are truth and justice.

The Magical Wave energy today is a 13, Ooxlajun. Its gift is the power of transcendence. This is the cosmic wild card, the place of synchronicities and magic!

Intention: Magical synchronicities are putting my heart at ease.

🦋 Today is a good day to:

- Pursue or deliver truth and knowledge
- Deliver and receive justice
- Find or bring balance
- Pursue inner peace
- Enjoy great sex
- Take fast and direction action
- Beware of fast and direct action
- Stay on guard against anger in both yourself and others

Color & Direction: Lak'in, the Red East
Ritual: The Day Ceremony is Lak'in: unity, beginnings, and creation. This is a powerful day. It is a day to go to the mountains and commune with them. Light a fire and speak directly to the earth and ask for protection. You can also ask for justice, truth, peace, and balance.
Power Places: Mountains, volcanoes, pyramids, starry night
Amulet: Jade, snake, or pyramid—especially the one at Chichen Itza (where the temple of Kukulkan is). An especially powerful totem for today is a jade pyramid.
Element: Fire

Notes, Reflections, and Synchronicities:

_____

_____

_____

_____

_____

_____

_____

_____

_____

Thoughts About this Past Trecena

_____

_____

_____

_____

_____

_____

_____

_____

_____

_____

_____

_____

_____

_____

_____

_____

_____

_____

_____

_____

_____

_____

_____

_____

_____

_____

_____

_____

_____

What to Expect During Kimi

Focus: What do you want to transform over the next 13 days?

Kimi is the day of Death. That being said, it is nothing to fear, for the death of one thing means there is space for the birth of another. Perhaps you would prefer to think of this as the day of change. It is this cycle of birth, death, and birth that keeps us moving through life, growing and evolving. If there were no transformation, life would quickly become very stale.

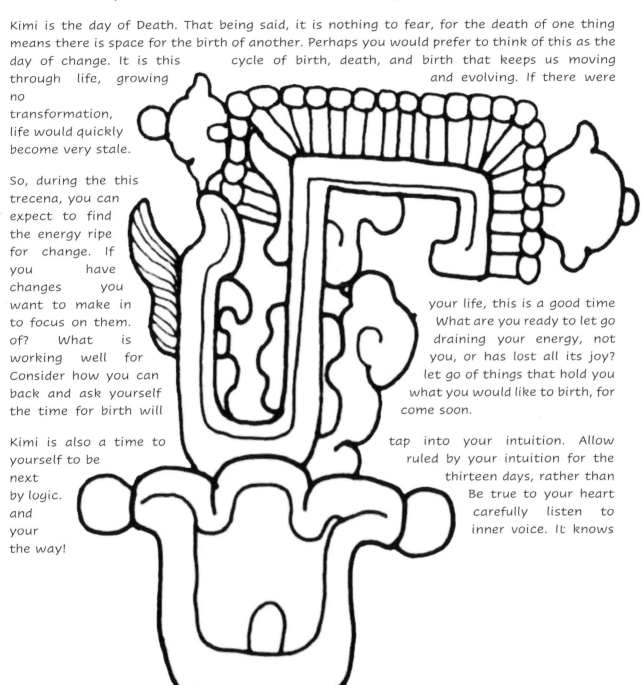

So, during the this trecena, you can expect to find the energy ripe for change. If you have changes you want to make in to focus on them. of? What is working well for Consider how you can back and ask yourself the time for birth will

your life, this is a good time What are you ready to let go draining your energy, not you, or has lost all its joy? let go of things that hold you what you would like to birth, for come soon.

Kimi is also a time to yourself to be next by logic. and your the way!

tap into your intuition. Allow ruled by your intuition for the thirteen days, rather than Be true to your heart carefully listen to inner voice. It knows

White flower associated with death, Palenque

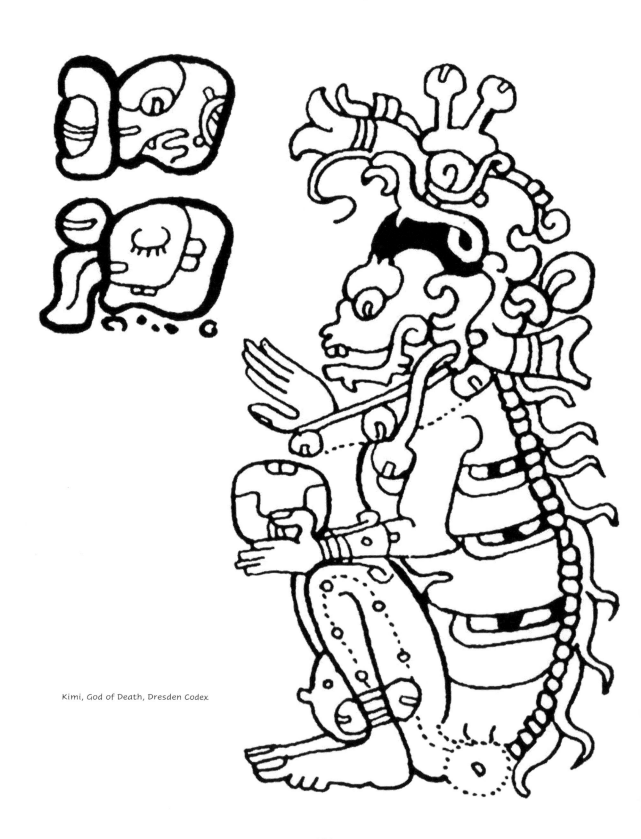

Kimi, God of Death, Dresden Codex

Kimi the White World Bringer
Trecena Planner

White flower, Palenque

1 Kimi the White World Bringer - Day/Date:

_____
_____
_____
_____
_____
_____
_____

2 Manik the Blue Deer – Day/Date:

_____
_____
_____
_____
_____
_____

3 Lamat the Yellow Seed – Day/Date:

_____

_____

_____

_____

_____

_____

_____

4 Muluk the Red Moon – Day/Date:

_____

_____

_____

_____

_____

_____

_____

5 Ok the White Dog – Day/Date:

_____

_____

_____

_____

_____

_____

_____

6 Chuwen the Blue Monkey – Day/Date:

_____
_____
_____
_____
_____
_____
_____
_____

7 Eb' the Yellow Path – Day/Date:

_____
_____
_____
_____
_____
_____
_____
_____

8 Ben the Red Corn Stalk - Day/Date:

_____
_____
_____
_____
_____
_____
_____

9 Ix the White Jaguar - Day/Date:

_____

_____

_____

_____

_____

_____

_____

10 Men the Blue Eagle - Day/Date:

_____

_____

_____

_____

_____

_____

_____

11 Kib the Yellow Owl - Day/Date:

_____

_____

_____

_____

_____

_____

_____

12 Kaban the Red Earth - Day/Date:

_____
_____
_____
_____
_____
_____
_____

13 Etz'nab the White Knife - Day/Date:

_____
_____
_____
_____
_____
_____

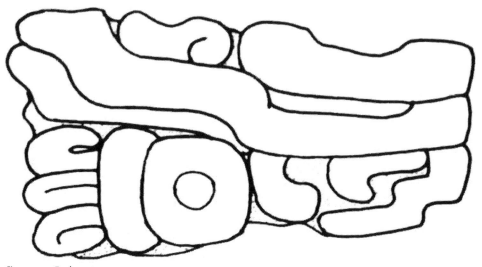

White death flower, Palenque

1 Kimi: White World Bringer – Date:

The god of death and the lords of the underworld. Kimi is all about transformation and change. This usually applies to things like a job, relationship, living location, or some other part of your life that is in flux. Energies end and others begin. Change is an integral part of life and, if we harness it correctly, can keep moving us toward becoming more enlightened beings.

The Magical Wave is Jun, the energy of one, today. Jun is a strong and balanced energy because it is the beginning. It is magnetic, purposeful, and attracting.

Intention: I am attracting transformation for the purpose of moving forward.

🦋 Today is a good day to:

Call in the 4 Directions

- A great day to make or think about changes
- End relationships (business, friendships, or romantic)
- Work towards tranquility among friends and colleagues, both living and dead
- Both give and ask for forgiveness
- Remember the dead
- Do up-keep on and take care of equipment
- A tranquil day to be patient and conservative in your energy

Color & Direction: Xaman, the White North
Ritual: The Day Ceremony today is for Xaman, the North who brings Transparency, clarity and truth. During your day ceremony you can give thanks to the ancestors who continue to give you guidance and ask for peace, love, money, health, and forgiveness.
Energetic Power Places: Pyramids, sacred sites, ceremonial sites, the fireplace, temples
Amulet: Skull, butterfly (transformation), corn seed, skeleton
Element: Air

Notes, Reflections, and Synchronicities:

_____

_____

_____

_____

_____

_____

_____

2 Manik: Blue Deer – Date:

Balance, support, and the game of life. Manik is a very important day to focus on balance. Without balance, support cannot function properly. Think of the four legs of a table. If all the legs are different heights (unbalanced) how good is the table? Manik is the deer and the Lord of the hunt. It is a day to get into the game of life. You can think of hunting in our modern world as doing any activities that involve the pursuit of sustenance and strength. That makes Manik a good day for business. It is also a good day for long range travel. (Deer travel vast distances.)

The Magical Wave energy is that of Ka'a, duality and the number 2. Its gift is the power of opposing forces bringing balance. Today is a balanced day with a balanced energy!

Intention: I am finding balance in opposing forces today.

🦋 Today is good for:

- Teamwork & meetings
- Business pursuits, getting out "in the field" and talking to customers
- Long range travel
- Staying alert for traps in business and the game of life
- An excellent day for diviners

Color & Direction: Chik'in, the Blue West
Ritual: The Day Ceremony is for Chik'in, the West. Chik'in brings you duality, cooperation, and change. As you perform your Day Ceremony, consider asking Chik'in to bless your finances and business.
Energetic Power Places are forests, and fields (places where you might find deer)
Amulet: Anything to do with the deer, anything with the number 4 or four parts to it.
Element: Water

Notes, Reflections, and Synchronicities:

_____

_____

_____

_____

_____

_____

_____

3 Lamat: Yellow Star Flower – Date:

Today is all about abundance and growing! It's a wonderful day to plant something, be it friendships, project ideas, or actual flowers. Lamat is also about fertility and is represented by the planet (star) Venus and the color gold.

The Magical Wave energy today is at a 3, Oox in Mayan. This is the energy of taking creative action.

Intention: I am taking creative action to grow wonderful things!

Today is good for:

- Planting new things: flowers, friendships, projects
- Honoring past works
- Tending to your crops (in our modern times, that also means tending to business or whatever it is that sustains you)
- Star gazing (Lamat is also associated with Venus)
- Thinking about the Universe
- Feeding the world
- Fertility

Color: Yellow
Direction: Today the wind is blowing from the south. It brings harvest, abundance, and endings.
Ritual: The Day Ceremony today is Nohol, the South. Try placing some wildflowers, especially yellow ones, or seeds around your candle today.
Energetic Power Places today are forests, places where wildflowers grow, rivers and lakes
Amulet: Flowers (especially yellow ones), stars, or Venus
Element: Earth

Notes, Reflections, and Synchronicities:

_____

_____

_____

_____

_____

_____

_____

_____

4 Muluk: Red Moon – Date:

A day to make payments, give offerings, and ask for dark things to come to light. Muluk is also about emotions and using your intuition. This is a day of cycles, rhythms and water since water is intrinsically connected to the moon.

The Magical Wave energy of Kan, the number 4, rules this day. Kan is all about things taking form, finding balance, and becoming stable.

Intention: I am understanding my intuition and finding stability as I use it.

Today is good for:

- Paying off debts (financial, relational, societal, spiritual)
- Asking people to pay you back for their debts to you
- Working to end suffering
- Giving offerings to the earth
- Asking for rain
- Asking for dark things to come to light
- Pay attention to your dreams
- Use your intuition

Color & Direction: Lak'in the Red East
Ritual: The day ceremony for today is Lak'in the East. You can also cleanse your candles and other alter items under the moon today.
Energetic Power Places today are the beach, big rocks, oceans, rivers, and lakes
Amulets: Shark or whale or other large aquatic creature, jade, the moon
Element: Fire

Notes, Reflections, and Synchronicities:

_____

_____

_____

_____

_____

_____

_____

_____

_____

_____

5 Ok: White Dog ~ Date:

The one who guides the night sun through the underworld. Ok is about guidance and protection. Your guides are with you today in a powerful way to guide you through the underworld. This is also a day about justice and truth. On the lighter side, Ok is the most sexually charged day of the Nawales.

The Magical Wave energy that wants to work with you today is Jo'o, the number 5. Jo'o is the energy of empowerment. The wave is strengthening and beginning to stabilize.

Intention: I am empowered and guided.

Today is good for:

- Asking for guidance
- Giving guidance
- Short distance travel (like around your town)
- Being alert for dangers/update home security
- Having great sex
- Looking for hidden truth

Color & Direction: Xaman, the White North.
Element: Air
Ritual: The Day Ceremony for today is for Xaman, the North. Consider asking the energy of Xaman to guide you today. Xaman brings transparency, clarity and truth.
Energetic Power Places today are mountains and beaches. If you don't live near these places, try a watching a video with beautiful scenery to add a little nature energy to your day.
Amulets: Anything related to dogs
Element: Air

Notes, Reflections, and Synchronicities:

_____

_____

_____

_____

_____

_____

_____

_____

6 Chuwen: Blue Monkey – Date:

The great craftsman, patron of the arts, the thread of that symbolizes destiny and maintains the continuity the past, the present, and the future. Monkey is all about being creative and having fun! It is a highly positive day that is full of energy that is friendly and happy!

The Magical Wave energy of 6, Wak in Mayan, is here to work with you today. Wak is all about getting in the flow and letting go of control. Trust that the energy will take you where you need to go!

Intention: I am in the flow of creativity and fun!

🦋 Today is good for:

- Partying and celebrating
- Dancing, singing, writing, painting
- Getting married
- Studying the sacred calendar
- Taking time to look for patterns in life
- Starting projects
- Watch for synchronicities today!

Color & Direction: Chik'in the Blue/Black West
Ritual: This is a great day for burning incense, especially copal or frankincense. The Day Ceremony for today is Chik'in, the West.
Element: Water
Energetic Power Places where the energy is strong today are lakes and forests.
Amulet: Try wearing something woven today, especially a cloth wrist band or bracelet or something made from woven threads. Something that reminds you of monkeys.
Element: Water

Notes, Reflections, and Synchronicities:

_____

_____

_____

_____

_____

_____

_____

_____

7 Eb: Yellow Path – Date:

Travel and destiny...your path in life. This is a great day to travel or to consider what direction you want to go in life. This day can also be about following the path of the sacred calendar. It is a day when the ancestors are ready to listen.

The Magical Wave energy today is Ku, the number 7. Its gift is the practical application of your mystical powers! Think about channeling, my dear!

Intention: I am aligned with my path in life.

Today is good for:

- Travel or making plans to travel
- Spending time considering your path in life
- Making changes in your path in life
- Starting a new business or making a business plan
- Asking for good luck in both spiritual and material pursuits
- Being careful of dangers along the way

Color & Direction: Nohol, the Yellow South
Ritual: The Day Ceremony for today is Nohol, the south. Nohol bring abundance, increase and harvest!
Energetic Power Places: Mountains and Woods and paths, especially ancient ones.
Amulets: Good amulets for today are pyramid, ladder, tooth (there is a tooth in the glyph to remind you to be careful of dangers along the road), compass or globe. Anything else that you associate with travel or your path in life.
Element: Earth

Notes, Reflections, and Synchronicities:

_____

_____

_____

_____

_____

_____

_____

_____

8 Ben: Red Corn Stalk – Date:

Ben is the rod of virtues of divine power! It is the corn stalk and is associated with harvest and success! The energy is both growing & surging upward like corn stalks after a heavy rain. It is a very meaningful day, associated with triumph! ALSO, the staff (stalk) symbolizes the spine and the internal fire which moves upward and activates the secret powers. (I love this stuff!)

The Magical Wave is the energy of Waxak is the number 8. Waxak is the most balanced place on the wave. It is strong and stable and is all about being in harmony!

Intention: I am in harmony with harvest and success!

Today is a good day to:

Call in the 4 Directions

- Plant a seed or start a project
- Spend time with family or friends
- Follow your intuition and listen to your dreams
- Ask the ancestors for help in teaching and caretaking
- Study and investigate things
- Ask for rain and growth

Color & Direction: Lak'in the Red East
Ritual: The day ceremony for today is Lak'in the East. Consider requesting help from the ancestors in caring for your home and family or ask for help in starting a new business or project or help with your finances.
Amulet: Carry with you or wear small seeds (especially corn seeds), a small stone (used for grinding corn), whisky, bourbon, or rum. . .also sugar, and yellow clothes or jewelry.
Energetic Power Places: fields, meadows, forests, beaches
Element: Fire

Notes, Reflections, and Synchronicities:

_____

_____

_____

_____

_____

_____

_____

_____

9 Ix: White Jaguar – Date:

Ix (pronounced *Ish*) is feminine energy and all things related to the earth, strength, and vitality. Think of the qualities of a jaguar. They are stealthy, strong, and hunt at night. This energy is powerful and wise and is related to the goddess Ixchel.

The Magical Wave energy of Bolon, the number 9, rules this day. It is the divine feminine and is about expansion and mastery.

Intention: I am mastering working with the powerful and wise energy of Mother earth.

🦋 Today is a good day to:

- Meditate on the Earth as our home and how-to live-in harmony with Her.
- Use magic powers
- Take care of your home, especially by getting rid of things that no longer serve you.
- Use feminine energy
- Get pregnant
- Hunt for things such as knowledge, truth, wisdom
- Any ecological projects

Color & Direction: Xaman, the White North.
Ritual: The Day Ceremony is for Xaman, the North. Xaman brings transparency, clarity and truth. After asking this energy to work with you today, give thanks to the ancestors for all things related to the earth. Consider placing some treasures from the earth around your candle today.
Energetic Power Places: Ceremonial places (especially the pyramids), forests, and mountains (high places)
Amulet: Jaguar, pyramid, or something with a jaguar or spotted design.
Element: Air

Notes, Reflections, and Synchronicities:

_____

_____

_____

_____

_____

_____

_____

_____

10 Men: Blue Eagle – Date:

Men the eagle is all about flying high, ambition, and vision. This is a day of Men the eagle is all about flying high, ambition, and vision. This is a day of good fortune, a day of freedom and of spiritual advancement! It is also about financial advancement. Men is the day of business, merchants, and money. So, this is also the day to dream big and reach for the sky in regard to your business ideas and dreams.

The Magical Wave energy of Lajun is the number 10. It is the power of manifestation!

Intention: I am manifesting vision!

This is a good day to:

- Communicate with Heart of Sky, the creator god
- Ask for money for buying things
- Consider the big picture
- Focus on goals and consider how to best meet them
- Pursue goals that have already been set
- Spiritual elevation
- Work on self-improvement

Color & Direction: Chik'in, the Blue West
Ritual: The Day Ceremony is Chik'in the West. Chik'in brings cooperation, duality, and change. This is a very important day for a sacrificial ritual to give thanks for money. The required offering is CHOCOLATE! Simply thank the gods and your ancestors for providing material goods and money, offer them some chocolate. When you finish, then eat it!
Energetic Power Places: Mountains, lakes, misty places, upland forests
Amulet: Bird feathers, dream catchers, anything with a bird, eagle, or quetzal on it
Element: Water

Notes, Reflections, and Synchronicities:

_____

_____

_____

_____

_____

_____

_____

_____

11 Kib: Yellow Owl – Date:

Kib, the warrior owl, is all about taking it easy, relaxation, patience, and timing. The warrior is careful in his timing. He is patient, not rushed. Like the warrior, today is about choosing your timing carefully. This day is also about the illusion of the material world. The night birds Today is a very spiritual day, indeed!

The Magical Wave energy is a level 11 today and is called Buluk in Mayan. It is about letting go! The wave has crested and broken and can no longer be controlled.

Intention: I am letting go and allowing myself to just be.

This is a good day to:

- Go with the flow
- Relax
- Commune with the ancestors
- Wash your clothes, especially your good clothes
- Be a spiritual guide
- Ask for forgiveness for ignoring moral teachings
- This is a very special day to spend time preventing mistakes
- Kib is not a good day to start a new project because the energy is low.

Color & Direction: Nohol, the Yellow South
Ritual: The day ceremony is for Nohol which brings increase, abundance, and harvest. Consider taking time to commune with your ancestors during your Day Ceremony today.
Energetic Power Places: Mountains, volcanoes, tropical forests, lakes
Amulet: The earth, any rocks or crystals
Element: Earth

Notes, Reflections, and Synchronicities:

_____
_____
_____
_____
_____
_____
_____
_____

12 Kaban: Red Earth – Date:

Kaban, the earth is the energy of thoughts, logic, ideas, and science. It is movement and sweeping change. Kaban is the earthquake: A day of formidable power and wisdom, a day of shaking the foundations and sudden revelations

The Magical Wave energy of Lajka'a is the number 12 and is all about understanding. You have created something, let go of control, and now you can observe and understand it!

Intention: I am gaining understanding as grand ideas flow to me.

🦋 Today is good for:

- Thinking creativity
- Working with others
- Scientific investigation
- Being connected to the earth
- Coming into agreement with the creator
- Movement, travel
- Travel on the spiritual plane
- Shaking things up/sudden revelation/revelations that shake your foundations

Color & Direction: Lak'in, the Red East
Ritual: The Day Ceremony is for Lak'in. Lak'in bring the energy of beginnings, creation, and unity. As you ask Lak'in to work with you today, consider adding some rocks or crystals to your altar space.
Energetic Power Places: Mountains, volcanoes, tropical forests, lakes
Amulet: The earth, any rocks or crystals
Element: Fire

Notes, Reflections, and Synchronicities:

_____

_____

_____

_____

_____

_____

_____

_____

13 Etznab: White Knife – Date:

The obsidian sacrificial blade. A day to cut to the core of things. This is a day to reduce, clean out, and cleanse. Its energy is also about healing because the knife can both cut and heal. The obsidian blade is shined to the point of reflection and so the energy of the mirror also comes into play today.

The Magical Wave energy of Ooxlajun, the number 13, rules this day. It is transcendence, the cosmic wild card! It is a day of chaos when anything is possible. Will you use its magic?

Intention: I am embracing transcendence as I cleanse my life!

Today is a good day to:

- Clean out your closet
- Do some editing (writing, song writing)
- Sort things out
- End an unproductive relationship
- Have a sale
- Let go of the past
- Diagnose and cure illness (physical, mental, and spiritual)
- Make predictions about the future

NOTE: Today is not a good day for travel or to start something new.

Color & Direction: Xaman, the White North.
Ritual: The Day Ceremony is for Xaman, the North. Xaman brings transparency, clarity and truth. Today is a good day to make up for things you neglected to do or should not have done and to receive forgiveness. You can also ask for protection from disease and accidents. No other ceremonies are performed on a knife day.
Energetic Power Places: Pyramids, cliffs, waterfalls, lightning storms
Amulet: Obsidian stone, jade, a knife, a pyramid (the glyph has a pyramid on it) or a mirror
Element: Air

Notes, Reflections, and Synchronicities:

_____

_____

_____

_____

_____

_____

_____

Thoughts About this Past Trecena

_____

_____

_____

_____

_____

_____

_____

_____

_____

_____

_____

_____

_____

_____

_____

_____

_____

_____

_____

_____

_____

_____

_____

_____

_____

_____

What to Expect During Kawak

Focus: How do you want to embrace the comforts of home during the next 13 days?

Kawak is the raging storm. But don't worry. That doesn't mean this trecena will be filled with raging energy. Think of what it feels like when a storm is coming. Everything becomes still and then the temperature drops and the wind whips up. You feel a rush of energy, wild and enticing. And as the first raindrops begin to fall, what do you do? You run for safety. You run inside and feel the warmth and welcome of the arms of your home or whatever sanctuary you have found. That is the energy of Kawak. It is both the exhilaration and the feeling of protection, the embrace of your haven. Expect this trecena to bring you the opportunity to find yourself enjoying the comforts of home. Take time to thank the people in your life who help make this possible. This is the perfect time to work on creating a welcoming feeling in your home. During Kawak, the energy of nesting is with you. You can make use of it by rearranging furniture and art in your house and paying attention to color schemes and creating lovely fragrances. You can add

incense to your daily routine and cook the yummiest food you can think of. Each day's energy will have something specific you can do to bring the energy of Kawak into your life in a deeper way. On Ak'bal, the night, focus on your bedroom or on soft nighttime lighting or candles. On Kan, the seed, think about flowers or plants you might want to add to your home! What a fun and comforting way to spend your days during this trecena!

A Mosaic Mirror found in the temple to Chac, the Rain god.

Kawak the Blue Storm

Trecena Planner

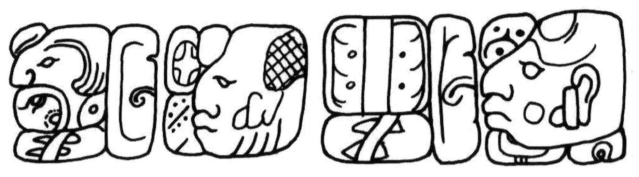

Glyphs from the Grolier Codex

1 Kawak the Blue Storm - Day/Date:

_____
_____
_____
_____
_____
_____
_____

2 Ahaw the Yellow Sun – Day/Date:

_____
_____
_____
_____
_____
_____
_____

3 Imix the Red Crocodile – Day/Date:

_____

_____

_____

_____

_____

_____

_____

4 Ik the White Wind – Day/Date:

_____

_____

_____

_____

_____

_____

_____

5 Ak'bal the Blue Night – Day/Date:

_____

_____

_____

_____

_____

_____

_____

6 K'an the Yellow Seed – Day/Date:

_____

_____

_____

_____

_____

_____

_____

7 Chikchan the Red Feathered Serpent – Day/Date:

_____

_____

_____

_____

_____

_____

_____

8 Kimi the White World Bringer - Day/Date:

_____

_____

_____

_____

_____

_____

_____

9 Manik the Blue Deer - Day/Date:

_____

_____

_____

_____

_____

_____

_____

_____

10 Lamat the Yellow Star Flower - Day/Date:

_____

_____

_____

_____

_____

_____

_____

_____

11 Muluk the Red Moon - Day/Date:

_____

_____

_____

_____

_____

_____

_____

_____

12 Ok the White Dog - Day/Date:

_____

_____

_____

_____

_____

_____

_____

13 Chuwen the Blue Monkey - Day/Date:

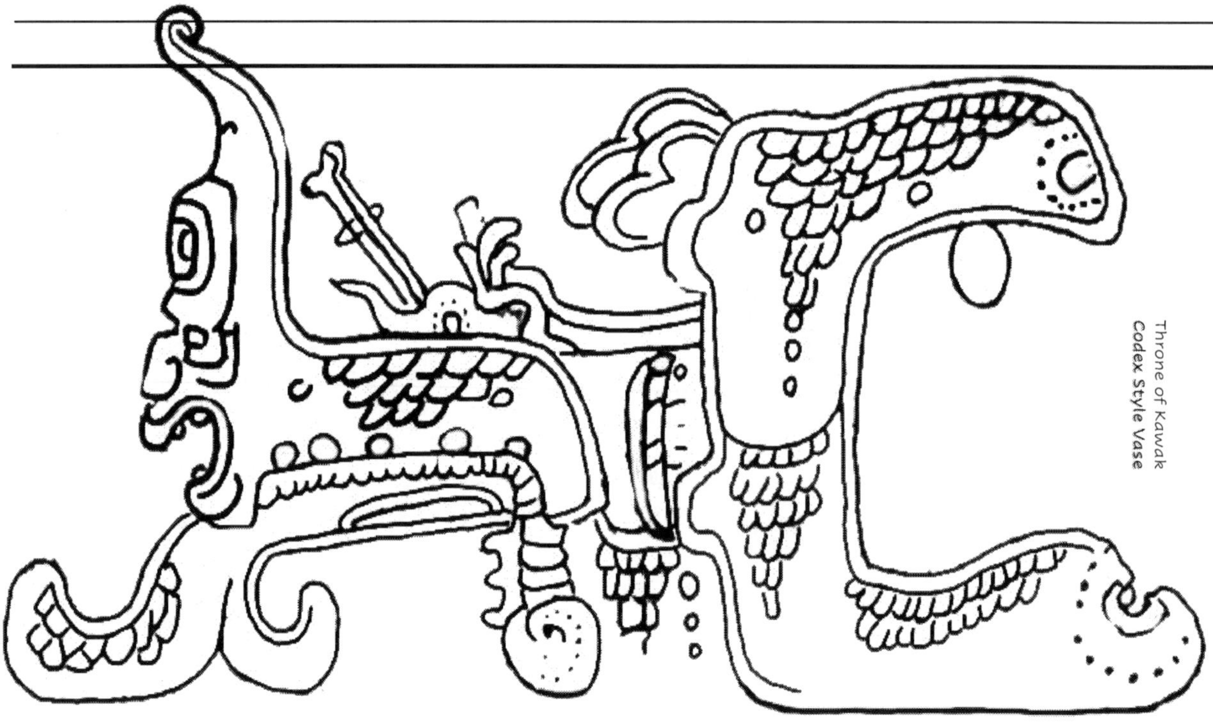

_____

_____

_____

_____

_____

Throne of Kawak
Codex Style Vase

1 Kawak: Blue Storm – Date:

Storm is the Nawal of women and strength. It is the lightening flash of inspiration, the warmth and safety of the home, and the cleansing and purification of the rain. Imagine what it feels like to run inside as a storm approaches. That is the energy of Kawak. The rage of the wind and the comfort of home and the care of the woman who wraps loved ones in her arms.

The Magical Wave energy of Jun, the number 1, is with you today. One is a powerful energy. It is all about unity and attracting. It is magnetic!

Intention: I am attracting strength and inspiration.

Call in the 4 Directions

🦋 Today is a good day to:

- Tend to your family and home
- Do volunteer work
- Use your authority
- Ask for the actions of your enemies to turn against them
- Be prepared for trouble
- Heal mental illness
- Receive flashes of inspiration

Color & Direction: Chik'in, the Blue West
Ritual: The Day Ceremony is Chik'in the West. Chik'in brings cooperation, duality and change. As you ask the energy of Chik'in to work with you today, you can also give thanks for the women in your life.
Energetic Power Places: Pine and cypress forests
Amulet: Storm cloud, lightening, Mayan goddess, or pyramid
Element: Water

Notes, Reflections, and Synchronicities:

_____

_____

_____

_____

_____

_____

_____

2 Ahaw: Yellow Sun – Date:

Illumination and growth. The most powerful and positive nawal, radiating energy in all things. Its light not only lights up the day and the night (the moon is a reflection of the sun) but it also brings enlightenment and vision!

The Magical Wave energy of Ka'a, the number 2, is the power of opposing forces bringing balance. Day and night, sun and rain, male and female. All life is about working in balance.

Intention: I am allowing the dual forces in my life to bring illumination

Today is a good day to:

- Contact the dead
- Be brave against things that scare you
- Ask for illumination
- Build a house
- Start or continue projects
- Have a party
- Reflect on the positive things in life
- Place flowers on the graves of loved ones
- Seek spiritual illumination

Color & Direction: Nohol, the Yellow South
Ritual: The day ceremony is for Nohol which brings increase, abundance, and harvest. Consider doing this at sunrise or sunset today.
Energetic Power Places: Sunrise and sunset, find a beautiful view, especially on the beach or in a field of flowers
Amulet: Anything that shows the sun or flowers (especially yellow)
Element: Earth

Notes, Reflections, and Synchronicities:

_____

_____

_____

_____

_____

_____

_____

3 Imix: Red Crocodile – Date:

Imix is a day of turbulent, stirring waters, of birth, new beginnings, and nurturing. It is a day of raw creative power. Because the crocodile lives in the mangroves, water lilies are associated with this day.

The Magical Wave number 3, Oox, carries the energy of creative action. It is lifting, rising and in benefit to all.

Intention: I am taking creative action to start something new!

🦋 **Today is a good day to:**

- Ask for water/rain
- Start the day with grounding exercises and/or meditation
- Make sweeping changes and lay new foundations
- Stay aware of the tendency to take wild and unpredictable actions.
- Be creative
- Develop your powers of intuition
- Receive messages from beyond
- Cleanse yourself from negative energy
- Ask for the calming of mental issues, spiritual problems, climate change

Color & Direction: Lak'in, the Red East
Ritual: The wind is blowing from the east today, so the Day Ceremony for is Lak'in. Lak'in brings new beginnings, unity, and creation. During your Day Ceremony, you can ask for guidance as you align with this powerful energy of creation!
Power Places: Lakes, lagoons, and other in-land bodies of water
Amulet: Crocodile, lotus blossom, crystals and images associated with the sea.
Element: Fire

Notes, Reflections, and Synchronicities:

_____

_____

_____

_____

_____

_____

_____

_____

4 Ik: White Wind – Date:

The breath of life and creativity. It is also a day of air, heavy showers, and hurricanes. The wind can carry news, bring change, and inspire creativity. It is a day to use your voice and is good for communication and letting your "voice" be heard.

The Magical Wave Energy of Kan, the number 4, is about taking form and finding stability. It is a defining energy and is rising and gentle.

Intention: The breath of life and creativity are taking form and finding balance in my life!

Today is a good day to:

- Use your voice, let your voice be heard.
- This is the best day for writing!
- Do something creative
- Cure respiratory illness
- Work on spiritual growth
- Go on a picnic or hike
- Do some gardening

Color & Direction: Xaman, the White North
Ritual: Burn pine or copal incense. This is the sacred day of stone alters. You can place stones around your altar or in a special place at home. Then perform the day ceremony for Xaman the North. Xaman brings transparency, clarity, and truth. During the day ceremony, you can ask for protection for friends and family and ask for protection against the rage of overly strong human emotions.
Energetic Power Places: Canyons, mountains, valleys, forests, and stone alters
Amulet: Hang wind chimes, a tree or branch, the beautiful quetzal bird
Element: Air

Notes, Reflections, and Synchronicities:

_____

_____

_____

_____

_____

_____

_____

_____

April 20 2021

5 Ak'bal: Blue Night ~ Date:

Ak'bal is the night house, the underworld, and the realm of the eternal jaguar sun (the night sun). It is the darkness before the dawn. It is a day of good luck, especially in love! Ak'bal, the night, is generally, this is a tranquil and happy day.

The Magical Wave Energy of 5, Jo'o, is the power to look at your creation and take delight in it. It is empowering!

Intention: I am empowered as things come out of the darkness and into the light.

🦋 Today's energy is good for:

- Declaring your love: This is a lucky day for love!
- Looking within to find answers.
- Seeking anything: jobs, lovers, friends, answers, knowledge
- Discovering the underlying causes of problems
- Face personal challenges with intuition rather than strength
- Ask for light to reach all things
- Acknowledge feelings from the heart
- Getting a fresh start or new beginning

Color & Direction: Chik'in, the Blue West
Ritual: Make a fire at dusk or dawn and ask for renewal. The Day Ceremony for today is Chik'in the West. Chik'in brings the energies or cooperation, duality, adjusting, and change. During your Day Ceremony, you can ask the energy of Chik'in to help you find the answers you are looking for.
Energetic Power Places: Caves, pyramids, mountains, and valleys especially at dusk and dawn.
Amulet/Totem: Jaguar, pyramid, the color black
Element: Water

Notes, Reflections, and Synchronicities:

_____

_____

_____

_____

_____

_____

_____

6 K'an: Yellow Seed ~ Date:

A day of gathering, collecting, harvest, and abundance. An abundant harvest is indicated here. The meaning is also linked to the net that is traditionally used to gather the corn and can represent tangling or untangling.

Magical Wave Energy today is 6, Wak in Mayan. This is the energy of being in the flow. It is rhythmic and organized and is the power to move forward.

Intention: I am flowing and moving forward with the energy of harvest!

🦋 Today is good for:

- Paying off debts
- Collecting things (even collecting your thoughts)
- Reaping the rewards of your work
- Piecing things together
- Do something associated with the interNET
- Witchy stuff (casting spells like one might cast a net)
- Disentangling things

Color & Direction: Nohol, the Yellow South
Element: Earth
Ritual: The Day Ceremony is Nohol, the south. Place seeds or yellow flowers around your candle. Nohol brings the energy of harvest, increase, and abundance! As you burn your candle, let it send prayers to the Heart of Sky and ask to be freed (untangled) from anything that prevents you from receiving the harvest you have worked for.
Energetic Power Places: The sea, farmer's fields, gardens
Amulet: Seeded jewelry or accessories, dream catcher (net).
Element: Earth

Notes, Reflections, and Synchronicities:

_____

_____

_____

_____

_____

_____

_____

_____

7 Chikchan: Red Feathered Serpent – Date:

The sky serpent, the cosmological snake, also known as Kukulkan. Chikchan is Framer and shaper of the Universe. This is an extremely powerful sign. It is the fire at the base of the spine, the Kundalini. It is associated with sexual magic and the rain gods. Key elements for this day are truth and justice.

The Magical Wave energy today is Uk, the number 7. The gift of Uk is the practical application of your mystical powers! It is inspiring, balanced, and in alignment!

Intention: I am in alignment with wisdom.

🦋 Today is a good day to:

- Pursue or deliver truth and knowledge
- Deliver and receive justice
- Find or bring balance
- Pursue inner peace
- Enjoy great sex
- Take fast and direction action
- Beware of fast and direct action
- Stay on guard against anger in both yourself and others

Color & Direction: Lak'in, the Red East
Ritual: The Day Ceremony is Lak'in: unity, beginnings, and creation. This is a powerful day. It is a day to go to the mountains and commune with them. Light a fire and speak directly to the earth and ask for protection. You can also ask for justice, truth, peace, and balance.
Power Places: Mountains, volcanoes, pyramids, starry night
Amulet: Jade, snake, or pyramid—especially the one at Chichen Itza (where the temple of Kukulkan is). An especially powerful totem for today is a jade pyramid.
Element: Fire

Notes, Reflections, and Synchronicities:

_____

_____

_____

_____

_____

_____

_____

_____

8 Kimi: White World Bringer – Date:

The god of death and the lords of the underworld. Kimi is all about transformation and change. This usually applies to things like a job, relationship, living location, or some other part of your life that is in flux. Energies end and others begin. Change is an integral part of life and, if we harness it correctly, can keep moving us toward becoming more enlightened beings.

The Magical Wave is an 8 today. Waxak (8) is the gift of harmonizing with integrity all parts of your true self!

Intention: I am moving in harmony with transformation as it benefits my true self.

Call in the 4 Directions

Today is a good day to:

- A great day to make or think about changes
- End relationships (business, friendships, or romantic)
- Work towards tranquility among friends and colleagues, both living and dead
- Both give and ask for forgiveness
- Remember the dead
- Do up-keep on and take care of equipment
- A tranquil day to be patient and conservative in your energy

Color & Direction: Xaman, the White North
Ritual: The Day Ceremony today is for Xaman, the North who brings Transparency, clarity and truth. During your day ceremony you can give thanks to the ancestors who continue to give you guidance and ask for peace, love, money, health, and forgiveness.
Energetic Power Places: Pyramids, sacred sites, ceremonial sites, the fireplace, temples
Amulet: Skull, butterfly (transformation), corn seed, skeleton
Element: Air

Notes, Reflections, and Synchronicities:

_____

_____

_____

_____

_____

_____

_____

_____

9 Manik: Blue Deer – Date:

Balance, support, and the game of life. Manik is a very important day to focus on balance. Without balance, support cannot function properly. Think of the four legs of a table. If all the legs are different heights (unbalanced) how good is the table? Manik is the deer and the Lord of the hunt. It is a day to get into the game of life. You can think of hunting in our modern world as doing any activities that involve the pursuit of sustenance and strength. That makes Manik a good day for business. It is also a good day for long range travel. (Deer travel vast distances.)

The Magical Wave energy is a 9 today. Nine, Bolon in Mayan, is the divine feminine. It is about walking in mastery.

Intention: I am mastering balance.

Today is good for:

- Teamwork & meetings
- Business pursuits, getting out "in the field" and talking to customers
- Long range travel
- Staying alert for traps in business and the game of life
- An excellent day for diviners

Color & Direction: Chik'in, the Blue West
Ritual: The Day Ceremony is for Chik'in, the West. Chik'in brings you duality, cooperation, and change. As you perform your Day Ceremony, consider asking Chik'in to bless your finances and business.
Energetic Power Places are forests, and fields (places where you might find deer)
Amulet: Anything to do with the deer, anything with the number 4 or four parts to it.
Element: Water

Notes, Reflections, and Synchronicities:

_____

_____

_____

_____

_____

_____

_____

_____

 ## 10 Lamat: Yellow Star Flower – Date:

Today is all about abundance and growing! It's a wonderful day to plant something, be it friendships, project ideas, or actual flowers. Lamat is also about fertility and is represented by the planet (star) Venus and the color gold.

The Magical Wave energy today is Lajun, the power of ten. It is the peak of the wave and is the git of manifestation!

Intention: I am in manifesting the ability to grow beautiful things.

Today is good for:

- Planting new things: flowers, friendships, projects
- Honoring past works
- Tending to your crops (in our modern times, that also means tending to business or whatever it is that sustains you)
- Star gazing (Lamat is also associated with Venus)
- Thinking about the Universe
- Feeding the world
- Fertility

Color: Yellow
Direction: Today the wind is blowing from the south. It brings harvest, abundance, and endings.
Ritual: The Day Ceremony today is Nohol, the South. Try placing some wildflowers, especially yellow ones, or seeds around your candle today.
Energetic Power Places today are forests, places where wildflowers grow, rivers and lakes
Amulet: Flowers (especially yellow ones), stars, or Venus
Element: Earth

Notes, Reflections, and Synchronicities:

_____

_____

_____

_____

_____

_____

_____

_____

11 Muluk: Red Moon - Date:

A day to make payments, give offerings, and ask for dark things to come to light. Muluk is also about emotions and using your intuition. This is a day of cycles, rhythms and water since water is intrinsically connected to the moon.

The Magical Wave energy of 11, Buluk, rules this day. Buluk is the point of letting go. The wave has crested and become too powerful for you to control!

Intention: I am letting go and allowing my intuition to have its way!

🦋 Today is good for:

- Paying off debts (financial, relational, societal, spiritual)
- Asking people to pay you back for their debts to you
- Working to end suffering
- Giving offerings to the earth
- Asking for rain
- Asking for dark things to come to light
- Pay attention to your dreams
- Use your intuition

Color & Direction: Lak'in the Red East
Ritual: The day ceremony for today is Lak'in the East. You can also cleanse your candles and other alter items under the moon today.
Energetic Power Places today are the beach, big rocks, oceans, rivers, and lakes
Amulets: Shark or whale or other large aquatic creature, jade, the moon
Element: Fire

Notes, Reflections, and Synchronicities:

_____

_____

_____

_____

_____

_____

_____

_____

_____

12 Ok: White Dog – Date:

The one who guides the night sun through the underworld. Ok is about guidance and protection. Your guides are with you today in a powerful way to guide you through the underworld. This is also a day about justice and truth. On the lighter side, Ok is the most sexually charged day of the Nawales.

The Magical Wave energy that wants to work with you today is 12, which is Lajka'a in Mayan. Lajka'a is the power of crystalizing. It is the point when understanding comes!

Intention: Guidance is now becoming crystal clear to me.

🦋 Today is good for:

- Asking for guidance
- Giving guidance
- Short distance travel (like around your town)
- Being alert for dangers/update home security
- Having great sex
- Looking for hidden truth

Color & Direction: Xaman, the White North.
Element: Air
Ritual: The Day Ceremony for today is for Xaman, the North. Consider asking the energy of Xaman to guide you today. Xaman brings transparency, clarity and truth.
Energetic Power Places today are mountains and beaches. If you don't live near these places, try a watching a video with beautiful scenery to add a little nature energy to your day.
Amulets: Anything related to dogs
Element: Air

Notes, Reflections, and Synchronicities:

_____

_____

_____

_____

_____

_____

_____

13 Chuwen: Blue Monkey – Date:

The great craftsman, patron of the arts, the thread of that symbolizes destiny and maintains the continuity the past, the present, and the future. Monkey is all about being creative and having fun! It is a highly positive day that is full of energy that is friendly and happy!

The Magical Wave energy of 13 is here to work with you today. Ooxlajun is the power of transcendence! It is the cosmic wild card, chaos, the point where everything is up in the air. Expect synchronicities and magic today!

Intention: I am finding transcendence in creativity and fun today!

🦋 Today is good for:

- Partying and celebrating
- Dancing, singing, writing, painting
- Getting married
- Studying the sacred calendar
- Taking time to look for patterns in life
- Starting projects
- Watch for synchronicities today!

Color & Direction: Chik'in the Blue/Black West
Ritual: This is a great day for burning incense, especially copal or frankincense. The Day Ceremony for today is Chik'in, the West.
Element: Water
Energetic Power Places where the energy is strong today are lakes and forests.
Amulet: Try wearing something woven today, especially a cloth wrist band or bracelet or something made from woven threads. Something that reminds you of monkeys.
Element: Water

Notes, Reflections, and Synchronicities:

_____

_____

_____

_____

_____

_____

_____

_____

Thoughts About this Past Trecena

Maize God, Subterranean Vault, Palenque

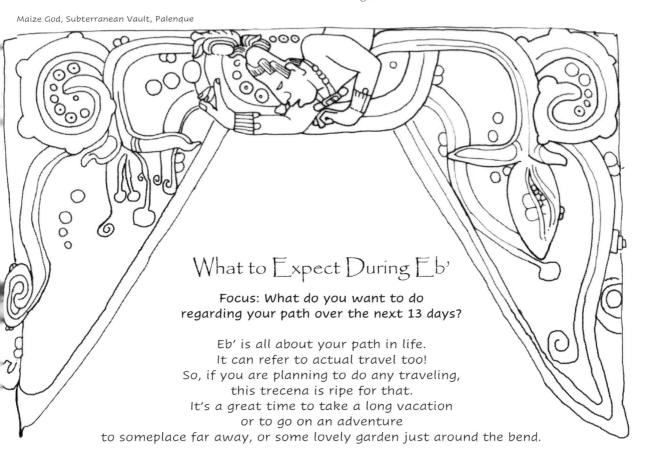

What to Expect During Eb'

Focus: What do you want to do
regarding your path over the next 13 days?

Eb' is all about your path in life.
It can refer to actual travel too!
So, if you are planning to do any traveling,
this trecena is ripe for that.
It's a great time to take a long vacation
or to go on an adventure
to someplace far away, or some lovely garden just around the bend.

Your path in life is something you work out as you move through time and space. It is something to consider carefully and to check in with yourself often to see how you are doing. So, expect things to come up during Eb' that will help you reflect on your life's direction and/or give you opportunities to make adjustments or refinements to the direction you are walking in this world.

The energy is strong now for re-evaluating your hopes and dreams. Perhaps you made a plan and are moving in a way that you thought you wanted, but as Eb' begins to unfold, it comes to you that you don't really love what you are doing in life. Now is the time to ask yourself questions and do some self-exploration about this manner. What do you want in life? What experiences will benefit both you and those around you? Are there things you want to let go of or things you want to add?

Take some time during the next 13 days to explore your path in life. After all, it is vital. When someone who is Maya greets you by saying, "Bix a bel?" they are asking you, "How is your path?"

The Vision Serpent: Lid of a Cache Vessel

Eb' the Yellow Path

Trecena Planner

Glyphs from the Grolier Codex

1 Eb' the Yellow Path - Day/Date:

_____

_____

_____

_____

_____

_____

_____

2 Ben the Red Corn Stalk – Day/Date:

_____

_____

_____

_____

_____

_____

3 Ix the White Jaguar – Day/Date:

_____

_____

_____

_____

_____

_____

_____

4 Men the Blue Eagle – Day/Date:

_____

_____

_____

_____

_____

_____

_____

5 Kib the Yellow Owl – Day/Date:

_____

_____

_____

_____

_____

_____

_____

6 Kaban the Red Earth – Day/Date:

_____

_____

_____

_____

_____

_____

_____

7 Etz'nab the White Knife – Day/Date:

_____

_____

_____

_____

_____

_____

_____

8 Kawak the Blue Storm - Day/Date:

_____

_____

_____

_____

_____

_____

_____

9 Ahaw the Yellow Sun - Day/Date:

_____

_____

_____

_____

_____

_____

_____

10 Imix the Red Crocodile - Day/Date:

_____

_____

_____

_____

_____

_____

_____

11 Ik the White Wind - Day/Date:

_____

_____

_____

_____

_____

_____

_____

12 Ak'bal the Blue Night - Day/Date:

_____

_____

_____

_____

_____

_____

_____

13 K'an the Yellow Seed - Day/Date:

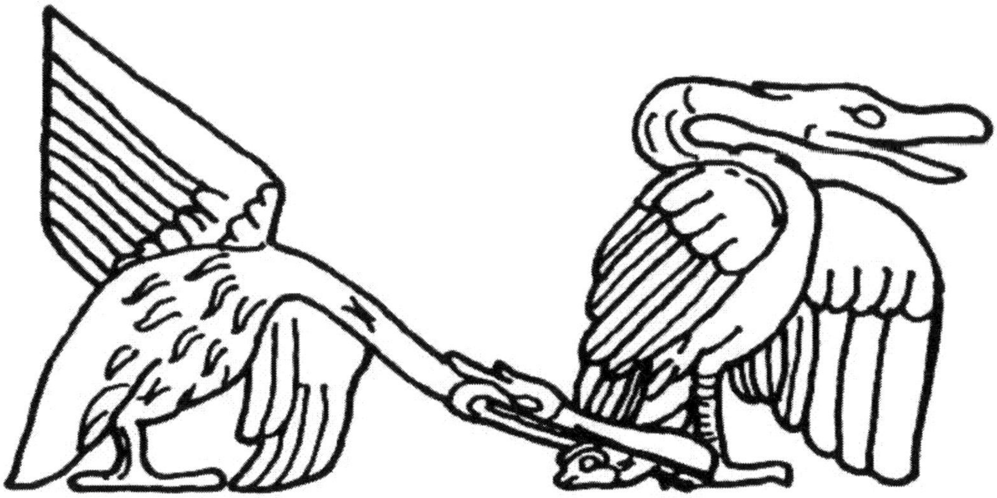

_____

_____

_____

_____

_____

_____

Water Birds

1 Eb: Yellow Path ~ Date:

Travel and destiny...your path in life. This day can also be about following the path of the sacred calendar. It is a day when the ancestors are ready to listen.

The Magical Wave energy today is a one, Jun in Mayan. The energy of today is strong because it is the day Eb' in the trecena of Eb'. So, its double Eb'! One is the energy of attracting. It is magnetic and unifying.

Intention: I am attracting everything I need to walk my path!

Call in the 4 Directions

Today is good for:

- Travel or making plans to travel
- Spending time considering your path in life
- Making changes in your path in life
- Starting a new business or making a business plan
- Asking for good luck in both spiritual and material pursuits
- Being careful of dangers along the way

Color & Direction: Nohol, the Yellow South

Ritual: The Day Ceremony for today is Nohol, the south. Nohol bring abundance, increase and harvest!

Energetic Power Places: Mountains and Woods and paths, especially ancient ones.

Amulets: Good amulets for today are pyramid, ladder, tooth (there is a tooth in the glyph to remind you to be careful of dangers along the road), compass or globe. Anything else that you associate with travel or your path in life.

Element: Earth

Notes, Reflections, and Synchronicities:

_____

_____

_____

_____

_____

_____

_____

2 Ben: Red Corn Stalk – Date:

Ben is the rod of virtues of divine power! It is the corn stalk and is associated with harvest and success! The energy is both growing & surging upward like corn stalks after a heavy rain. It is a very meaningful day, associated with triumph! ALSO, the staff (stalk) symbolizes the spine and the internal fire which moves upward and activates the secret powers. (I love this stuff!)

The Magical Wave is the energy of Ka'a in the number 2. It is polarizing and balancing. Like the sun and moon, or male and female. It brings opposites into balance.

Intention: I am balancing the secret powers of harvest magic!

🦋,Today is a good day to:

- Plant a seed or start a project
- Spend time with family or friends
- Follow your intuition and listen to your dreams
- Ask the ancestors for help in teaching and caretaking
- Study and investigate things
- Ask for rain and growth

Color & Direction: Lak'in the Red East
Ritual: The day ceremony for today is Lak'in the East. Consider requesting help from the ancestors in caring for your home and family or ask for help in starting a new business or project or help with your finances.
Amulet: Carry with you or wear small seeds (especially corn seeds), a small stone (used for grinding corn) ... hahaha....you will like the next one....whisky, bourbon, or rum. . .also sugar, and yellow clothes or jewelry.
Energetic Power Places: fields, meadows, forests, beaches
Element: Fire

Notes, Reflections, and Synchronicities:

_____

_____

_____

_____

_____

_____

_____

3 Ix: White Jaguar – Date:

Ix (pronounced *Ish*) is feminine energy and all things related to the earth, strength, and vitality. Think of the qualities of a jaguar. They are stealthy, strong, and hunt at night. This energy is powerful and wise and is related to the goddess Ixchel.

The Magical Wave energy of O'ox, the number 3, rules this day. It is the gift of taking creative action for the benefit of all.

Intention: I am taking creative action to work with the earth's energy today!

🦋 Today is a good day to:

- Meditate on the Earth as our home and how-to live-in harmony with Her.
- Use magic powers
- Take care of your home, especially by getting rid of things that no longer serve you.
- Use feminine energy
- Get pregnant
- Hunt for things such as knowledge, truth, wisdom
- Any ecological projects

Color & Direction: Xaman, the White North.
Ritual: The Day Ceremony is for Xaman, the North. Xaman brings transparency, clarity and truth. After asking this energy to work with you today, give thanks to the ancestors for all things related to the earth. Consider placing some treasures from the earth around your candle today.
Energetic Power Places: Ceremonial places (especially the pyramids), forests, and mountains (high places)
Amulet: Jaguar, pyramid, or something with a jaguar or spotted design.
Element: Air

Notes, Reflections, and Synchronicities:

_____

_____

_____

_____

_____

_____

_____

_____

4 Men: Blue Eagle ~ Date:

Men the eagle is all about flying high, ambition, and vision. This is a day of good fortune, a day of freedom and of spiritual advancement! It is also about financial advancement. Men is the day of business, merchants, and money. So, this is also the day to dream big and reach for the sky in regard to your business ideas and dreams.

The Magical Wave energy of Kan is the defining energy of the number 4. Think of the 4 legs of a table. As you find balance, you find stability.

Intention: Flying high vision is taking form in my mind and heart today!

This is a good day to:

- Communicate with Heart of Sky, the creator god
- Ask for money for buying things
- Consider the big picture
- Focus on goals and consider how to best meet them
- Pursue goals that have already been set
- Spiritual elevation
- Work on self-improvement

Color & Direction: Chik'in, the Blue West
Ritual: The Day Ceremony is Chik'in the West. Chik'in brings cooperation, duality, and change. This is a very important day for a sacrificial ritual to give thanks for money. The required offering is CHOCOLATE! Simply thank the gods and your ancestors for providing material goods and money, offer them some chocolate. When you finish, then eat it!
Energetic Power Places: Mountains, lakes, misty places, upland forests
Amulet: Bird feathers, dream catchers, anything with a bird, eagle, or quetzal on it
Element: Water

Notes, Reflections, and Synchronicities:

_____

_____

_____

_____

_____

_____

_____

_____

5 Kib: Yellow Owl - Date:

Kib, the warrior owl, is all about taking it easy, relaxation, patience, and timing. The warrior is careful in his timing. He is patient, not rushed. Like the warrior, today is about choosing your timing carefully. This day is also about the illusion of the material world. The night birds Today is a very spiritual day, indeed!

The Magical Wave energy is a level 5 today and is called Jo'o in Mayan. Jo'o is the radiant energy of finding your purpose and taking delight in it!

Intention: I am relaxed and patient as revelation of my purpose in life unfolds for me.

This is a good day to:

- Go with the flow
- Relax
- Commune with the ancestors
- Wash your clothes, especially your good clothes
- Be a spiritual guide
- Ask for forgiveness for ignoring moral teachings
- This is a very special day to spend time preventing mistakes
- Kib is not a good day to start a new project because the energy is low.

Color & Direction: Nohol, the Yellow South
Ritual: The day ceremony is for Nohol which brings increase, abundance, and harvest. Consider taking time to commune with your ancestors during your Day Ceremony today.
Energetic Power Places: Mountains, volcanoes, tropical forests, lakes
Amulet: The earth, any rocks or crystals
Element: Earth

Notes, Reflections, and Synchronicities:

_____

_____

_____

_____

_____

_____

_____

_____

6 Kaban: Red Earth – Date:

Kaban, the earth is the energy of thoughts, logic, ideas, and science. It is movement and sweeping change. Kaban is the earthquake: A day of formidable power and wisdom, a day of shaking the foundations and sudden revelations

The Magical Wave energy of Wak, the number 6, is here to work with you today. It is moving forward and flowing!

Intention: I am moving forward and in the flow of sweeping change and wisdom!

Today is good for:

- Thinking creativity
- Working with others
- Scientific investigation
- Being connected to the earth
- Coming into agreement with the creator
- Movement, travel
- Travel on the spiritual plane
- Shaking things up/sudden revelation/revelations that shake your foundations

Color & Direction: Lak'in, the Red East
Ritual: The Day Ceremony is for Lak'in. Lak'in bring the energy of beginnings, creation, and unity. As you ask Lak'in to work with you today, consider adding some rocks or crystals to your altar space.
Energetic Power Places: Mountains, volcanoes, tropical forests, lakes
Amulet: The earth, any rocks or crystals
Element: Fire

Notes, Reflections, and Synchronicities:

_____

_____

_____

_____

_____

_____

_____

_____

7 Etznab: White Knife ~ Date:

The obsidian sacrificial blade. A day to cut to the core of things. This is a day to reduce, clean out, and cleanse. Its energy is also about healing because the knife can both cut and heal. The obsidian blade is shined to the point of reflection and so the energy of the mirror also comes into play today.

The Magical Wave energy of Uk, the number 7, rules this day. It is about coming into mystical alignment, becoming attuned, and applying your mystical powers!

Intention: I am attuned with the ability to cleanse and fine-tune my life.

Today is a good day to:

- Clean out your closet
- Do some editing (writing, song writing)
- Sort things out
- End an unproductive relationship
- Have a sale
- Let go of the past
- Diagnose and cure illness (physical, mental, and spiritual)
- Make predictions about the future

NOTE: Today is not a good day for travel or to start something new.

Color & Direction: Xaman, the White North.
Ritual: The Day Ceremony is for Xaman, the North. Xaman brings transparency, clarity and truth. Today is a good day to make up for things you neglected to do or should not have done and to receive forgiveness. You can also ask for protection from disease and accidents. No other ceremonies are performed on a knife day.
Energetic Power Places: Pyramids, cliffs, waterfalls, lightning storms
Amulet: Obsidian stone, jade, a knife, a pyramid (the glyph has a pyramid on it) or a mirror
Element: Air

Notes, Reflections, and Synchronicities:

_____

_____

_____

_____

_____

_____

_____

_____

8 Kawak: Blue Storm ~ Date:

Storm is the Nawal of women and strength. It is the lightening flash of inspiration, the warmth and safety of the home, and the cleansing and purification of the rain. Imagine what it feels like to run inside as a storm approaches. That is the energy of Kawak. The rage of the wind and the comfort of home and the care of the woman who wraps loved ones in her arms.

The Magical Wave energy is an 8 today. Waxak, the energy of 8, is the most balanced. It is about being in harmony with your authentic self. Today is a good day for rituals!

Intention: I am in harmony with strength and inspiration.

Call in the 4 Directions

🦋 Today is a good day to:

- Tend to your family and home
- Do volunteer work
- Use your authority
- Ask for the actions of your enemies to turn against them
- Be prepared for trouble
- Heal mental illness
- Receive flashes of inspiration

Color & Direction: Chik'in, the Blue West
Ritual: The Day Ceremony is Chik'in the West. Chik'in brings cooperation, duality and change. As you ask the energy of Chik'in to work with you today, you can also give thanks for the women in your life.
Energetic Power Places: Pine and cypress forests
Amulet: Storm cloud, lightening, Mayan goddess, or pyramid
Element: Water

Notes, Reflections, and Synchronicities:

_____

_____

_____

_____

_____

_____

_____

_____

9 Ahaw: Yellow Sun – Date:

Illumination and growth. The most powerful and positive nawal, radiating energy in all things. Its light not only lights up the day and the night (the moon is a reflection of the sun) but it also brings enlightenment and vision!

The Magical Wave energy of Bolon, the number 9, is the power of the divine feminine. It is all about expansion and mastery!

Intention: I am expanding in and mastering the energy of illumination!

🦋 Today is a good day to:

- Contact the dead
- Be brave against things that scare you
- Ask for illumination
- Build a house
- Start or continue projects
- Have a party
- Reflect on the positive things in life
- Place flowers on the graves of loved ones
- Seek spiritual illumination

Color & Direction: Nohol, the Yellow South
Ritual: The day ceremony is for Nohol which brings increase, abundance, and harvest. Consider doing this at sunrise or sunset today.
Energetic Power Places: Sunrise and sunset, find a beautiful view, especially on the beach or in a field of flowers
Amulet: Anything that shows the sun or flowers (especially yellow)
Element: Earth

Notes, Reflections, and Synchronicities:

_____

_____

_____

_____

_____

_____

_____

_____

10 Imix: Red Crocodile – Date:

Imix is a day of turbulent, stirring waters, of birth, new beginnings, and nurturing. It is a day of raw creative power. Because the crocodile lives in the mangroves, water lilies are associated with this day.

The Magical Wave number 10, Lajun, carries the energy of manifestation!! This is the point where the magical wave crests. It is the highest point on the wave and is perfect in power! What do you want to manifest today?

Intention: I am manifesting wonderful energy for new beginnings.

🦋 Today is a good day to:

- Ask for water/rain
- Start the day with grounding exercises and/or meditation
- Make sweeping changes and lay new foundations
- Stay aware of the tendency to take wild and unpredictable actions.
- Be creative
- Develop your powers of intuition
- Receive messages from beyond
- Cleanse yourself from negative energy
- Ask for the calming of mental issues, spiritual problems, climate change

Color & Direction: Lak'in, the Red East
Ritual: The wind is blowing from the east today, so the Day Ceremony for is Lak'in. Lak'in brings new beginnings, unity, and creation. During your Day Ceremony, you can ask for guidance as you align with this powerful energy of creation!
Power Places: Lakes, lagoons, and other in-land bodies of water
Amulet: Crocodile, lotus blossom, crystals and images associated with the sea.
Element: Fire

Notes, Reflections, and Synchronicities:

_____

_____

_____

_____

_____

_____

_____

11 Ik: White Wind – Date:

The breath of life and creativity. It is also a day of air, heavy showers, and hurricanes. The wind can carry news, bring change, and inspire creativity. It is a day to use your voice and is good for communication and letting your "voice" be heard.

The Magical Wave Energy of 11 is about letting go. The wave has crested and broken and now the water is rushing up on shore. You can no longer control it!

Intention: I am letting go and allowing the wind to come to me as it will, for my highest good!

🦋 Today is a good day to:

- Use your voice, let your voice be heard.
- This is the best day for writing!
- Do something creative
- Cure respiratory illness
- Work on spiritual growth
- Go on a picnic or hike
- Do some gardening

Color & Direction: Xaman, the White North
Ritual: Burn pine or copal incense. This is the sacred day of stone alters. You can place stones around your altar or in a special place at home. Then perform the day ceremony for Xaman the North. Xaman brings transparency, clarity, and truth. During the day ceremony, you can ask for protection for friends and family and ask for protection against the rage of overly strong human emotions.
Energetic Power Places: Canyons, mountains, valleys, forests, and stone alters
Amulet: Hang wind chimes, a tree or branch, the beautiful quetzal bird
Element: Air

Notes, Reflections, and Synchronicities:

_____
_____
_____
_____
_____
_____
_____
_____

12 Ak'bal: Blue Night – Date:

Ak'bal is the night house, the underworld, and the realm of the eternal jaguar sun (the night sun). It is the darkness before the dawn. It is a day of good luck, especially in love! Ak'bal, the night, is generally, this is a tranquil and happy day.

The Magical Wave Energy of 12, Lajka'a is crystalizing.

Intention: I am finding understanding as things are revealed to me today.

🦋 **Today's energy is good for:**

- Declaring your love: This is a lucky day for love!
- Looking within to find answers.
- Seeking anything: jobs, lovers, friends, answers, knowledge
- Discovering the underlying causes of problems
- Face personal challenges with intuition rather than strength
- Ask for light to reach all things
- Acknowledge feelings from the heart
- Getting a fresh start or new beginning

Color & Direction: Chik'in, the Blue West
Ritual: Make a fire at dusk or dawn and ask for renewal. The Day Ceremony for today is Chik'in the West. Chik'in brings the energies or cooperation, duality, adjusting, and change. During your Day Ceremony, you can ask the energy of Chik'in to help you find the answers you are looking for.
Energetic Power Places: Caves, pyramids, mountains, and valleys especially at dusk and dawn.
Amulet/Totem: Jaguar, pyramid, the color black
Element: Water

Notes, Reflections, and Synchronicities:

_____

_____

_____

_____

_____

_____

_____

_____

13 K'an: Yellow Seed – Date:

A day of gathering, collecting, harvest, and abundance. An abundant harvest is indicated here. The meaning is also linked to the net that is traditionally used to gather the corn and can represent tangling or untangling.

Magical Wave Energy today is 13, Ooxlajun. It is chaos, the point where anything can happen. It is powerful and a day for magic!

Intention: I am open to magic regarding an abundant harvest!

🦋 Today is good for:

- Paying off debts
- Collecting things (even collecting your thoughts)
- Reaping the rewards of your work
- Piecing things together
- Do something associated with the interNET
- Witchy stuff (casting spells like one might cast a net)
- Disentangling things

Color & Direction: Nohol, the Yellow South
Element: Earth
Ritual: The Day Ceremony is Nohol, the south. Place seeds or yellow flowers around your candle. Nohol brings the energy of harvest, increase, and abundance! As you burn your candle, let it send prayers to the Heart of Sky and ask to be freed (untangled) from anything that prevents you from receiving the harvest you have worked for.
Energetic Power Places: The sea, farmer's fields, gardens
Amulet: Seeded jewelry or accessories, dream catcher (net).
Element: Earth

Notes, Reflections, and Synchronicities:

_____

_____

_____

_____

_____

_____

_____

_____

Thoughts About this Past Trecena

_____

_____

_____

_____

_____

_____

_____

_____

_____

_____

_____

_____

_____

_____

_____

_____

_____

_____

_____

_____

_____

_____

_____

_____

_____

What Chikchan Brings

Focus: How do you want to experience the vision serpent over the next 13 days?

Chikchan is the vision serpent, the feathered snake. He is Kukulkan and the great plumed serpent who was there at the time of creation when the earth was formed in the primordial sea.

The Maya say he comes to you in the way you envision him. He is a being of great power and life is in him. If you hold your hands up to the sky and open and close them and send your mind out to the cosmos, he will come to you. And when he comes, are you you will feel the glory of his presence. If you afraid, he may appear as frightening. But if know that the serpent brings wisdom and justice and if you are full of light, he will come to you sparkling, shining and gifting you with the revelation of his great power and presence!

Expect energies to flow to you this trecena. Be open and not afraid and truth will come to you and you will receive the justice you seek.

Expect synchronicities to abound and your

Vision Serpent: Grolier Codex

dreams
to be rich and vivid.
Pay attention closely for you will find messages in your dreams. The vision serpent, Chikchan, will be with you for the next 13 days, so stay aware and open, for he has a message for you and it is one that supports you in truth, purity and unaltered revelation!

The Vision Serpent: Kukulkan Carving

Chikchan the Red Feathered Serpent

Trecena Planner

Vision Serpent, façade nunnary quadrangle, Uxmal

1 Chikchan the Red Serpent - Day/Date:

_____
_____
_____
_____
_____
_____
_____

2 Kimi the White World Bringer – Day/Date:

_____
_____
_____
_____
_____
_____
_____

3 Manik the Blue Deer – Day/Date:

_____

_____

_____

_____

_____

_____

_____

4 Lamat the Yellow Star Flower – Day/Date:

_____

_____

_____

_____

_____

_____

_____

5 Muluk the Red Moon – Day/Date:

_____

_____

_____

_____

_____

_____

_____

6 Ok the White Dog – Day/Date:

_____

_____

_____

_____

_____

_____

_____

7 Chuwen the Blue Monkey – Day/Date:

_____

_____

_____

_____

_____

_____

_____

8 Eb' the Yellow Path - Day/Date:

_____

_____

_____

_____

_____

_____

9 B'en the Red Corn Stalk - Day/Date:

_____

_____

_____

_____

_____

_____

_____

10 Ix the White Jaguar - Day/Date:

_____

_____

_____

_____

_____

_____

_____

11 Men the Blue Eagle - Day/Date:

_____

_____

_____

_____

_____

_____

12 Kib the Yellow Owl - Day/Date:

_____

_____

_____

_____

_____

_____

_____

13 Kaban the Red Earth - Day/Date:

_____

_____

_____

_____

_____

_____

_____

Feathered Serpent

1 Chikchan: Red Feathered Serpent – Date:

The sky serpent, the cosmological snake, also known as Kukulkan. Chikchan is Framer and shaper of the Universe. This is an extremely powerful sign. It is the fire at the base of the spine, the Kundalini. It is associated with sexual magic and the rain gods. Key elements for this day are truth and justice.

The Magical Wave energy today is a 1, Jun in Mayan. It is the magnetic energy of attraction!

Intention: I am attracting wisdom, truth, and justice!

Call in the 4 Directions

🦋 Today is a good day to:

- Pursue or deliver truth and knowledge
- Deliver and receive justice
- Find or bring balance
- Pursue inner peace
- Enjoy great sex
- Take fast and direction action
- Beware of fast and direct action
- Stay on guard against anger in both yourself and others

Color & Direction: Lak'in, the Red East
Ritual: The Day Ceremony is Lak'in: unity, beginnings, and creation. This is a powerful day. It is a day to go to the mountains and commune with them. Light a fire and speak directly to the earth and ask for protection. You can also ask for justice, truth, peace, and balance.
Power Places: Mountains, volcanoes, pyramids, starry night
Amulet: Jade, snake, or pyramid—especially the one at Chichen Itza (where the temple of Kukulkan is). An especially powerful totem for today is a jade pyramid.
Element: Fire

Notes, Reflections, and Synchronicities:

_____

_____

_____

_____

_____

_____

_____

_____

2 Kimi: White World Bringer – Date:

The god of death and the lords of the underworld. Kimi is all about transformation and change. This usually applies to things like a job, relationship, living location, or some other part of your life that is in flux. Energies end and others begin. Change is an integral part of life and, if we harness it correctly, can keep moving us toward becoming more enlightened beings.

The Magical Wave is a 2 today. Ka'a the energy of 2, is the gift of polar opposites coming into balance!

Intention: I am finding balance as things transform in my life!

Today is a good day to:

- A great day to make or think about changes
- End relationships (business, friendships, or romantic)
- Work towards tranquility among friends and colleagues, both living and dead
- Both give and ask for forgiveness
- Remember the dead
- Do up-keep on and take care of equipment
- A tranquil day to be patient and conservative in your energy

Color & Direction: Xaman, the White North
Ritual: The Day Ceremony today is for Xaman, the North who brings Transparency, clarity, and truth. During your day ceremony you can give thanks to the ancestors who continue to give you guidance and ask for peace, love, money, health, and forgiveness.
Energetic Power Places: Pyramids, sacred sites, ceremonial sites, the fireplace, temples
Amulet: Skull, butterfly (transformation), corn seed, skeleton
Element: Air

Notes, Reflections, and Synchronicities:

_____

_____

_____

_____

_____

_____

_____

_____

3 Manik: Blue Deer – Date:

Balance, support, and the game of life. Manik is a very important day to focus on balance. Without balance, support cannot function properly. Think of the four legs of a table. If all the legs are different heights (unbalanced) how good is the table? Manik is the deer and the Lord of the hunt. It is a day to get into the game of life. You can think of hunting in our modern world as doing any activities that involve the pursuit of sustenance and strength. That makes Manik a good day for business. It is also a good day for long range travel. (Deer travel vast distances.)

The Magical Wave energy is a 3 today. Three, Oox in Mayan, is the energy of creative action!

Intention: I am taking creative action to get into the game!

🦋 Today is good for:

- Teamwork & meetings
- Business pursuits, getting out "in the field" and talking to customers
- Long range travel
- Staying alert for traps in business and the game of life
- An excellent day for diviners

Color & Direction: Chik'in, the Blue West
Ritual: The Day Ceremony is for Chik'in, the West. Chik'in brings you duality, cooperation, and change. As you perform your Day Ceremony, consider asking Chik'in to bless your finances and business.
Energetic Power Places are forests, and fields (places where you might find deer)
Amulet: Anything to do with the deer, anything with the number 4 or four parts to it.
Element: Water

Notes, Reflections, and Synchronicities:

_____

_____

_____

_____

_____

_____

_____

_____

_____

4 Lamat: Yellow Star Flower – Date:

Today is all about abundance and growing! It's a wonderful day to plant something, be it friendships, project ideas, or actual flowers. Lamat is also about fertility and is represented by the planet (star) Venus and the color gold.

The Magical Wave energy today is Kan, the number 4 and is everything about stability! Kan is things taking form and finding balance, becoming stable!

Intention: The energy of growing lovely things is taking form in my life!

🦋 Today is good for:

- Planting new things: flowers, friendships, projects
- Honoring past works
- Tending to your crops (in our modern times, that also means tending to business or whatever it is that sustains you)
- Star gazing (Lamat is also associated with Venus)
- Thinking about the Universe
- Feeding the world
- Fertility

Color: Yellow
Direction: Today the wind is blowing from the south. It brings harvest, abundance, and endings.
Ritual: The Day Ceremony today is Nohol, the South. Try placing some wildflowers, especially yellow ones, or seeds around your candle today.
Energetic Power Places today are forests, places where wildflowers grow, rivers and lakes
Amulet: Flowers (especially yellow ones), stars, or Venus
Element: Earth

Notes, Reflections, and Synchronicities:

_____

_____

_____

_____

_____

_____

_____

_____

 ## 5 Muluk: Red Moon – Date:

A day to make payments, give offerings, and ask for dark things to come to light. Muluk is also about emotions and using your intuition. This is a day of cycles, rhythms and water since water is intrinsically connected to the moon.

The Magical Wave energy of 5 rules this day. Jo'o, the number 5, is the power to look at your creation and take delight in it!

Intention: My intuition is radiant, and I take delight in it!

🦋 Today is good for:

- Paying off debts (financial, relational, societal, spiritual)
- Asking people to pay you back for their debts to you
- Working to end suffering
- Giving offerings to the earth
- Asking for rain
- Asking for dark things to come to light
- Pay attention to your dreams
- Use your intuition

Color & Direction: Lak'in the Red East
Ritual: The day ceremony for today is Lak'in the East. You can also cleanse your candles and other alter items under the moon today.
Energetic Power Places today are the beach, big rocks, oceans, rivers, and lakes
Amulets: Shark or whale or other large aquatic creature, jade, the moon
Element: Fire

Notes, Reflections, and Synchronicities:

_____

_____

_____

_____

_____

_____

_____

_____

_____

6 Ok: White Dog – Date:

The one who guides the night sun through the underworld. Ok is about guidance and protection. Your guides are with you today in a powerful way to guide you through the underworld. This is also a day about justice and truth. On the lighter side, Ok is the most sexually charged day of the Nawales.

The Magical Wave energy that wants to work with you today is 6, Wak, the flow! It is rhythmic, organized, and balanced. This is an energy for moving forward and flowing!

Intention: I am flowing easily as I trust my guides!

Today is good for:

- Asking for guidance
- Giving guidance
- Short distance travel (like around your town)
- Being alert for dangers/update home security
- Having great sex
- Looking for hidden truth

Color & Direction: Xaman, the White North.
Element: Air
Ritual: The Day Ceremony for today is for Xaman, the North. Consider asking the energy of Xaman to guide you today. Xaman brings transparency, clarity and truth.
Energetic Power Places today are mountains and beaches. If you don't live near these places, try a watching a video with beautiful scenery to add a little nature energy to your day.
Amulets: Anything related to dogs
Element: Air

Notes, Reflections, and Synchronicities:

_____

_____

_____

_____

_____

_____

_____

7 Chuwen: Blue Monkey – Date:

The great craftsman, patron of the arts, the thread of that symbolizes destiny and maintains the continuity the past, the present, and the future. Monkey is all about being creative and having fun! It is a highly positive day that is full of energy that is friendly and happy!

The Magical Wave energy of Uk, the number 7, is here to work with you today. Uk is you coming into alignment with your magical powers!

Intention: I am aligning with my magical power to have creative fun!

Today is good for:

- Partying and celebrating
- Dancing, singing, writing, painting
- Getting married
- Studying the sacred calendar
- Taking time to look for patterns in life
- Starting projects
- Watch for synchronicities today!

Color & Direction: Chik'in the Blue/Black West
Ritual: This is a great day for burning incense, especially copal or frankincense. The Day Ceremony for today is Chik'in, the West.
Element: Water
Energetic Power Places where the energy is strong today are lakes and forests.
Amulet: Try wearing something woven today, especially a cloth wrist band or bracelet or something made from woven threads. Something that reminds you of monkeys.
Element: Water

Notes, Reflections, and Synchronicities:

_____

_____

_____

_____

_____

_____

_____

_____

8 Eb: Yellow Path – Date:

Travel and destiny...your path in life. This day can also be about following the path of the sacred calendar. It is a day when the ancestors are ready to listen.

The Magical Wave energy today is the number 8, Waxak. Waxak is the most balance of all the energies. It is a powerful day to be in harmony with your authentic self and to do rituals and ceremonies!

Intention: I am in harmony with my authentic path!

Call in the 4 Directions

🦋 Today is good for:

- Travel or making plans to travel
- Spending time considering your path in life
- Making changes in your path in life
- Starting a new business or making a business plan
- Asking for good luck in both spiritual and material pursuits
- Being careful of dangers along the way

Color & Direction: Nohol, the Yellow South
Ritual: The Day Ceremony for today is Nohol, the south. Nohol bring abundance, increase and harvest!
Energetic Power Places: Mountains and Woods and paths, especially ancient ones.
Amulets: Good amulets for today are pyramid, ladder, tooth (there is a tooth in the glyph to remind you to be careful of dangers along the road), compass or globe. Anything else that you associate with travel or your path in life.
Element: Earth

Notes, Reflections, and Synchronicities:

_____

_____

_____

_____

_____

_____

_____

_____

9 Ben: Red Corn Stalk – Date:

Ben is the rod of virtues of divine power! It is the corn stalk and is associated with harvest and success! The energy is both growing & surging upward like corn stalks after a heavy rain. It is a very meaningful day, associated with triumph! ALSO, the staff (stalk) symbolizes the spine and the internal fire which moves upward and activates the secret powers. (I love this stuff!)

The Magical Wave is the energy of Bolon, the number 9. It is the ability to expand and find mastery and is the power of the divine feminine.

Intention: I am expanding and finding mastery in secret powers magic!

🦋 Today is a good day to:

- Plant a seed or start a project
- Spend time with family or friends
- Follow your intuition and listen to your dreams
- Ask the ancestors for help in teaching and caretaking
- Study and investigate things
- Ask for rain and growth

Color & Direction: Lak'in the Red East
Ritual: The day ceremony for today is Lak'in the East. Consider requesting help from the ancestors in caring for your home and family or ask for help in starting a new business or project or help with your finances.
Amulet: Carry with you or wear small seeds (especially corn seeds), a small stone (used for grinding corn) ... hahaha....you will like the next one....whisky, bourbon, or rum. . .also sugar, and yellow clothes or jewelry.
Energetic Power Places: fields, meadows, forests, beaches
Element: Fire

Notes, Reflections, and Synchronicities:

_____

_____

_____

_____

_____

_____

_____

_____

10 Ix: White Jaguar – Date:

Ix (pronounced *Ish*) is feminine energy and all things related to the earth, strength, and vitality. Think of the qualities of a jaguar. They are stealthy, strong, and hunt at night. This energy is powerful and wise and is related to the goddess Ixchel.

The Magical Wave energy of Lajun, the number 10, rules this day. This is the highest point of the wave and is the power to manifest!

Intention: I am manifesting all the power of the jaguar!

Today is a good day to:

- Meditate on the Earth as our home and how-to live-in harmony with Her.
- Use magic powers
- Take care of your home, especially by getting rid of things that no longer serve you.
- Use feminine energy
- Get pregnant
- Hunt for things such as knowledge, truth, wisdom
- Any ecological projects

Color & Direction: Xaman, the White North.
Ritual: The Day Ceremony is for Xaman, the North. Xaman brings transparency, clarity and truth. After asking this energy to work with you today, give thanks to the ancestors for all things related to the earth. Consider placing some treasures from the earth around your candle today.
Energetic Power Places: Ceremonial places (especially the pyramids), forests, and mountains (high places)
Amulet: Jaguar, pyramid, or something with a jaguar or spotted design.
Element: Air

Notes, Reflections, and Synchronicities:

_____

_____

_____

_____

_____

_____

_____

_____

11 Men: Blue Eagle – Date:

Men the eagle is all about flying high, ambition, and vision. This is a day of good fortune, a day of freedom and of spiritual advancement! It is also about financial advancement. Men is the day of business, merchants, and money. So, this is also the day to dream big and reach for the sky in regard to your business ideas and dreams.

The Magical Wave energy of Buluk, the number 11, is all about letting go! The wave has crested and broken and is rushing onto shore. It's too powerful now to control!

Intention: I am letting go and flying high!

🦋 This is a good day to:

- Communicate with Heart of Sky, the creator god
- Ask for money for buying things
- Consider the big picture
- Focus on goals and consider how to best meet them
- Pursue goals that have already been set
- Spiritual elevation
- Work on self-improvement

Color & Direction: Chik'in, the Blue West
Ritual: The Day Ceremony is Chik'in the West. Chik'in brings cooperation, duality and change. This is a very important day for a sacrificial ritual to give thanks for money. The required offering is CHOCOLATE! Simply thank the gods and your ancestors for providing material goods and money, offer them some chocolate. When you finish, then eat it!
Energetic Power Places: Mountains, lakes, misty places, upland forests
Amulet: Bird feathers, dream catchers, anything with a bird, eagle, or quetzal on it
Element: Water

Notes, Reflections, and Synchronicities:

_____

_____

_____

_____

_____

_____

_____

12 Kib: Yellow Owl – Date:

Kib, the warrior owl, is all about taking it easy, relaxation, patience, and timing. The warrior is careful in his timing. He is patient, not rushed. Like the warrior, today is about choosing your timing carefully. This day is also about the illusion of the material world. The night birds Today is a very spiritual day, indeed!

The Magical Wave energy is a level 12 today and is called Lajka'a in Mayan. It is the place where everything crystalizes and you really being to understand!

Intention: My ability to be patient and find perfect timing is crystalizing!

This is a good day to:

- Go with the flow
- Relax
- Commune with the ancestors
- Wash your clothes, especially your good clothes
- Be a spiritual guide
- Ask for forgiveness for ignoring moral teachings
- This is a very special day to spend time preventing mistakes
- Kib is not a good day to start a new project because the energy is low.

Color & Direction: Nohol, the Yellow South
Ritual: The day ceremony is for Nohol which brings increase, abundance, and harvest. Consider taking time to commune with your ancestors during your Day Ceremony today.
Energetic Power Places: Mountains, volcanoes, tropical forests, lakes
Amulet: The earth, any rocks or crystals
Element: Earth

Notes, Reflections, and Synchronicities:

_____

_____

_____

_____

_____

_____

_____

13 Kaban: Red Earth – Date:

Kaban, the earth is the energy of thoughts, logic, ideas and science. It is movement and sweeping change. Kaban is the earthquake: A day of formidable power and wisdom, a day of shaking the foundations and sudden revelations

The Magical Wave energy of Ooxlajun (13) is the wild card, the place of transcendence. It is where chaos causes synchronicities. What do YOU want to "magic" today?

Intention: Wild synchronicities are bringing great wisdom to me today!

🦋 Today is good for:

- Thinking creativity
- Working with others
- Scientific investigation
- Being connected to the earth
- Coming into agreement with the creator
- Movement, travel
- Travel on the spiritual plane
- Shaking things up/sudden revelation/revelations that shake your foundations

Color & Direction: Lak'in, the Red East
Ritual: The Day Ceremony is for Lak'in. Lak'in brings the energy of beginnings, creation and unity. As you ask Lak'in to work with you today, consider adding some rocks or crystals to your altar space.
Energetic Power Places: Mountains, volcanoes, tropical forests, lakes
Amulet: The earth, any rocks or crystals
Element: Fire

Notes, Reflections, and Synchronicities:

_____

_____

_____

_____

_____

_____

_____

Thoughts About this Past Trecena

_____

_____

_____

_____

_____

_____

_____

_____

_____

_____

_____

_____

_____

_____

_____

_____

_____

_____

_____

_____

_____

_____

_____

_____

_____

_____

_____

_____

_____

_____

What to Expect During Etz'nab

Focus: What life-editing do you want to work on over the next 13 days?

Etz'nab is the obsidian knife, the blade of sacrifice. Sounds a bit daunting, doesn't it? No worries! Remember, the idea is for all parts of life to come into balance. The knife is about removing things. It is also about healing. Think for a moment about the surgeon's knife. He removes things that are not good for you in order that you might heal. Now let's put that in perspective with everyday life.

Think about something as simple and mundane as your closet. If all you did was keep stuffing things in there (abundance, growth, that sort of thing) eventually your closet would be daunting! It would be filled with old things, things you never wear, things you don't like or that never really fit right. It feels great to clean out a closet in preparation for spring! You remove things you don't want or need so you have room for the new!

This trecena is all about that! It's a time to go through things, edit projects, weed gardens, clean out your junk drawer (I know you have one!) You can expect the energy over the next 13 days to bring clarity so that you can easily make decisions about what to keep in your life and what to let go of. This is a cleansing time, a healing time, a refreshing time! You might even want to trim your hair!

As you move through this trecena, keep in mind the energy of Etz'nab. For example: Kawak is a day to take care of your home and make it a haven from the storms of life. So, when Kawak arrives, ask yourself what you can do to prune away the clutter in your home so that it flourishes more.

Expect to feel lighter and lighter as this trecena progresses. Little by little you will be shaping the garden of your life until it is something beautiful, healthy, and full of vigor and life!

Offering, Grolier Codex

227

Offering, Codex Style Vase

Etz'nab the White Knife
Trecena Planner

Offering guy, Grolier Codex

1 Etz'nab the White Knife - Day/Date:

_____
_____
_____
_____
_____
_____
_____

2 Kawak the Blue Storm – Day/Date:

_____
_____
_____
_____
_____
_____

3 Ahaw the Yellow Sun – Day/Date:

_____

_____

_____

_____

_____

_____

_____

4 Imix the Red Crocodile – Day/Date:

_____

_____

_____

_____

_____

_____

_____

5 Ik the White Wind – Day/Date:

_____

_____

_____

_____

_____

_____

_____

6 Ak'bal the Blue Night – Day/Date:

_____

_____

_____

_____

_____

_____

_____

7 K'an the Yellow Seed – Day/Date:

_____

_____

_____

_____

_____

_____

_____

8 Chikchan the Red Serpent - Day/Date:

_____

_____

_____

_____

_____

_____

_____

9 Kimi the White World Bringer - Day/Date:

_____

_____

_____

_____

_____

_____

10 Manik the Blue Deer - Day/Date:

_____

_____

_____

_____

_____

_____

11 Lamat the Yellow Star Flower - Day/Date:

_____

_____

_____

_____

_____

_____

12 Muluk the Red Moon - Day/Date:

_____

_____

_____

_____

_____

_____

_____

13 Ok the White Dog - Day/Date:

_____

_____

_____

_____

_____

_____

_____

Offering, Grolier Codex

1 Etz'nab: White Knife – Date:

The obsidian sacrificial blade. A day to cut to the core of things. This is a day to reduce, clean out, and cleanse. Its energy is also about healing because the knife can both cut and heal. The obsidian blade is shined to the point of reflection and so the energy of the mirror also comes into play today.

The Magical Wave energy of Jun, the number 1 rules this day. It is all about attracting.

Intention: I am attracting the energy of cleansing.

Call in the 4 Directions

🦋 Today is a good day to:

- Clean out your closet
- Do some editing (writing, song writing)
- Sort things out
- End an unproductive relationship
- Have a sale
- Let go of the past
- Diagnose and cure illness (physical, mental, and spiritual)
- Make predictions about the future

NOTE: Today is not a good day for travel or to start something new.

Color & Direction: Xaman, the White North.
Ritual: The Day Ceremony is for Xaman, the North. Xaman brings transparency, clarity, and truth. Today is a good day to make up for things you neglected to do or should not have done and to receive forgiveness. You can also ask for protection from disease and accidents. No other ceremonies are performed on a knife day.
Energetic Power Places: Pyramids, cliffs, waterfalls, lightning storms
Amulet: Obsidian stone, jade, a knife, a pyramid (the glyph has a pyramid on it) or a mirror
Element: Air

Notes, Reflections, and Synchronicities:

_____

_____

_____

_____

_____

_____

_____

_____

2 Kawak: Blue Storm – Date:

Storm is the Nawal of women and strength. It is the lightening flash of inspiration, the warmth and safety of the home, and the cleansing and purification of the rain. Imagine what it feels like to run inside as a storm approaches. That is the energy of Kawak. The rage of the wind and the comfort of home and the care of the woman who wraps loved ones in her arms.

The Magical Wave energy is a 2. In Mayan it is known as Ka'a and it is all about duality. Think of opposite forces being in balance.

Intention: I am balancing the strength of the storm and the comfort of home.

Today is a good day to:

- Tend to your family and home
- Do volunteer work
- Use your authority
- Ask for the actions of your enemies to turn against them
- Be prepared for trouble
- Heal mental illness
- Receive flashes of inspiration

Color & Direction: Chik'in, the Blue West
Ritual: The Day Ceremony is Chik'in the West. Chik'in brings cooperation, duality, and change. As you ask the energy of Chik'in to work with you today, you can also give thanks for the women in your life.
Energetic Power Places: Pine and cypress forests
Amulet: Storm cloud, lightening, Mayan goddess, or pyramid
Element: Water

Notes, Reflections, and Synchronicities:

_____

_____

_____

_____

_____

_____

_____

_____

3 Ahaw: Yellow Sun – Date:

Illumination and growth. The most powerful and positive nawal, radiating energy in all things. Its light not only lights up the day and the night (the moon is a reflection of the sun) but it also brings enlightenment and vision!

The Magical Wave energy of Oox, the number 3, is the power to take creative action for the benefit of all.

Intention: I am taking creative action to embrace illumination.

🦋 Today is a good day to:

- Contact the dead
- Be brave against things that scare you
- Ask for illumination
- Build a house
- Start or continue projects
- Have a party
- Reflect on the positive things in life
- Place flowers on the graves of loved ones
- Seek spiritual illumination

Color & Direction: Nohol, the Yellow South
Ritual: The day ceremony is for Nohol which brings increase, abundance, and harvest. Consider doing this at sunrise or sunset today.
Energetic Power Places: Sunrise and sunset, find a beautiful view, especially on the beach or in a field of flowers
Amulet: Anything that shows the sun or flowers (especially yellow)
Element: Earth

Notes, Reflections, and Synchronicities:

_____

_____

_____

_____

_____

_____

_____

_____

4 Imix: Red Crocodile ~ Date:

Imix is a day of turbulent, stirring waters, of birth, new beginnings, and nurturing. It is a day of raw creative power. Because the crocodile lives in the mangroves, water lilies are associated with this day.

The Magical Wave number 4 carries the energy of stability. It is energy taking form.

Intention: Powerful new beginnings are taking form and becoming stable in my life.

Today is a good day to:

- Ask for water/rain
- Start the day with grounding exercises and/or meditation
- Make sweeping changes and lay new foundations
- Stay aware of the tendency to take wild and unpredictable actions.
- Be creative
- Develop your powers of intuition
- Receive messages from beyond
- Cleanse yourself from negative energy
- Ask for the calming of mental issues, spiritual problems, climate change

Color & Direction: Lak'in, the Red East
Ritual: The wind is blowing from the east today, so the Day Ceremony for is Lak'in. Lak'in brings new beginnings, unity, and creation. During your Day Ceremony, you can ask for guidance as you align with this powerful energy of creation!
Power Places: Lakes, lagoons, and other in-land bodies of water
Amulet: Crocodile, lotus blossom, crystals and images associated with the sea.
Element: Fire

Notes, Reflections, and Synchronicities:

_____

_____

_____

_____

_____

_____

_____

_____

5 Ik: White Wind – Date:

The breath of life and creativity. It is also a day of air, heavy showers, and hurricanes. The wind can carry news, bring change, and inspire creativity. It is a day to use your voice and is good for communication and letting your "voice" be heard.

The Magical Wave Energy of 5 (Jo'o) is about empowerment! Jo'o's gift is the ability to look at your creation and take delight in it.

Intention: I am taking delight in letting my voice be heard.

🦋 Today is a good day to:

- Use your voice, let your voice be heard.
- This is the best day for writing!
- Do something creative
- Cure respiratory illness
- Work on spiritual growth
- Go on a picnic or hike
- Do some gardening

Color & Direction: Xaman, the White North
Ritual: Burn pine or copal incense. This is the sacred day of stone alters. You can place stones around your altar or in a special place at home. Then perform the day ceremony for Xaman the North. Xaman brings transparency, clarity, and truth. During the day ceremony, you can ask for protection for friends and family and ask for protection against the rage of overly strong human emotions.
Energetic Power Places: Canyons, mountains, valleys, forests, and stone alters
Amulet: Hang wind chimes, a tree or branch, the beautiful quetzal bird
Element: Air

Notes, Reflections, and Synchronicities:

_____

_____

_____

_____

_____

_____

_____

_____

6 Ak'bal: Blue Night ~ Date:

Ak'bal is the night house, the underworld, and the realm of the eternal jaguar sun (the night sun). It is the darkness before the dawn. It is a day of good luck, especially in love! Ak'bal, the night, is generally, this is a tranquil and happy day.

The Magical Wave Energy of Wak, the number 6, is a flowing energy.

Intention: I am flowing in the energy of bringing things out of the darkness and into the light.

🦋 Today's energy is good for:

- Declaring your love: This is a lucky day for love!
- Looking within to find answers.
- Seeking anything: jobs, lovers, friends, answers, knowledge
- Discovering the underlying causes of problems
- Face personal challenges with intuition rather than strength
- Ask for light to reach all things
- Acknowledge feelings from the heart
- Getting a fresh start or new beginning

Color & Direction: Chik'in, the Blue West
Ritual: Make a fire at dusk or dawn and ask for renewal. The Day Ceremony for today is Chik'in the West. Chik'in brings the energies or cooperation, duality, adjusting, and change. During your Day Ceremony, you can ask the energy of Chik'in to help you find the answers you are looking for.
Energetic Power Places: Caves, pyramids, mountains, and valleys especially at dusk and dawn.
Amulet/Totem: Jaguar, pyramid, the color black
Element: Water

Notes, Reflections, and Synchronicities:

_____

_____

_____

_____

_____

_____

_____

_____

_____

7 K'an: Yellow Seed – Date:

A day of gathering, collecting, harvest, and abundance. An abundant harvest is indicated here. The meaning is also linked to the net that is traditionally used to gather the corn and can represent tangling or untangling.

Magical Wave Energy today is Uk, the number 7. It is the ability to harness your secret powers! It brings attunement and mystical alignment.

Intention: I am in alignment with gathering in a wonderful harvest.

🦋 Today is good for:

- Paying off debts
- Collecting things (even collecting your thoughts)
- Reaping the rewards of your work
- Piecing things together
- Do something associated with the interNET
- Witchy stuff (casting spells like one might cast a net)
- Disentangling things

Color & Direction: Nohol, the Yellow South
Element: Earth
Ritual: The Day Ceremony is Nohol, the south. Place seeds or yellow flowers around your candle. Nohol brings the energy of harvest, increase, and abundance! As you burn your candle, let it send prayers to the Heart of Sky and ask to be freed (untangled) from anything that prevents you from receiving the harvest you have worked for.
Energetic Power Places: The sea, farmer's fields, gardens
Amulet: Seeded jewelry or accessories, dream catcher (net).
Element: Earth

Notes, Reflections, and Synchronicities:

_____

_____

_____

_____

_____

_____

_____

_____

8 Chikchan: Red Feathered Serpent ~ Date:

The sky serpent, the cosmological snake, also known as Kukulkan. Chikchan is Framer and shaper of the Universe. This is an extremely powerful sign. It is the fire at the base of the spine, the Kundalini. It is associated with sexual magic and the rain gods. Key elements for this day are truth and justice.

The Magical Wave energy today is Waxak, (8). Waxak is powerful and balanced. A day for ritual and ceremony. Its energy brings the ability to harmonize with all parts of yourself.

Intention: I am in vibratory harmony with wisdom, truth, and justice.

🦋 Today is a good day to:

Call in the 4 Directions

- Pursue or deliver truth and knowledge
- Deliver and receive justice
- Find or bring balance
- Pursue inner peace
- Enjoy great sex
- Take fast and direction action
- Beware of fast and direct action
- Stay on guard against anger in both yourself and others

Color & Direction: Lak'in, the Red East
Ritual: The Day Ceremony is Lak'in: unity, beginnings, and creation. This is a powerful day. It is a day to go to the mountains and commune with them. Light a fire and speak directly to the earth and ask for protection. You can also ask for justice, truth, peace, and balance.
Power Places: Mountains, volcanoes, pyramids, starry night
Amulet: Jade, snake, or pyramid—especially the one at Chichen Itza (where the temple of Kukulkan is). An especially powerful totem for today is a jade pyramid.
Element: Fire

Notes, Reflections, and Synchronicities:

_____

_____

_____

_____

_____

_____

_____

_____

_____

9 Kimi: White World Bringer – Date:

The god of death and the lords of the underworld. Kimi is all about transformation and change. This usually applies to things like a job, relationship, living location, or some other part of your life that is in flux. Energies end and others begin. Change is an integral part of life and, if we harness it correctly, can keep moving us toward becoming more enlightened beings.

The Magical Wave is a 9, Bolon, today. Bolon is expanding and mastering. It is the energy of the divine feminine.

Intention: I have mastery of the expansion of transformation.

Today is a good day to:

- A great day to make or think about changes
- End relationships (business, friendships, or romantic)
- Work towards tranquility among friends and colleagues, both living and dead
- Both give and ask for forgiveness
- Remember the dead
- Do up-keep on and take care of equipment
- A tranquil day to be patient and conservative in your energy

Color & Direction: Xaman, the White North
Ritual: The Day Ceremony today is for Xaman, the North who brings Transparency, clarity and truth. During your day ceremony you can give thanks to the ancestors who continue to give you guidance and ask for peace, love, money, health, and forgiveness.
Energetic Power Places: Pyramids, sacred sites, ceremonial sites, the fireplace, temples
Amulet: Skull, butterfly (transformation), corn seed, skeleton
Element: Air

Notes, Reflections, and Synchronicities:

_____

_____

_____

_____

_____

_____

_____

_____

10 Manik: Blue Deer – Date:

Balance, support, and the game of life. Manik is a very important day to focus on balance. Without balance, support cannot function properly. Think of the four legs of a table. If all the legs are different heights (unbalanced) how good is the table? Manik is the deer and the Lord of the hunt. It is a day to get into the game of life. You can think of hunting in our modern world as doing any activities that involve the pursuit of sustenance and strength. That makes Manik a good day for business. It is also a good day for long range travel. (Deer travel vast distances.)

The Magical Wave energy is a 10 today! I love ten, Lajun, because it is all about manifesting!

Intention: I am manifesting balance in every area of my life.

🦋 Today is good for:

- Teamwork & meetings
- Business pursuits, getting out "in the field" and talking to customers
- Long range travel
- Staying alert for traps in business and the game of life
- An excellent day for diviners

Color & Direction: Chik'in, the Blue West
Ritual: The Day Ceremony is for Chik'in, the West. Chik'in brings you duality, cooperation, and change. As you perform your Day Ceremony, consider asking Chik'in to bless your finances and business.
Energetic Power Places are forests, and fields (places where you might find deer)
Amulet: Anything to do with the deer, anything with the number 4 or four parts to it.
Element: Water

Notes, Reflections, and Synchronicities:

_____

_____

_____

_____

_____

_____

_____

_____

11 Lamat: Yellow Star Flower – Date:

Today is all about abundance and growing! It's a wonderful day to plant something, be it friendships, project ideas, or actual flowers. Lamat is also about fertility and is represented by the planet (star) Venus and the color gold.

The Magical Wave energy today is Buluk, the number 11. Buluk is the power to let go. It is the point where the wave breaks and runs up on shore, too powerful to be contained!

Intention: I am letting go and allowing things to grow.

🦋 Today is good for:

- Planting new things: flowers, friendships, projects
- Honoring past works
- Tending to your crops (in our modern times, that also means tending to business or whatever it is that sustains you)
- Star gazing (Lamat is also associated with Venus)
- Thinking about the Universe
- Feeding the world
- Fertility

Color: Yellow
Direction: Today the wind is blowing from the south. It brings harvest, abundance, and endings.
Ritual: The Day Ceremony today is Nohol, the South. Try placing some wildflowers, especially yellow ones, or seeds around your candle today.
Energetic Power Places today are forests, places where wildflowers grow, rivers and lakes
Amulet: Flowers (especially yellow ones), stars, or Venus
Element: Earth

Notes, Reflections, and Synchronicities:

_____

_____

_____

_____

_____

_____

_____

12 Muluk: Red Moon – Date:

A day to make payments, give offerings, and ask for dark things to come to light. Muluk is also about emotions and using your intuition. This is a day of cycles, rhythms and water since water is intrinsically connected to the moon.

The Magical Wave energy of Lajk'a', the number 12 rules this day. Lajka'a is the energy of crystalizing. It is reaching the point of understanding.

Intention: My intuition is becoming crystal clear.

🦋 Today is good for:

- Paying off debts (financial, relational, societal, spiritual)
- Asking people to pay you back for their debts to you
- Working to end suffering
- Giving offerings to the earth
- Asking for rain
- Asking for dark things to come to light
- Pay attention to your dreams
- Use your intuition

Color & Direction: Lak'in the Red East
Ritual: The day ceremony for today is Lak'in the East. You can also cleanse your candles and other alter items under the moon today.
Energetic Power Places today are the beach, big rocks, oceans, rivers, and lakes
Amulets: Shark or whale or other large aquatic creature, jade, the moon
Element: Fire

Notes, Reflections, and Synchronicities:

_____

_____

_____

_____

_____

_____

_____

_____

_____

_____

13 Ok: White Dog – Date:

The one who guides the night sun through the underworld. Ok is about guidance and protection. Your guides are with you today in a powerful way to guide you through the underworld. This is also a day about justice and truth. On the lighter side, Ok is the most sexually charged day of the Nawales.

The Magical Wave energy that wants to work with you today is Ooxlajun, the number 13. It is the point where everything is possible, the cosmic wild card, the place of magic!

Intention: I am discovering synchronicities regarding guidance in my life!

🦋 Today is good for:

- Asking for guidance
- Giving guidance
- Short distance travel (like around your town)
- Being alert for dangers/update home security
- Having great sex
- Looking for hidden truth

Color & Direction: Xaman, the White North.
Element: Air
Ritual: The Day Ceremony for today is for Xaman, the North. Consider asking the energy of Xaman to guide you today. Xaman brings transparency, clarity, and truth.
Energetic Power Places today are mountains and beaches. If you don't live near these places, try a watching a video with beautiful scenery to add a little nature energy to your day.
Amulets: Anything related to dogs
Element: Air

Notes, Reflections, and Synchronicities:

_____

_____

_____

_____

_____

_____

_____

_____

Sacred Tzolk'in Daily Journal

Thoughts About this Past Trecena

Sacred Tzolk'in Daily Journal

Thoughts About this Past Trecena

Monkey, polychrome vase, Chama

What to Expect as Chuwen Comes to Play

Focus: How do you plan to have creative fun over the next 13 days?

Chuwen, the monkey, is the party animal! Monkey loves to be creative and have fun. Chuwen is the great patron of the arts! There is a time for everything and over the next thirteen days, the energy is great for planning parties, dancing, singing, and getting creative!

You can expect your creative juices to be flowing during this trecena, so go ahead and plan to make the best use of this energy. You might want to paint a room in your house. Or, create beautiful artwork to hang on the walls. Or, you might want to start a new dance class or get friends together to listen to great music and enjoy delicious food.

Creativity and fun come in so many colors and flavors. What do you love to do?

This is also a time to consider how the thread of time connects the past, the present, and the future. Perhaps you would like to make a scrapbook during the next two weeks. Or, go through old photos and make a beautiful collage. You might want to connect with old friends or make new ones. And when you do, don't forget to enjoy your time and have fun!

Take time to look through the upcoming days and make some plans that incorporate the energy of each day. For example: on Eb, the Path, you might want to go for a fun picnic. Or on Ben, the Corn Stalk, you might want to have a garden party. Perhaps on Ak'bal, the Night, you might want to go out for dinner and dancing. Maybe on Men, the Eagle, the day related to business, you might want to come up with some great creative business ideas! The sky's the limit. Make time to be creative and have fun!

Monkey Dancing, polychrome vase

Chuwen the Blue Monkey

Trecena Planner

Monkey Yui Creature: vase

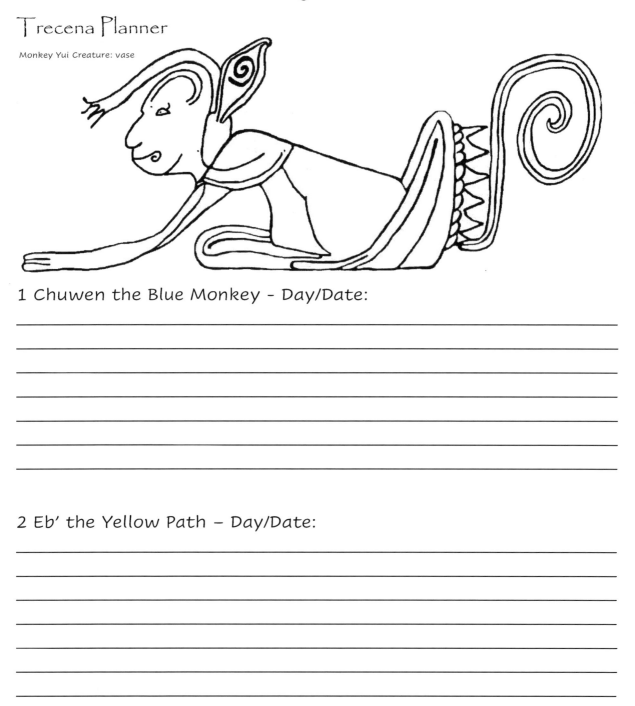

1 Chuwen the Blue Monkey - Day/Date:

_____
_____
_____
_____
_____
_____
_____

2 Eb' the Yellow Path – Day/Date:

_____
_____
_____
_____
_____
_____
_____

3 Ben the Red Corn Stalk– Day/Date:

_____
_____
_____
_____
_____
_____
_____

4 Ix the White Jaguar – Day/Date:

_____
_____
_____
_____
_____
_____
_____

5 Men the Blue Eagle – Day/Date:

_____
_____
_____
_____
_____
_____
_____

6 Kib the Yellow Owl – Day/Date:

_____

_____

_____

_____

_____

_____

_____

7 Kaban the Red Earth – Day/Date:

_____

_____

_____

_____

_____

_____

_____

8 Etz'nab the White Knife - Day/Date:

_____

_____

_____

_____

_____

_____

_____

9 Kawak the Blue Storm - Day/Date:

_____

_____

_____

_____

_____

_____

_____

10 Ahaw the Yellow Sun - Day/Date:

_____

_____

_____

_____

_____

_____

_____

11 Imix the Red Crocodile - Day/Date:

_____

_____

_____

_____

_____

_____

_____

12 Ik the White Wind - Day/Date:

_____
_____
_____
_____
_____
_____
_____

13 Ak'bal the Blue Night - Day/Date:

_____
_____
_____
_____
_____
_____
_____

Monkey: Nuttall Codex

1 Chuwen: Blue Monkey – Date:

The great craftsman, patron of the arts, the thread of that symbolizes destiny and maintains the continuity the past, the present, and the future. Monkey is all about being creative and having fun! It is a highly positive day that is full of energy that is friendly and happy!

The Magical Wave energy of Jun, the number 1, is here to work with you today. Jun is a strong energy and is all about attracting!

Intention: I am attracting creativity and fun!

🦋 Today is good for:

- Partying and celebrating
- Dancing, singing, writing, painting
- Getting married
- Studying the sacred calendar
- Taking time to look for patterns in life
- Starting projects
- Watch for synchronicities today!

Call in the 4 Directions

Color & Direction: Chik'in the Blue/Black West
Ritual: This is a great day for burning incense, especially copal or frankincense. The Day Ceremony for today is Chik'in, the West.
Element: Water
Energetic Power Places where the energy is strong today are lakes and forests.
Amulet: Try wearing something woven today, especially a cloth wrist band or bracelet or something made from woven threads. Something that reminds you of monkeys.
Element: Water

Notes, Reflections, and Synchronicities:

_____

_____

_____

_____

_____

_____

_____

_____

2 Eb: Yellow Path ~ Date:

Travel and destiny...your path in life. You may find yourself on a vacation, or you may find yourself considering your direction in life and asking yourself if you are satisfied with it. This day can also be about following the path of the sacred calendar. It is a day when the ancestors are ready to listen.

The Magical Wave energy today is Ka'a, the number 2. Ka'a is the duality of two opposing forces finding balance. Think of the light and the dark, or cold and heat. We need both to exist in our lives in balance.

Intention: I am considering my path from all sides in order to find balance.

🦋 Today is good for:

- Travel or making plans to travel
- Spending time considering your path in life
- Making changes in your path in life
- Starting a new business or making a business plan
- Asking for good luck in both spiritual and material pursuits
- Being careful of dangers along the way

Color & Direction: Nohol, the Yellow South
Ritual: The Day Ceremony for today is Nohol, the south. Nohol bring abundance, increase, and harvest!
Energetic Power Places: Mountains and Woods and paths, especially ancient ones.
Amulets: Good amulets for today are pyramid, ladder, tooth (there is a tooth in the glyph to remind you to be careful of dangers along the road), compass or globe. Anything else that you associate with travel or your path in life.
Element: Earth

Notes, Reflections, and Synchronicities:

_____

_____

_____

_____

_____

_____

_____

_____

3 Ben: Red Corn Stalk – Date:

Ben is the rod of virtues of divine power! It is the corn stalk and is associated with harvest and success! The energy is both growing & surging upward like corn stalks after a heavy rain. It is a very meaningful day, associated with triumph! ALSO, the staff (stalk) symbolizes the spine and the internal fire which moves upward and activates the secret powers. (I love this stuff!)

The Magical Wave is the energy of Oox, the number 3, is here to play today. It is about taking creative action.

Intention: I am taking creative action and seeing great harvest and success!

🦋 **Today is a good day to:**

- Plant a seed or start a project
- Spend time with family or friends
- Follow your intuition and listen to your dreams
- Ask the ancestors for help in teaching and caretaking
- Study and investigate things
- Ask for rain and growth

Color & Direction: Lak'in the Red East
Ritual: The day ceremony for today is Lak'in the East. Consider requesting help from the ancestors in caring for your home and family or ask for help in starting a new business or project or help with your finances.
Amulet: Carry with you or wear small seeds (especially corn seeds), a small stone (used for grinding corn), whisky, bourbon, or rum. . .also sugar, and yellow clothes or jewelry.
Energetic Power Places: fields, meadows, forests, beaches
Element: Fire

Notes, Reflections, and Synchronicities:

_____

_____

_____

_____

_____

_____

_____

4 Ix: White Jaguar – Date:

Ix (pronounced *Ish*) is feminine energy and all things related to the earth, strength, and vitality. Think of the qualities of a jaguar. They are stealthy, strong, and hunt at night. This energy is powerful and wise and is related to the goddess Ixchel.

The Magical Wave is the energy of Kan is the number 4. Kan is when things begin to take form and become stable.

Intention: The energy of vitality is taking form and becoming stable in my life!

Today is a good day to:

- Meditate on the Earth as our home and how to live in harmony with Her.
- Use magic powers
- Take care of your home, especially by getting rid of things that no longer serve you.
- Use feminine energy
- Get pregnant
- Hunt for things such as knowledge, truth, wisdom
- Any ecological projects

Color & Direction: Xaman, the White North.
Ritual: The Day Ceremony is for Xaman, the North. Xaman brings transparency, clarity, and truth. After asking this energy to work with you today, give thanks to the ancestors for all things related to the earth. Consider placing some treasures from the earth around your candle today.
Energetic Power Places: Ceremonial places (especially the pyramids), forests, and mountains (high places)
Amulet: Jaguar, pyramid, or something with a jaguar or spotted design.
Element: Air

Notes, Reflections, and Synchronicities:

_____

_____

_____

_____

_____

_____

_____

_____

5 Men: Blue Eagle – Date:

Men the eagle is all about flying high, ambition, and vision. This is a day of good fortune, a day of freedom and of spiritual advancement! It is also about financial advancement. Men is the day of business, merchants, and money. So, this is also the day to dream big and reach for the sky in regard to your business ideas and dreams.

The Magical Wave energy of Jo'o, the umber 5, rules this day. This energy is empowering and focused on your core purpose.

Intention: I am empowered to reach for the stars!

🦋 This is a good day to:

- Communicate with Heart of Sky, the creator god
- Ask for money for buying things
- Consider the big picture
- Focus on goals and consider how to best meet them
- Pursue goals that have already been set
- Spiritual elevation
- Work on self-improvement

Color & Direction: Chik'in, the Blue West
Ritual: The Day Ceremony is Chik'in the West. Chik'in brings cooperation, duality, and change. This is a very important day for a sacrificial ritual to give thanks for money. The required offering is CHOCOLATE! Simply thank the gods and your ancestors for providing material goods and money, offer them some chocolate. When you finish, then eat it!
Energetic Power Places: Mountains, lakes, misty places, upland forests
Amulet: Bird feathers, dream catchers, anything with a bird, eagle, or quetzal on it
Element: Water

Notes, Reflections, and Synchronicities:

_____

_____

_____

_____

_____

_____

_____

_____

6 Kib: Yellow Owl – Date:

Kib, the warrior owl, is all about taking it easy, relaxation, patience, and timing. The warrior is careful in his timing. He is patient, not rushed. Like the warrior, today is about choosing your timing carefully. This day is also about the illusion of the material world. The night birds Today is a very spiritual day, indeed!

The Magical Wave energy of Wak (6) is all about moving forward and getting into the flow.

Intention: I am feeling easy and relaxed as I go with the flow.

This is a good day to:

- Go with the flow
- Relax
- Commune with the ancestors
- Wash your clothes, especially your good clothes
- Be a spiritual guide
- Ask for forgiveness for ignoring moral teachings
- This is a very special day to spend time preventing mistakes
- Kib is not a good day to start a new project because the energy is low.

Color & Direction: Nohol, the Yellow South
Ritual: The day ceremony is for Nohol which brings increase, abundance, and harvest. Consider taking time to commune with your ancestors during your Day Ceremony today.
Energetic Power Places: Mountains, volcanoes, tropical forests, lakes
Amulet: The earth, any rocks or crystals
Element: Earth

Notes, Reflections, and Synchronicities:

_____

_____

_____

_____

_____

_____

_____

_____

7 Kaban: Red Earth – Date:

Kaban, the earth is the energy of thoughts, logic, ideas and science. It is movement and sweeping change. Kaban is the earthquake: A day of formidable power and wisdom, a day of shaking the foundations and sudden revelations

The Magical Wave energy of Uk, the number 7, is inspiring and balanced. It is you coming into alignment or being in tune with the practical application of your mystic powers!

Intention: I am channeling earth-shaking ideas!

🦋 Today is good for:

- Thinking creativity
- Working with others
- Scientific investigation
- Being connected to the earth
- Coming into agreement with the creator
- Movement, travel
- Travel on the spiritual plane
- Shaking things up/sudden revelation/revelations that shake your foundations

Color & Direction: Lak'in, the Red East
Ritual: The Day Ceremony is for Lak'in. Lak'in bring the energy of beginnings, creation, and unity. As you ask Lak'in to work with you today, consider adding some rocks or crystals to your altar space.
Energetic Power Places: Mountains, volcanoes, tropical forests, lakes
Amulet: The earth, any rocks or crystals
Element: Fire

Notes, Reflections, and Synchronicities:

_____

_____

_____

_____

_____

_____

_____

_____

8 Etznab: White Knife – Date:

The obsidian sacrificial blade. A day to cut to the core of things. This is a day to reduce, clean out, and cleanse. Its energy is also about healing because the knife can both cut and heal. The obsidian blade is shined to the point of reflection and so the energy of the mirror also comes into play today.

The Magical Wave energy of Waxak (8) rules this day. It is all about harmony.

Intention: I am harmonizing with the energy of cleansing in my life today.

🦋 Today is a good day to:

Call in the 4 Directions

- Clean out your closet
- Do some editing (writing, song writing)
- Sort things out
- End an unproductive relationship
- Have a sale
- Let go of the past
- Diagnose and cure illness (physical, mental, and spiritual)
- Make predictions about the future

NOTE: Today is not a good day for travel or to start something new.

Color & Direction: Xaman, the White North.
Ritual: The Day Ceremony is for Xaman, the North. Xaman brings transparency, clarity, and truth. Today is a good day to make up for things you neglected to do or should not have done and to receive forgiveness. You can also ask for protection from disease and accidents. No other ceremonies are performed on a knife day.
Energetic Power Places: Pyramids, cliffs, waterfalls, lightning storms
Amulet: Obsidian stone, jade, a knife, a pyramid (the glyph has a pyramid on it) or a mirror
Element: Air

Notes, Reflections, and Synchronicities:

_____

_____

_____

_____

_____

_____

_____

_____

9 Kawak: Blue Storm – Date:

Storm is the Nawal of women and strength. It is the lightening flash of inspiration, the warmth and safety of the home, and the cleansing and purification of the rain. Imagine what it feels like to run inside as a storm approaches. That is the energy of Kawak. The rage of the wind and the comfort of home and the care of the woman who wraps loved ones in her arms.

The Magical Wave energy Bolon (9) is the power of the divine feminine. It is about mastery!

Intention: I am mastering caring for my home.

🦋 Today is a good day to:

- Tend to your family and home
- Do volunteer work
- Use your authority
- Ask for the actions of your enemies to turn against them
- Be prepared for trouble
- Heal mental illness
- Receive flashes of inspiration

Color & Direction: Chik'in, the Blue West
Ritual: The Day Ceremony is Chik'in the West. Chik'in brings cooperation, duality, and change. As you ask the energy of Chik'in to work with you today, you can also give thanks for the women in your life.
Energetic Power Places: Pine and cypress forests
Amulet: Storm cloud, lightening, Mayan goddess, or pyramid
Element: Water

Notes, Reflections, and Synchronicities:

_____

_____

_____

_____

_____

_____

_____

_____

10 Ahaw: Yellow Sun – Date:

Illumination and growth. The most powerful and positive nawal, radiating energy in all things. Its light not only lights up the day and the night (the moon is a reflection of the sun) but it also brings enlightenment and vision!

The Magical Wave energy of Lajun (10) is the power of manifesting!

Intention: I am manifesting illumination and growth!

🦋 Today is a good day to:

- Contact the dead
- Be brave against things that scare you
- Ask for illumination
- Build a house
- Start or continue projects
- Have a party
- Reflect on the positive things in life
- Place flowers on the graves of loved ones
- Seek spiritual illumination

Color & Direction: Nohol, the Yellow South
Ritual: The day ceremony is for Nohol which brings increase, abundance, and harvest. Consider doing this at sunrise or sunset today.
Energetic Power Places: Sunrise and sunset, find a beautiful view, especially on the beach or in a field of flowers
Amulet: Anything that shows the sun or flowers (especially yellow)
Element: Earth

Notes, Reflections, and Synchronicities:

_____

_____

_____

_____

_____

_____

_____

_____

11 Imix: Red Crocodile ~ Date:

Imix is a day of turbulent, stirring waters, of birth, new beginnings, and nurturing. It is a day of raw creative power. Because the crocodile lives in the mangroves, water lilies are associated with this day.

The Magical Wave number Buluk (11) is about letting go. The energy is too strong to handle now, so stand back and watch what it is becoming!

Intention: I am letting go of control as new things are birthed in my life.

🦋 **Today is a good day to:**

- Ask for water/rain
- Start the day with grounding exercises and/or meditation
- Make sweeping changes and lay new foundations
- Stay aware of the tendency to take wild and unpredictable actions.
- Be creative
- Develop your powers of intuition
- Receive messages from beyond
- Cleanse yourself from negative energy
- Ask for the calming of mental issues, spiritual problems, climate change

Color & Direction: Lak'in, the Red East
Ritual: The wind is blowing from the east today, so the Day Ceremony for is Lak'in. Lak'in brings new beginnings, unity, and creation. During your Day Ceremony, you can ask for guidance as you align with this powerful energy of creation!
Power Places: Lakes, lagoons, and other in-land bodies of water
Amulet: Crocodile, lotus blossom, crystals and images associated with the sea.
Element: Fire

Notes, Reflections, and Synchronicities:

_____
_____
_____
_____
_____
_____
_____
_____

12 Ik: White Wind – Date:

The breath of life and creativity. It is also a day of air, heavy showers, and hurricanes. The wind can carry news, bring change, and inspire creativity. It is a day to use your voice and is good for communication and letting your "voice" be heard.

The Magical Wave Energy of 12, Lajka'a, is the energy of crystalizing.

Intention: The energy of understanding what I want to say has crystalized in my life!

🦋 Today is a good day to:

- Use your voice, let your voice be heard.
- This is the best day for writing!
- Do something creative
- Cure respiratory illness
- Work on spiritual growth
- Go on a picnic or hike
- Do some gardening

Color & Direction: Xaman, the White North
Ritual: Burn pine or copal incense. This is the sacred day of stone alters. You can place stones around your altar or in a special place at home. Then perform the day ceremony for Xaman the North. Xaman brings transparency, clarity, and truth. During the day ceremony, you can ask for protection for friends and family and ask for protection against the rage of overly strong human emotions.
Energetic Power Places: Canyons, mountains, valleys, forests, and stone alters
Amulet: Hang wind chimes, a tree or branch, the beautiful quetzal bird
Element: Air

Notes, Reflections, and Synchronicities:

_____

_____

_____

_____

_____

_____

_____

_____

13 Ak'bal: Blue Night – Date:

Ak'bal is the night house, the underworld, and the realm of the eternal jaguar sun (the night sun). It is the darkness before the dawn. It is a day of good luck, especially in love! Ak'bal, the night, is generally, this is a tranquil and happy day.

The Magical Wave Energy of Ooxlajun (13) is the cosmic wild card! Anything is possible today!

Intention: I am in awe as the Universe brings things to light!

🦋 **Today's energy is good for:**

- Declaring your love: This is a lucky day for love!
- Looking within to find answers.
- Seeking anything: jobs, lovers, friends, answers, knowledge
- Discovering the underlying causes of problems
- Face personal challenges with intuition rather than strength
- Ask for light to reach all things
- Acknowledge feelings from the heart
- Getting a fresh start or new beginning

Color & Direction: Chik'in, the Blue West
Ritual: Make a fire at dusk or dawn and ask for renewal. The Day Ceremony for today is Chik'in the West. Chik'in brings the energies or cooperation, duality, adjusting, and change. During your Day Ceremony, you can ask the energy of Chik'in to help you find the answers you are looking for.
Energetic Power Places: Caves, pyramids, mountains, and valleys especially at dusk and dawn.
Amulet/Totem: Jaguar, pyramid, the color black
Element: Water

Notes, Reflections, and Synchronicities:

_____

_____

_____

_____

_____

_____

_____

_____

Thoughts About this Past Trecena

What K'an Brings

Focus: What harvest do you want to bring in over the next 13 days?

K'an is the seed. This is a time for harvest, collecting and gathering in! You might think of seeds as being about planting, but here they are the corn that comes in the fall. Think of them, golden and yellow and sweet! During the next thirteen days you can expect the energy of abundance and harvest to be with you! Is there something you have been working diligently on? Now is the time to finish it and reap the rewards! Or perhaps you could take time to look back over your past successes and remind yourself of how much you have done and let that inspire you. If you have been waiting for your harvest to come in, now is the time. So, make preparations to receive it. After all, you worked hard and now you get to enjoy the fruit of your labors!

Celestial bird, detail from altar, Kaminaljuyu

K'an the Yellow Seed

Trecena Planner

Glyphs from the Grolier Codex

1 K'an the Yellow Seed - Day/Date:

_____

_____

_____

_____

_____

_____

_____

2 Chikchan the Red Serpent – Day/Date:

_____

_____

_____

_____

_____

_____

3 Kimi the White World Bringer – Day/Date:

_____

_____

_____

_____

_____

_____

_____

4 Manik the Blue Deer – Day/Date:

_____

_____

_____

_____

_____

_____

_____

5 Lamat the Yellow Star Flower – Day/Date:

_____

_____

_____

_____

_____

_____

_____

6 Muluk the Red Moon – Day/Date:

_____

_____

_____

_____

_____

_____

_____

7 Ok the White Dog – Day/Date:

_____

_____

_____

_____

_____

_____

_____

8 Chuwen the Blue Monkey - Day/Date:

_____

_____

_____

_____

_____

_____

_____

9 Eb' the Yellow Path - Day/Date:

_____

_____

_____

_____

_____

_____

10 Ben the Red Corn Stalk - Day/Date:

_____

_____

_____

_____

_____

_____

11 Ix the White Jaguar - Day/Date:

_____

_____

_____

_____

_____

_____

12 Men the Blue Eagle - Day/Date:

_____

_____

_____

_____

_____

_____

_____

13 Kib the Yellow Owl - Day/Date:

_____

_____

_____

_____

_____

_____

Corn God in a celestial canoe Codex Style Vase

1 K'an: Yellow Seed – Date:

A day of gathering, collecting, harvest, and abundance. An abundant harvest is indicated here. The meaning is also linked to the net that is traditionally used to gather the corn and can represent tangling or untangling.

Magical Wave Energy of Jun (1) rules this day. Jun is the energy of beginnings. It is a strong energy and brings the gifts of magnetism and attraction.

Intention: I am an abundance magnet!

Call in the 4 Directions

🦋 Today is good for:

- Paying off debts
- Collecting things (even collecting your thoughts)
- Reaping the rewards of your work
- Piecing things together
- Do something associated with the interNET
- Witchy stuff (casting spells like one might cast a net)
- Disentangling things

Color & Direction: Nohol, the Yellow South
Element: Earth
Ritual: The Day Ceremony is Nohol, the south. Place seeds or yellow flowers around your candle. Nohol brings the energy of harvest, increase, and abundance! As you burn your candle, let it send prayers to the Heart of Sky and ask to be freed (untangled) from anything that prevents you from receiving the harvest you have worked for.
Energetic Power Places: The sea, farmer's fields, gardens
Amulet: Seeded jewelry or accessories, dream catcher (net).
Element: Earth

Notes, Reflections, and Synchronicities:

_____

_____

_____

_____

_____

_____

_____

_____

2 Chikchan: Red Feathered Serpent – Date:

The sky serpent, the cosmological snake, also known as Kukulkan. Chikchan is Framer and shaper of the Universe. This is an extremely powerful sign. It is the fire at the base of the spine, the Kundalini. It is associated with sexual magic and the rain gods. Key elements for this day are truth and justice.

The Magical Wave energy of Ka'a (2) is with you today. Think of tow opposite things balancing on a scale. This is Ka'a's energy, the polarizing energy of duality in balance.

Intention: I am balancing truth and wisdom.

Today is a good day to:

- Pursue or deliver truth and knowledge
- Deliver and receive justice
- Find or bring balance
- Pursue inner peace
- Enjoy great sex
- Take fast and direction action
- Beware of fast and direct action
- Stay on guard against anger in both yourself and others

Color & Direction: Lak'in, the Red East
Ritual: The Day Ceremony is Lak'in: unity, beginnings, and creation. This is a powerful day. It is a day to go to the mountains and commune with them. Light a fire and speak directly to the earth and ask for protection. You can also ask for justice, truth, peace, and balance.
Power Places: Mountains, volcanoes, pyramids, starry night
Amulet: Jade, snake, or pyramid—especially the one at Chichen Itza (where the temple of Kukulkan is). An especially powerful totem for today is a jade pyramid.
Element: Fire

Notes, Reflections, and Synchronicities:

_____

_____

_____

_____

_____

_____

_____

_____

3 Kimi: White World Bringer – Date:

The god of death and the lords of the underworld. Kimi is all about transformation and change. This usually applies to things like a job, relationship, living location, or some other part of your life that is in flux. Energies end and others begin. Change is an integral part of life and, if we harness it correctly, can keep moving us toward becoming more enlightened beings.

The Magical Wave energy of Oox (3) is here to play! It brings the power for taking creative action!

Intention: I am taking creative action to make the transformations that I want to make!

🦋 Today is a good day to:

- A great day to make or think about changes
- End relationships (business, friendships, or romantic)
- Work towards tranquility among friends and colleagues, both living and dead
- Both give and ask for forgiveness
- Remember the dead
- Do up-keep on and take care of equipment
- A tranquil day to be patient and conservative in your energy

Color & Direction: Xaman, the White North
Ritual: The Day Ceremony today is for Xaman, the North who brings Transparency, clarity, and truth. During your day ceremony you can give thanks to the ancestors who continue to give you guidance and ask for peace, love, money, health, and forgiveness.
Energetic Power Places: Pyramids, sacred sites, ceremonial sites, the fireplace, temples
Amulet: Skull, butterfly (transformation), corn seed, skeleton
Element: Air

Notes, Reflections, and Synchronicities:

_____

_____

_____

_____

_____

_____

_____

_____

4 Manik: Blue Deer – Date:

Balance, support, and the game of life. Manik is a very important day to focus on balance. Without balance, support cannot function properly. Think of the four legs of a table. If all the legs are different heights (unbalanced) how good is the table? Manik is the deer and the Lord of the hunt. It is a day to get into the game of life. You can think of hunting in our modern world as doing any activities that involve the pursuit of sustenance and strength. That makes Manik a good day for business. It is also a good day for long range travel. (Deer travel vast distances.)

The Magical Wave energy of Kan (4) brings stability as things take form. Because this is a balancing energy on a balanced day, this day is excellent for getting into the game of life!

Intention: I am successfully getting into the game of life!

🦋 Today is good for:

- Teamwork & meetings
- Business pursuits, getting out "in the field" and talking to customers
- Long range travel
- Staying alert for traps in business and the game of life
- An excellent day for diviners

Color & Direction: Chik'in, the Blue West
Ritual: The Day Ceremony is for Chik'in, the West. Chik'in brings you duality, cooperation, and change. As you perform your Day Ceremony, consider asking Chik'in to bless your finances and business.
Energetic Power Places are forests, and fields (places where you might find deer)
Amulet: Anything to do with the deer, anything with the number 4 or four parts to it.
Element: Water

Notes, Reflections, and Synchronicities:

_____

_____

_____

_____

_____

_____

_____

_____

5 Lamat: Yellow Star Flower – Date:

Today is all about abundance, growing, and harvest! It's a wonderful day to plant something, be it friendships, project ideas, or actual flowers. Lamat is also about fertility and is represented by the planet (star) Venus and the color gold.

The Magical Wave energy of Jo'o (5) empowers you. It is inspiring and encourages you to celebrate the things you are creating!

Intention: I am celebrating an abundant harvest!

Today is good for:

- Planting new things: flowers, friendships, projects
- Honoring past works
- Tending to your crops (in our modern times, that also means tending to business or whatever it is that sustains you)
- Star gazing (Lamat is also associated with Venus)
- Thinking about the Universe
- Feeding the world
- Fertility

Color: Yellow
Direction: Today the wind is blowing from the south. It brings harvest, abundance, and endings.
Ritual: The Day Ceremony today is Nohol, the South. Try placing some wildflowers, especially yellow ones, or seeds around your candle today.
Energetic Power Places today are forests, places where wildflowers grow, rivers and lakes
Amulet: Flowers (especially yellow ones), stars, or Venus
Element: Earth

Notes, Reflections, and Synchronicities:

_____

_____

_____

_____

_____

_____

_____

6 Muluk: Red Moon ~ Date:

A day to make payments, give offerings, and ask for dark things to come to light. Muluk is also about emotions and using your intuition. This is a day of cycles, rhythms and water since water is intrinsically connected to the moon.

The Magical Wave energy of Wak (6) is flowing today and helping you move forward. Relax and let her have her course!

Intention: I am in the flow of bringing dark things into the light!

🦋 Today is good for:

- Paying off debts (financial, relational, societal, spiritual)
- Asking people to pay you back for their debts to you
- Working to end suffering
- Giving offerings to the earth
- Asking for rain
- Asking for dark things to come to light
- Pay attention to your dreams
- Use your intuition

Color & Direction: Lak'in the Red East
Ritual: The day ceremony for today is Lak'in the East. You can also cleanse your candles and other alter items under the moon today.
Energetic Power Places today are the beach, big rocks, oceans, rivers, and lakes
Amulets: Shark or whale or other large aquatic creature, jade, the moon
Element: Fire

Notes, Reflections, and Synchronicities:

_____

_____

_____

_____

_____

_____

_____

_____

_____

7 Ok: White Dog ~ Date:

The one who guides the night sun through the underworld. Ok is about guidance and protection. Your guides are with you today in a powerful way to guide you through the underworld. This is also a day about justice and truth. On the lighter side, Ok is the most sexually charged day of the nawales.

The Magical Wave energy of Uk (7) brings you into alignment with your mystical powers!

Intention: My guides are helping me harness my mystical powers!

🦋 Today is good for:

- Asking for guidance
- Giving guidance
- Short distance travel (like around your town)
- Being alert for dangers/update home security
- Having great sex
- Looking for hidden truth

Color & Direction: Xaman, the White North.
Element: Air
Ritual: The Day Ceremony for today is for Xaman, the North. Consider asking the energy of Xaman to guide you today. Xaman brings transparency, clarity and truth.
Energetic Power Places today are mountains and beaches. If you don't live near these places, try a watching a video with beautiful scenery to add a little nature energy to your day.
Amulets: Anything related to dogs
Element: Air

Notes, Reflections, and Synchronicities:

_____

_____

_____

_____

_____

_____

_____

_____

8 Chuwen: Blue Monkey – Date:

The great craftsman, patron of the arts, the thread of that symbolizes destiny and maintains the continuity the past, the present, and the future. Monkey is all about being creative and having fun! It is a highly positive day that is full of energy that is friendly and happy!

The Magical Wave energy of Waxak (8) brings harmony to your inner self. Waxak is a good day for rituals and ceremonies because the energy is both strong and balanced.

Intention: I am finding harmony in play!

🦋 **Today is good for:**

Call in the 4 Directions

- Partying and celebrating
- Dancing, singing, writing, painting
- Getting married
- Studying the sacred calendar
- Taking time to look for patterns in life
- Starting projects
- Watch for synchronicities today!

Color & Direction: Chik'in the Blue/Black West
Ritual: This is a great day for burning incense, especially copal or frankincense. The Day Ceremony for today is Chik'in, the West.
Element: Water
Energetic Power Places where the energy is strong today are lakes and forests.
Amulet: Try wearing something woven today, especially a cloth wrist band or bracelet or something made from woven threads. Something that reminds you of monkeys.
Element: Water

Notes, Reflections, and Synchronicities:

_____
_____
_____
_____
_____
_____
_____
_____

9 Eb: Yellow Path – Date:

Travel and destiny...your path in life. This is a powerful day to consider your path. Do you like where you are headed? If not, this is a great day to make a change! This day can also be about following the path of the sacred calendar. It is a day when the ancestors are ready to listen.

The Magical Wave energy of Bolon (9) brings you expansion and mastery as you harness the power of the divine feminine!

Intention: I am expanding into the journey of my destiny!

Today is good for:

- Travel or making plans to travel
- Spending time considering your path in life
- Making changes in your path in life
- Starting a new business or making a business plan
- Asking for good luck in both spiritual and material pursuits
- Being careful of dangers along the way

Color & Direction: Nohol, the Yellow South
Ritual: The Day Ceremony for today is Nohol, the south. Nohol bring abundance, increase and harvest!
Energetic Power Places: Mountains and Woods and paths, especially ancient ones.
Amulets: Good amulets for today are pyramid, ladder, tooth (there is a tooth in the glyph to remind you to be careful of dangers along the road), compass or globe. Anything else that you associate with travel or your path in life.
Element: Earth

Notes, Reflections, and Synchronicities:

_____

_____

_____

_____

_____

_____

_____

_____

10 Ben: Red Corn Stalk – Date:

Ben is the rod of virtues of divine power! It is the corn stalk and is associated with harvest and success! The energy is both growing & surging upward like corn stalks after a heavy rain. It is a very meaningful day, associated with triumph! ALSO, the staff (stalk) symbolizes the spine and the internal fire which moves upward and activates the secret powers. (I love this stuff!)

The Magical Wave energy of Lajun (10) is the power of manifestation! It is a motivating, producing, and powerful energy.

Intention: I am manifesting harvest, success, and great triumph!

Today is a good day to:

- Plant a seed or start a project
- Spend time with family or friends
- Follow your intuition and listen to your dreams
- Ask the ancestors for help in teaching and caretaking
- Study and investigate things
- Ask for rain and growth

Color & Direction: Lak'in the Red East
Ritual: The day ceremony for today is Lak'in the East. Consider requesting help from the ancestors in caring for your home and family or ask for help in starting a new business or project or help with your finances.
Amulet: Carry with you or wear small seeds (especially corn seeds), a small stone (used for grinding corn) ... hahaha....you will like the next one....whisky, bourbon, or rum. . .also sugar, and yellow clothes or jewelry.
Energetic Power Places: fields, meadows, forests, beaches
Element: Fire

Notes, Reflections, and Synchronicities:

_____
_____
_____
_____
_____
_____
_____
_____

11 Ix: White Jaguar – Date:

Ix (pronounced *Ish*) is feminine energy and all things related to the earth, strength, and vitality. Think of the qualities of a jaguar. They are stealthy, strong, and hunt at night. This energy is powerful and wise and is related to the goddess Ixchel.

The Magical Wave energy of Buluk (11) brings the ability to release. You have done your work, now it is time to let go and see what it will become!

Intention: I am letting go of control and allowing the energy of the divine feminine to come!

🦋 Today is a good day to:

- Meditate on the Earth as our home and how to live in harmony with Her.
- Use magic powers
- Take care of your home, especially by getting rid of things that no longer serve you.
- Use feminine energy
- Get pregnant
- Hunt for things such as knowledge, truth, wisdom
- Any ecological projects

Color & Direction: Xaman, the White North.
Ritual: The Day Ceremony is for Xaman, the North. Xaman brings transparency, clarity, and truth. After asking this energy to work with you today, give thanks to the ancestors for all things related to the earth. Consider placing some treasures from the earth around your candle today.
Energetic Power Places: Ceremonial places (especially the pyramids), forests, and mountains (high places)
Amulet: Jaguar, pyramid, or something with a jaguar or spotted design.
Element: Air

Notes, Reflections, and Synchronicities:

_____

_____

_____

_____

_____

_____

_____

12 Men: Blue Eagle ~ Date:

Men the eagle is all about flying high, ambition, and vision. This is a day of good fortune, a day of freedom and of spiritual advancement! It is also about financial advancement. Men is the day of business, merchants, and money. So, this is also the day to dream big and reach for the sky in regard to your business ideas and dreams.

The Magical Wave energy of Lajka'a crystalizes. Understanding is now glowing brightly.

Intention: My vision is crystalizing!

This is a good day to:

- Communicate with Heart of Sky, the creator god
- Ask for money for buying things
- Consider the big picture
- Focus on goals and consider how to best meet them
- Pursue goals that have already been set
- Spiritual elevation
- Work on self-improvement

Color & Direction: Chik'in, the Blue West
Ritual: The Day Ceremony is Chik'in the West. Chik'in brings cooperation, duality, and change. This is a very important day for a sacrificial ritual to give thanks for money. The required offering is CHOCOLATE! Simply thank the gods and your ancestors for providing material goods and money, offer them some chocolate. When you finish, then eat it!
Energetic Power Places: Mountains, lakes, misty places, upland forests
Amulet: Bird feathers, dream catchers, anything with a bird, eagle, or quetzal on it
Element: Water

Notes, Reflections, and Synchronicities:
_____
_____
_____
_____
_____
_____
_____
_____

13 Kib: Yellow Owl – Date:

Kib, the warrior owl, is all about taking it easy, relaxation, patience, and timing. The warrior is careful in his timing. He is patient, not rushed. Like the warrior, today is about choosing your timing carefully. This day is also about the illusion of the material world. The night birds Today is a very spiritual day, indeed!

The Magical Wave energy of Ooxlajun (13) brings a higher vibration, a place where the impossible becomes possible! Today is the cosmic wild card. Watch for synchronicities!

Intention: My careful and patient timing is allowing magical synchronicities!

🦋 This is a good day to:

- Go with the flow
- Relax
- Commune with the ancestors
- Wash your clothes, especially your good clothes
- Be a spiritual guide
- Ask for forgiveness for ignoring moral teachings
- This is a very special day to spend time preventing mistakes
- Kib is not a good day to start a new project because the energy is low.

Color & Direction: Nohol, the Yellow South
Ritual: The day ceremony is for Nohol which brings increase, abundance, and harvest. Consider taking time to commune with your ancestors during your Day Ceremony today.
Energetic Power Places: Mountains, volcanoes, tropical forests, lakes
Amulet: The earth, any rocks or crystals
Element: Earth

Notes, Reflections, and Synchronicities:

_____

_____

_____

_____

_____

_____

_____

_____

Thoughts About this Past Trecena

_____

_____

_____

_____

_____

_____

_____

_____

_____

_____

_____

_____

_____

_____

_____

_____

_____

_____

_____

_____

_____

_____

_____

_____

_____

_____

_____

_____

What Kaban Has in Store For YOU!

Focus: What revelations would you like to uncover and discover over the next 13 days?

Get ready for sweeping change and earth-shattering revelations that will shake foundations! Kaban is a very powerful nawal and this Earth energy will be with you for the next thirteen days. Kaban's power comes in the form of logic, ideas, and science. So, this is a time to let your intuition take a backseat and let the scientific method take the stage. To come into alignment with Kaban's energy, start asking questions. There are answers you have been looking for and they are on the way. In fact, they will blow your socks off! They will change the way you think and the way you perceive the world. But you need to know where to find them.

This is a trecena to do research. It's a time to apply your logical mind to your questions. You may be used to using your intuition to get revelation, but this is a time for finding out what the facts are, digging deep into reasoning, and opening your mind to new ideas and new ways of thinking!

As you move through this trecena, pay attention to how you can apply this approach to each day. For example: You might want to do some stargazing on Ak'bal, the Night, and consider the vastness of the universe. Or take time on Ik, the Wind, to study how different breathing techniques can influence your well-being. Whatever you choose to do this trecena, make science, reasoning, and logic your friend!

Cave as the mouth of the Witz Monster

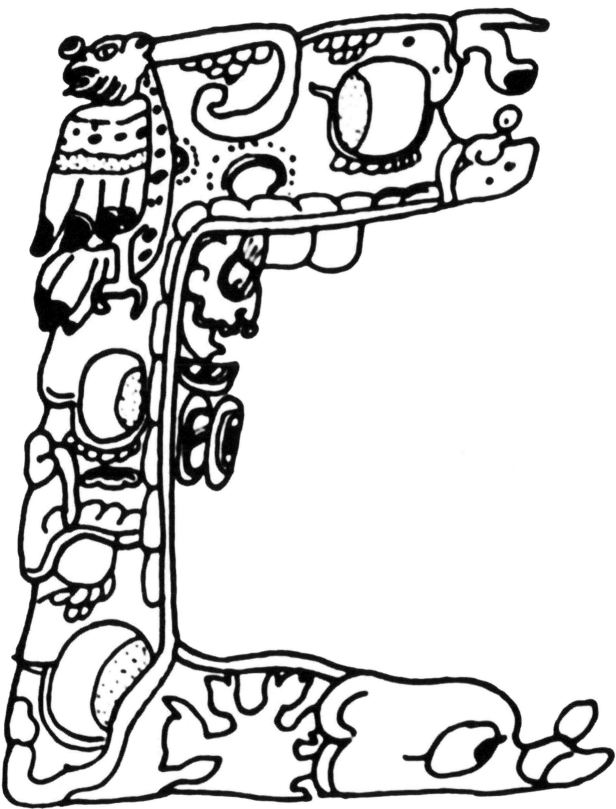

Kaban the Red Earth
Trecena Planner

Cave in Earth Detail

1 Kaban the red Earth - Day/Date:

_____
_____
_____
_____
_____
_____
_____

2 Etz'nab the White Knife – Day/Date:

_____
_____
_____
_____
_____
_____
_____

3 Kawak the Blue Storm – Day/Date:

_____
_____
_____
_____
_____
_____
_____

4 Ahaw the Yellow Sun – Day/Date:

_____
_____
_____
_____
_____
_____
_____

5 Imix the Red Crocodile – Day/Date:

_____
_____
_____
_____
_____
_____

6 Ik the White Wind – Day/Date:

_____

_____

_____

_____

_____

_____

_____

7 Ak'bal the Blue Night – Day/Date:

_____

_____

_____

_____

_____

_____

_____

8 K'an the Yellow Seed - Day/Date:

_____

_____

_____

_____

_____

_____

_____

9 Chikchan the Red Serpent - Day/Date:

_____

_____

_____

_____

_____

_____

_____

10 Kimi the White World Bringer - Day/Date:

_____

_____

_____

_____

_____

_____

_____

11 Manik the Blue Deer - Day/Date:

_____

_____

_____

_____

_____

_____

_____

12 Lamat the Yellow Star Flower - Day/Date:

_____

_____

_____

_____

_____

_____

_____

13 Muluk the Red Moon - Day/Date:

_____

_____

_____

_____

_____

_____

_____

Cave detail

1 Kaban: Red Earth – Date:

Kaban, the earth is the energy of thoughts, logic, ideas and science. It is movement and sweeping change. Kaban is the earthquake: A day of formidable power and wisdom, a day of shaking the foundations and sudden revelations

The Magical Wave energy of Jun (1) is that of attracting. It is strong and magnetic.

Intention: I am attracting sudden revelations!

🦋 Today is good for:

Call in the 4 Directions

- Thinking creativity
- Working with others
- Scientific investigation
- Being connected to the earth
- Coming into agreement with the creator
- Movement, travel
- Travel on the spiritual plane
- Shaking things up/sudden revelation/revelations that shake your foundations

Color & Direction: Lak'in, the Red East
Ritual: The Day Ceremony is for Lak'in. Lak'in bring the energy of beginnings, creation, and unity. As you ask Lak'in to work with you today, consider adding some rocks or crystals to your altar space.
Energetic Power Places: Mountains, volcanoes, tropical forests, lakes
Amulet: The earth, any rocks or crystals
Element: Fire

Notes, Reflections, and Synchronicities:

_____
_____
_____
_____
_____
_____
_____
_____

2 Etz'nab: White Knife – Date:

The obsidian sacrificial blade. A day to cut to the core of things. This is a day to reduce, clean out, and cleanse. Its energy is also about healing because the knife can both cut and heal. The obsidian blade is shined to the point of reflection and so the energy of the mirror also comes into play today.

The Magical Wave energy of Ka'a (2) rules this day. Ka'a is the power of duality finding balance.

Intention: I am finding balance as I remove things from my life that do not serve me.

🦋 Today is a good day to:

- Clean out your closet
- Do some editing (writing, song writing)
- Sort things out
- End an unproductive relationship
- Have a sale
- Let go of the past
- Diagnose and cure illness (physical, mental, and spiritual)
- Make predictions about the future

NOTE: Today is not a good day for travel or to start something new.

Color & Direction: Xaman, the White North.
Ritual: The Day Ceremony is for Xaman, the North. Xaman brings transparency, clarity, and truth. Today is a good day to make up for things you neglected to do or should not have done and to receive forgiveness. You can also ask for protection from disease and accidents. No other ceremonies are performed on a knife day.
Energetic Power Places: Pyramids, cliffs, waterfalls, lightning storms
Amulet: Obsidian stone, jade, a knife, a pyramid (the glyph has a pyramid on it) or a mirror
Element: Air

Notes, Reflections, and Synchronicities:

_____

_____

_____

_____

_____

_____

_____

_____

3 Kawak: Blue Storm ~ Date:

Storm is the Nawal of women and strength. It is the lightening flash of inspiration, the warmth and safety of the home, and the cleansing and purification of the rain. Imagine what it feels like to run inside as a storm approaches. That is the energy of Kawak. The rage of the wind and the comfort of home and the care of the woman who wraps loved ones in her arms.

The Magical Wave energy of Oox (3) is the power of taking creative action.

Intention: I am taking creative action to make my home a haven.

Today is a good day to:

- Tend to your family and home
- Do volunteer work
- Use your authority
- Ask for the actions of your enemies to turn against them
- Be prepared for trouble
- Heal mental illness
- Receive flashes of inspiration

Color & Direction: Chik'in, the Blue West
Ritual: The Day Ceremony is Chik'in the West. Chik'in brings cooperation, duality, and change. As you ask the energy of Chik'in to work with you today, you can also give thanks for the women in your life.
Energetic Power Places: Pine and cypress forests
Amulet: Storm cloud, lightening, Mayan goddess, or pyramid
Element: Water

Notes, Reflections, and Synchronicities:

_____

_____

_____

_____

_____

_____

_____

_____

4 Ahaw: Yellow Sun – Date:

Illumination and growth. The most powerful and positive nawal, radiating energy in all things. Its light not only lights up the day and the night (the moon is a reflection of the sun) but it also brings enlightenment and vision!

The Magical Wave energy of Kan (4) is the gift of things taking form and stabilizing.

Intention: The power of Illumination is taking form and stabilizing in my life.

🦋 Today is a good day to:

- Contact the dead
- Be brave against things that scare you
- Ask for illumination
- Build a house
- Start or continue projects
- Have a party
- Reflect on the positive things in life
- Place flowers on the graves of loved ones
- Seek spiritual illumination

Color & Direction: Nohol, the Yellow South
Ritual: The day ceremony is for Nohol which brings increase, abundance, and harvest. Consider doing this at sunrise or sunset today.
Energetic Power Places: Sunrise and sunset, find a beautiful view, especially on the beach or in a field of flowers
Amulet: Anything that shows the sun or flowers (especially yellow)
Element: Earth

Notes, Reflections, and Synchronicities:

_____

_____

_____

_____

_____

_____

_____

_____

5 Imix: Red Crocodile – Date:

Imix is a day of turbulent, stirring waters, of birth, new beginnings, and nurturing. It is a day of raw creative power. Because the crocodile lives in the mangroves, water lilies are associated with this day.

The Magical Wave energy of Jo'o (5) brings empowerment as you take joy in your creation!

Intention: I take joy in the things I create.

🦋 **Today is a good day to:**

- Ask for water/rain
- Start the day with grounding exercises and/or meditation
- Make sweeping changes and lay new foundations
- Stay aware of the tendency to take wild and unpredictable actions.
- Be creative
- Develop your powers of intuition
- Receive messages from beyond
- Cleanse yourself from negative energy
- Ask for the calming of mental issues, spiritual problems, climate change

Color & Direction: Lak'in, the Red East
Ritual: The wind is blowing from the east today, so the Day Ceremony for is Lak'in. Lak'in brings new beginnings, unity, and creation. During your Day Ceremony, you can ask for guidance as you align with this powerful energy of creation!
Power Places: Lakes, lagoons, and other in-land bodies of water
Amulet: Crocodile, lotus blossom, crystals and images associated with the sea.
Element: Fire

Notes, Reflections, and Synchronicities:

_____

_____

_____

_____

_____

_____

_____

_____

6 Ik: White Wind – Date:

The breath of life and creativity. It is also a day of air, heavy showers, and hurricanes. The wind can carry news, bring change, and inspire creativity. It is a day to use your voice and is good for communication and letting your "voice" be heard.

The Magical Wave Energy of Wak (6) brings the ability to get in the flow and move forward.

Intention: I am in the flow of creative expression.

🦋 **Today is a good day to:**

- Use your voice, let your voice be heard.
- This is the best day for writing!
- Do something creative
- Cure respiratory illness
- Work on spiritual growth
- Go on a picnic or hike
- Do some gardening

Color & Direction: Xaman, the White North
Ritual: Burn pine or copal incense. This is the sacred day of stone alters. You can place stones around your altar or in a special place at home. Then perform the day ceremony for Xaman the North. Xaman brings transparency, clarity, and truth. During the day ceremony, you can ask for protection for friends and family and ask for protection against the rage of overly strong human emotions.
Energetic Power Places: Canyons, mountains, valleys, forests, and stone alters
Amulet: Hang wind chimes, a tree or branch, the beautiful quetzal bird
Element: Air

Notes, Reflections, and Synchronicities:

_____

_____

_____

_____

_____

_____

_____

_____

7 Ak'bal: Blue Night – Date:

Ak'bal is the night house, the underworld, and the realm of the eternal jaguar sun (the night sun). It is the darkness before the dawn. It is a day of good luck, especially in love! Ak'bal, the night, is generally, this is a tranquil and happy day.

The Magical Wave Energy of Uk (7) brings the power of channeling.

Intention: I am channeling the power to bring things out of the darkness and into the light.

🦋 Today's energy is good for:

- Declaring your love: This is a lucky day for love!
- Looking within to find answers.
- Seeking anything: jobs, lovers, friends, answers, knowledge
- Discovering the underlying causes of problems
- Face personal challenges with intuition rather than strength
- Ask for light to reach all things
- Acknowledge feelings from the heart
- Getting a fresh start or new beginning

Color & Direction: Chik'in, the Blue West
Ritual: Make a fire at dusk or dawn and ask for renewal. The Day Ceremony for today is Chik'in the West. Chik'in brings the energies or cooperation, duality, adjusting, and change. During your Day Ceremony, you can ask the energy of Chik'in to help you find the answers you are looking for.
Energetic Power Places: Caves, pyramids, mountains, and valleys especially at dusk and dawn.
Amulet/Totem: Jaguar, pyramid, the color black
Element: Water

Notes, Reflections, and Synchronicities:

_____

_____

_____

_____

_____

_____

_____

_____

8 K'an: Yellow Seed – Date:

A day of gathering, collecting, harvest, and abundance. An abundant harvest is indicated here. The meaning is also linked to the net that is traditionally used to gather the corn and can represent tangling or untangling.

Magical Wave Energy of Waxak (8) is the most balanced of all the energies. It is about being in harmony with your most authentic self.

Intention: I am in harmony with abundance!

🦋 Today is good for:

Call in the 4 Directions

- Paying off debts
- Collecting things (even collecting your thoughts)
- Reaping the rewards of your work
- Piecing things together
- Do something associated with the interNET
- Witchy stuff (casting spells like one might cast a net)
- Disentangling things

Color & Direction: Nohol, the Yellow South
Element: Earth
Ritual: The Day Ceremony is Nohol, the south. Place seeds or yellow flowers around your candle. Nohol brings the energy of harvest, increase, and abundance! As you burn your candle, let it send prayers to the Heart of Sky and ask to be freed (untangled) from anything that prevents you from receiving the harvest you have worked for.
Energetic Power Places: The sea, farmer's fields, gardens
Amulet: Seeded jewelry or accessories, dream catcher (net).
Element: Earth

Notes, Reflections, and Synchronicities:

_____

_____

_____

_____

_____

_____

_____

_____

9 Chikchan: Red Feathered Serpent – Date:

The sky serpent, the cosmological snake, also known as Kukulkan. Chikchan is Framer and shaper of the Universe. This is an extremely powerful sign. It is the fire at the base of the spine, the Kundalini. It is associated with sexual magic and the rain gods. Key elements for this day are truth and justice.

The Magical Wave energy of Bolon (9) is the power of the divine feminine. It shows expansion and mastery!

Intention: I am expanding in wisdom.

🦋 Today is a good day to:

- Pursue or deliver truth and knowledge
- Deliver and receive justice
- Find or bring balance
- Pursue inner peace
- Enjoy great sex
- Take fast and direction action
- Beware of fast and direct action
- Stay on guard against anger in both yourself and others

Color & Direction: Lak'in, the Red East
Ritual: The Day Ceremony is Lak'in: unity, beginnings, and creation. This is a powerful day. It is a day to go to the mountains and commune with them. Light a fire and speak directly to the earth and ask for protection. You can also ask for justice, truth, peace, and balance.
Power Places: Mountains, volcanoes, pyramids, starry night
Amulet: Jade, snake, or pyramid—especially the one at Chichen Itza (where the temple of Kukulkan is). An especially powerful totem for today is a jade pyramid.
Element: Fire

Notes, Reflections, and Synchronicities:

_____

_____

_____

_____

_____

_____

_____

_____

10 Kimi: White World Bringer – Date:

The god of death and the lords of the underworld. Kimi is all about transformation and change. This usually applies to things like a job, relationship, living location, or some other part of your life that is in flux. Energies end and others begin. Change is an integral part of life and, if we harness it correctly, can keep moving us toward becoming more enlightened beings.

The Magical Wave energy of Lajun (10) brings the gift of manifestation!

Intention: I am manifesting transformation.

Today is a good day to:

- A great day to make or think about changes
- End relationships (business, friendships, or romantic)
- Work towards tranquility among friends and colleagues, both living and dead
- Both give and ask for forgiveness
- Remember the dead
- Do up-keep on and take care of equipment
- A tranquil day to be patient and conservative in your energy

Color & Direction: Xaman, the White North
Ritual: The Day Ceremony today is for Xaman, the North who brings Transparency, clarity, and truth. During your day ceremony you can give thanks to the ancestors who continue to give you guidance and ask for peace, love, money, health, and forgiveness.
Energetic Power Places: Pyramids, sacred sites, ceremonial sites, the fireplace, temples
Amulet: Skull, butterfly (transformation), corn seed, skeleton
Element: Air

Notes, Reflections, and Synchronicities:

_____
_____
_____
_____
_____
_____
_____
_____

11 Manik: Blue Deer – Date:

Balance, support, and the game of life. Manik is a very important day to focus on balance. Without balance, support cannot function properly. Think of the four legs of a table. If all the legs are different heights (unbalanced) how good is the table? Manik is the deer and the Lord of the hunt. It is a day to get into the game of life. You can think of hunting in our modern world as doing any activities that involve the pursuit of sustenance and strength. That makes Manik a good day for business. It is also a good day for long range travel. (Deer travel vast distances.)

The Magical Wave energy of Buluk (11) is all about letting go!

Intention: I am letting go and finding balance.

Today is good for:

- Teamwork & meetings
- Business pursuits, getting out "in the field" and talking to customers
- Long range travel
- Staying alert for traps in business and the game of life
- An excellent day for diviners

Color & Direction: Chik'in, the Blue West
Ritual: The Day Ceremony is for Chik'in, the West. Chik'in brings you duality, cooperation, and change. As you perform your Day Ceremony, consider asking Chik'in to bless your finances and business.
Energetic Power Places are forests, and fields (places where you might find deer)
Amulet: Anything to do with the deer, anything with the number 4 or four parts to it.
Element: Water

Notes, Reflections, and Synchronicities:

_____

_____

_____

_____

_____

_____

_____

_____

12 Lamat: Yellow Star Flower – Date:

Today is all about abundance and growing! It's a wonderful day to plant something, be it friendships, project ideas, or actual flowers. Lamat is also about fertility and is represented by the planet (star) Venus and the color gold.

The Magical Wave energy of Lajka'a (12) brings things into focus, it is crystalizing and brings the ability to understand.

Intention: The ability to grow things is crystallizing in my life.

🦋 Today is good for:

- Planting new things: flowers, friendships, projects
- Honoring past works
- Tending to your crops (in our modern times, that also means tending to business or whatever it is that sustains you)
- Star gazing (Lamat is also associated with Venus)
- Thinking about the Universe
- Feeding the world
- Fertility

Color: Yellow
Direction: Today the wind is blowing from the south. It brings harvest, abundance, and endings.
Ritual: The Day Ceremony today is Nohol, the South. Try placing some wildflowers, especially yellow ones, or seeds around your candle today.
Energetic Power Places today are forests, places where wildflowers grow, rivers and lakes
Amulet: Flowers (especially yellow ones), stars, or Venus
Element: Earth

Notes, Reflections, and Synchronicities:

_____

_____

_____

_____

_____

_____

_____

_____

13 Muluk: Red Moon ~ Date:

A day to make payments, give offerings, and ask for dark things to come to light. Muluk is also about emotions and using your intuition. This is a day of cycles, rhythms and water since water is intrinsically connected to the moon.

The Magical Wave energy of Ooxlajun is transcendence! This is the day when the Universe takes the stage, and anything can happen!

Intention: I am in awe as I view synchronicities in the cycles of nature.

🦋 Today is good for:

- Paying off debts (financial, relational, societal, spiritual)
- Asking people to pay you back for their debts to you
- Working to end suffering
- Giving offerings to the earth
- Asking for rain
- Asking for dark things to come to light
- Pay attention to your dreams
- Use your intuition

Color & Direction: Lak'in the Red East
Ritual: The day ceremony for today is Lak'in the East. You can also cleanse your candles and other alter items under the moon today.
Energetic Power Places today are the beach, big rocks, oceans, rivers, and lakes
Amulets: Shark or whale or other large aquatic creature, jade, the moon
Element: Fire

Notes, Reflections, and Synchronicities:

_____

_____

_____

_____

_____

_____

_____

_____

_____

Thoughts About this Past Trecena

What Ok Brings

Focus: What guidance would you like to receive over the next 13 days?

Ok (Oc) is the faithful dog who guides you. He guides the night sun through the underworld, and he will be with you too! You can expect the next thirteen days to be a time when you can access guidance to help you find your way through the darkness. Perhaps there are things you are feeling confused about or things you don't understand. Maybe you are looking for spiritual answers or want guidance from your ancestors. Ok is the one who knows the way through Xibalba, the Maya underworld! He can help reveal the path and help you to navigate it safely.

Ok is also about justice, so if there is something you have been seeking justice about, expect

Dog from the Grolier Codex

this trecena to be a time of finding it!

In addition, there is a little something fun about Ok. Imagine a dog at play! He cares not who is looking. So, you can expect yourself to be feeling like a kid again, not afraid to dance in the rain. You also might find yourself feeling very sexually free during the next thirteen days because Ok is the most sexually dynamic of all the Nawales!

Wow! So much to expect during this trecena! Guidance, justice, and a sense of hedonism all come into play here. So, let go of your inhibitions and move forward in your search. Who knows what you might find!

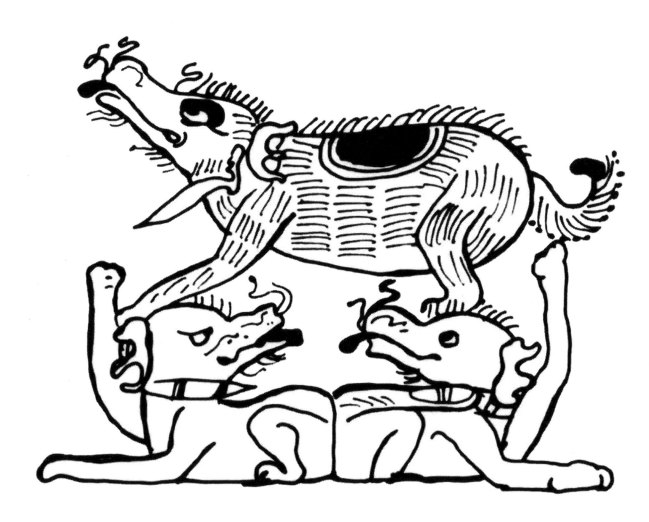

3 dog yui (pronounced way), supernatural shapeshifting creature
From a ceramic vessel

OK the White Dog

Trecena Planner

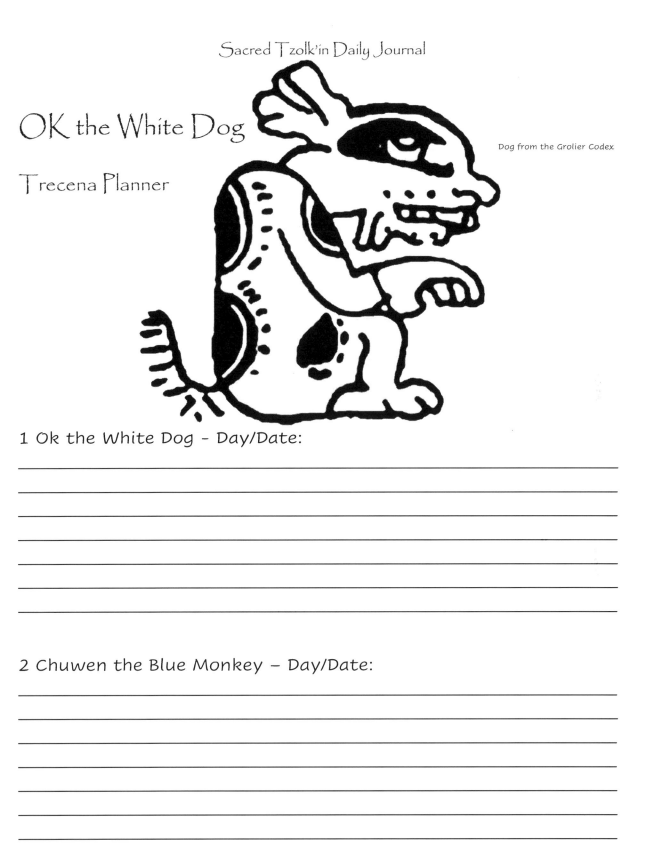

Dog from the Grolier Codex

1 Ok the White Dog - Day/Date:

_____
_____
_____
_____
_____
_____
_____

2 Chuwen the Blue Monkey – Day/Date:

_____
_____
_____
_____
_____
_____
_____

3 Eb' the Yellow Path – Day/Date:

_____

_____

_____

_____

_____

_____

_____

4 Ben the Red Corn Stalk – Day/Date:

_____

_____

_____

_____

_____

_____

_____

5 Ix the White Jaguar – Day/Date:

_____

_____

_____

_____

_____

_____

_____

6 Men the Blue Eagle – Day/Date:

_____

_____

_____

_____

_____

_____

_____

7 Kib the Yellow Path – Day/Date:

_____

_____

_____

_____

_____

_____

_____

8 Kaban the Red Earth - Day/Date:

_____

_____

_____

_____

_____

_____

_____

9 Etz'nab the White Knife - Day/Date:

_____
_____
_____
_____
_____
_____
_____

10 Kawak the Blue Storm - Day/Date:

_____
_____
_____
_____
_____
_____
_____

11 Ahaw the Yellow Sun - Day/Date:

_____
_____
_____
_____
_____
_____
_____

12 Imix the Red Crocodile - Day/Date:

_____
_____
_____
_____
_____
_____
_____

13 Ik the White Wind - Day/Date:

_____
_____
_____
_____
_____
_____
_____

Dog from the Grolier Codex

1 Ok: White Dog - Date:

The one who guides the night sun through the underworld. Ok is about guidance and protection. Your guides are with you today in a powerful way to guide you through the underworld. This is also a day about justice and truth. On the lighter side, Ok is the most sexually charged day of the Nawales.

The Magical Wave energy of Jun (1) is strong today. It is magnetic and attracting.

Intention: I am attracting guidance, justice, and fun!

🦋 Today is good for:

- Asking for guidance
- Giving guidance
- Short distance travel (like around your town)
- Being alert for dangers/update home security
- Having great sex
- Looking for hidden truth

Call in the 4 Directions

Color & Direction: Xaman, the White North.
Element: Air
Ritual: The Day Ceremony for today is for Xaman, the North. Consider asking the energy of Xaman to guide you today. Xaman brings transparency, clarity, and truth.
Energetic Power Places today are mountains and beaches. If you don't live near these places, try a watching a video with beautiful scenery to add a little nature energy to your day.
Amulets: Anything related to dogs
Element: Air

Notes, Reflections, and Synchronicities:

_____

_____

_____

_____

_____

_____

_____

_____

2 Chuwen: Blue Monkey – Date:

The great craftsman, patron of the arts, the thread of that symbolizes destiny and maintains the continuity the past, the present, and the future. Monkey is all about being creative and having fun! It is a highly positive day that is full of energy that is friendly and happy!

The Magical Wave energy of Ka'a is that of opposites finding balance.

Intention: I am finding balance as I indulge in creative fun!

🦋 Today is good for:

- Partying and celebrating
- Dancing, singing, writing, painting
- Getting married
- Studying the sacred calendar
- Taking time to look for patterns in life
- Starting projects
- Watch for synchronicities today!

Color & Direction: Chik'in the Blue/Black West
Ritual: This is a great day for burning incense, especially copal or frankincense. The Day Ceremony for today is Chik'in, the West.
Element: Water
Energetic Power Places where the energy is strong today are lakes and forests.
Amulet: Try wearing something woven today, especially a cloth wrist band or bracelet or something made from woven threads. Something that reminds you of monkeys.
Element: Water

Notes, Reflections, and Synchronicities:

_____

_____

_____

_____

_____

_____

_____

_____

3 Eb: Yellow Path - Date:

Travel and destiny...your path in life. This day can be about physical travel or about your direction in life. It can also be about following the path of the sacred calendar. It is a day when the ancestors are ready to listen.

The Magical Wave energy of Oox (3) is about taking creative action.

Intention: I am taking creative action regarding my path!

🦋 Today is good for:

- Travel or making plans to travel
- Spending time considering your path in life
- Making changes in your path in life
- Starting a new business or making a business plan
- Asking for good luck in both spiritual and material pursuits
- Being careful of dangers along the way

Color & Direction: Nohol, the Yellow South
Ritual: The Day Ceremony for today is Nohol, the south. Nohol bring abundance, increase, and harvest!
Energetic Power Places: Mountains and Woods and paths, especially ancient ones.
Amulets: Good amulets for today are pyramid, ladder, tooth (there is a tooth in the glyph to remind you to be careful of dangers along the road), compass or globe. Anything else that you associate with travel or your path in life.
Element: Earth

Notes, Reflections, and Synchronicities:

_____

_____

_____

_____

_____

_____

_____

_____

4 Ben: Red Corn Stalk – Date:

Ben is the rod of virtues of divine power! It is the corn stalk and is associated with harvest and success! The energy is both growing & surging upward like corn stalks after a heavy rain. It is a very meaningful day, associated with triumph! ALSO, the staff (stalk) symbolizes the spine and the internal fire which moves upward and activates the secret powers. (I love this stuff!)

The Magical Wave is the energy of Kan is balance. It is things becoming stable and taking form.

Intention: Great success is taking form in my life!

🦋 Today is a good day to:

- Plant a seed or start a project
- Spend time with family or friends
- Follow your intuition and listen to your dreams
- Ask the ancestors for help in teaching and caretaking
- Study and investigate things
- Ask for rain and growth

Color & Direction: Lak'in the Red East
Ritual: The day ceremony for today is Lak'in the East. Consider requesting help from the ancestors in caring for your home and family or ask for help in starting a new business or project or help with your finances.
Amulet: Carry with you or wear small seeds (especially corn seeds), a small stone (used for grinding corn), .whisky, bourbon, or rum. . .also sugar, and yellow clothes or jewelry.
Energetic Power Places: fields, meadows, forests, beaches
Element: Fire

Notes, Reflections, and Synchronicities:

_____

_____

_____

_____

_____

_____

_____

_____

5 Ix: White Jaguar – Date:

Ix (pronounced *Ish*) is feminine energy and all things related to the earth, strength, and vitality. Think of the qualities of a jaguar. They are stealthy, strong, and hunt at night. This energy is powerful and wise and is related to the goddess Ixchel.

The Magical Wave energy of Jo'o is the energy of empowerment!

Intention: I am empowered and full of vitality!

🦋 Today is a good day to:

- Meditate on the Earth as our home and how to live in harmony with Her.
- Use magic powers
- Take care of your home, especially by getting rid of things that no longer serve you.
- Use feminine energy
- Get pregnant
- Hunt for things such as knowledge, truth, wisdom
- Any ecological projects

Color & Direction: Xaman, the White North.
Ritual: The Day Ceremony is for Xaman, the North. Xaman brings transparency, clarity, and truth. After asking this energy to work with you today, give thanks to the ancestors for all things related to the earth. Consider placing some treasures from the earth around your candle today.
Energetic Power Places: Ceremonial places (especially the pyramids), forests, and mountains (high places)
Amulet: Jaguar, pyramid, or something with a jaguar or spotted design.
Element: Air

Notes, Reflections, and Synchronicities:

_____
_____
_____
_____
_____
_____
_____
_____

6 Men: Blue Eagle – Date:

Men the eagle is all about flying high, ambition, and vision. This is a day of good fortune, a day of freedom and of spiritual advancement! It is also about financial advancement. Men is the day of business, merchants, and money. So, this is also the day to dream big and reach for the sky in regard to your business ideas and dreams.

The Magical Wave energy of Wak (6) is about getting in the flow and moving forward.

Intention: I am in the flow of casting vision.

🦋 This is a good day to:

- Communicate with Heart of Sky, the creator god
- Ask for money for buying things
- Consider the big picture
- Focus on goals and consider how to best meet them
- Pursue goals that have already been set
- Spiritual elevation
- Work on self-improvement

Color & Direction: Chik'in, the Blue West
Ritual: The Day Ceremony is Chik'in the West. Chik'in brings cooperation, duality, and change. This is a very important day for a sacrificial ritual to give thanks for money. The required offering is CHOCOLATE! Simply thank the gods and your ancestors for providing material goods and money, offer them some chocolate. When you finish, then eat it!
Energetic Power Places: Mountains, lakes, misty places, upland forests
Amulet: Bird feathers, dream catchers, anything with a bird, eagle, or quetzal on it
Element: Water

Notes, Reflections, and Synchronicities:

_____

_____

_____

_____

_____

_____

_____

_____

7 Kib: Yellow Owl – Date:

Kib, the warrior owl, is all about taking it easy, relaxation, patience, and timing. The warrior is careful in his timing. He is patient, not rushed. Like the warrior, today is about choosing your timing carefully. This day is also about the illusion of the material world. The night birds Today is a very spiritual day, indeed!

The Magical Wave energy of Uk (7) is the ability to channel.

Intention: I am channeling the energy of perfect timing.

🦋 This is a good day to:

- Go with the flow
- Relax
- Commune with the ancestors
- Wash your clothes, especially your good clothes
- Be a spiritual guide
- Ask for forgiveness for ignoring moral teachings
- This is a very special day to spend time preventing mistakes
- Kib is not a good day to start a new project because the energy is low.

Color & Direction: Nohol, the Yellow South
Ritual: The day ceremony is for Nohol which brings increase, abundance, and harvest. Consider taking time to commune with your ancestors during your Day Ceremony today.
Energetic Power Places: Mountains, volcanoes, tropical forests, lakes
Amulet: The earth, any rocks or crystals
Element: Earth

Notes, Reflections, and Synchronicities:

_____

_____

_____

_____

_____

_____

_____

_____

8 Kaban: Red Earth ~ Date:

Kaban, the earth is the energy of thoughts, logic, ideas, and science. It is movement and sweeping change. Kaban is the earthquake: A day of formidable power and wisdom, a day of shaking the foundations and sudden revelations

The Magical Wave energy of Waxak (8) is all about being in harmony!

Intention: I am in harmony with the earth.

🦋 Today is good for:

Call in the 4 Directions

- Thinking creativity
- Working with others
- Scientific investigation
- Being connected to the earth
- Coming into agreement with the creator
- Movement, travel
- Travel on the spiritual plane
- Shaking things up/sudden revelation/revelations that shake your foundations

Color & Direction: Lak'in, the Red East
Ritual: The Day Ceremony is for Lak'in. Lak'in bring the energy of beginnings, creation, and unity. As you ask Lak'in to work with you today, consider adding some rocks or crystals to your altar space.
Energetic Power Places: Mountains, volcanoes, tropical forests, lakes
Amulet: The earth, any rocks or crystals
Element: Fire

Notes, Reflections, and Synchronicities:

_____

_____

_____

_____

_____

_____

_____

_____

9 Etznab: White Knife ~ Date:

The obsidian sacrificial blade. A day to cut to the core of things. This is a day to reduce, clean out, and cleanse. Its energy is also about healing because the knife can both cut and heal. The obsidian blade is shined to the point of reflection and so the energy of the mirror also comes into play today.

The Magical Wave energy of Bolon (9) is about finding mastery!

Intention: I am finding mastery as I cleanse my life.

Today is a good day to:

- Clean out your closet
- Do some editing (writing, song writing)
- Sort things out
- End an unproductive relationship
- Have a sale
- Let go of the past
- Diagnose and cure illness (physical, mental, and spiritual)
- Make predictions about the future

NOTE: Today is not a good day for travel or to start something new.

Color & Direction: Xaman, the White North.
Ritual: The Day Ceremony is for Xaman, the North. Xaman brings transparency, clarity and truth. Today is a good day to make up for things you neglected to do or should not have done and to receive forgiveness. You can also ask for protection from disease and accidents. No other ceremonies are performed on a knife day.
Energetic Power Places: Pyramids, cliffs, waterfalls, lightning storms
Amulet: Obsidian stone, jade, a knife, a pyramid (the glyph has a pyramid on it) or a mirror
Element: Air

Notes, Reflections, and Synchronicities:

_____

_____

_____

_____

_____

_____

_____

_____

10 Kawak: Blue Storm – Date:

Storm is the Nawal of women and strength. It is the lightening flash of inspiration, the warmth and safety of the home, and the cleansing and purification of the rain. Imagine what it feels like to run inside as a storm approaches. That is the energy of Kawak. The rage of the wind and the comfort of home and the care of the woman who wraps loved ones in her arms.

The Magical Wave energy of Lajun (10) is the ability to manifest!

Intention: I am manifesting a feeling of security in my home.

Today is a good day to:

- Tend to your family and home
- Do volunteer work
- Use your authority
- Ask for the actions of your enemies to turn against them
- Be prepared for trouble
- Heal mental illness
- Receive flashes of inspiration

Color & Direction: Chik'in, the Blue West
Ritual: The Day Ceremony is Chik'in the West. Chik'in brings cooperation, duality, and change. As you ask the energy of Chik'in to work with you today, you can also give thanks for the women in your life.
Energetic Power Places: Pine and cypress forests
Amulet: Storm cloud, lightening, Mayan goddess, or pyramid
Element: Water

Notes, Reflections, and Synchronicities:

_____
_____
_____
_____
_____
_____
_____

 ## 11 Ahaw: Yellow Sun – Date:

Illumination and growth. The most powerful and positive nawal, radiating energy in all things. Its light not only lights up the day and the night (the moon is a reflection of the sun) but it also brings enlightenment and vision!

The Magical Wave energy of Buluk (11) is that of letting go!

Intention: I am letting go so illumination can come to me.

Today is a good day to:

- Contact the dead
- Be brave against things that scare you
- Ask for illumination
- Build a house
- Start or continue projects
- Have a party
- Reflect on the positive things in life
- Place flowers on the graves of loved ones
- Seek spiritual illumination

Color & Direction: Nohol, the Yellow South
Ritual: The day ceremony is for Nohol which brings increase, abundance, and harvest. Consider doing this at sunrise or sunset today.
Energetic Power Places: Sunrise and sunset, find a beautiful view, especially on the beach or in a field of flowers
Amulet: Anything that shows the sun or flowers (especially yellow)
Element: Earth

Notes, Reflections, and Synchronicities:

_____

_____

_____

_____

_____

_____

_____

_____

12 Imix: Red Crocodile – Date:

Imix is a day of turbulent, stirring waters, of birth, new beginnings, and nurturing. It is a day of raw creative power. Because the crocodile lives in the mangroves, water lilies are associated with this day.

The Magical Wave energy of Lajka'a (12) is about understanding.

Intention: I understand what it is I want to birth!

🦋 Today is a good day to:

- Ask for water/rain
- Start the day with grounding exercises and/or meditation
- Make sweeping changes and lay new foundations
- Stay aware of the tendency to take wild and unpredictable actions.
- Be creative
- Develop your powers of intuition
- Receive messages from beyond
- Cleanse yourself from negative energy
- Ask for the calming of mental issues, spiritual problems, climate change

Color & Direction: Lak'in, the Red East
Ritual: The wind is blowing from the east today, so the Day Ceremony for is Lak'in. Lak'in brings new beginnings, unity, and creation. During your Day Ceremony, you can ask for guidance as you align with this powerful energy of creation!
Power Places: Lakes, lagoons, and other in-land bodies of water
Amulet: Crocodile, lotus blossom, crystals and images associated with the sea.
Element: Fire

Notes, Reflections, and Synchronicities:

_____

_____

_____

_____

_____

_____

_____

_____

13 Ik: White Wind ~ Date:

The breath of life and creativity. It is also a day of air, heavy showers, and hurricanes. The wind can carry news, bring change, and inspire creativity. It is a day to use your voice and is good for communication and letting your "voice" be heard.

The Magical Wave Energy of Ooxlajun (13) is the cosmic wild card. Today anything can happen! Watch for synchronicities!

Intention: I am in awe as the Universe speaks to me!

🦋 Today is a good day to:

- Use your voice, let your voice be heard.
- This is the best day for writing!
- Do something creative
- Cure respiratory illness
- Work on spiritual growth
- Go on a picnic or hike
- Do some gardening

Color & Direction: Xaman, the White North
Ritual: Burn pine or copal incense. This is the sacred day of stone alters. You can place stones around your altar or in a special place at home. Then perform the day ceremony for Xaman the North. Xaman brings transparency, clarity, and truth. During the day ceremony, you can ask for protection for friends and family and ask for protection against the rage of overly strong human emotions.
Energetic Power Places: Canyons, mountains, valleys, forests, and stone alters
Amulet: Hang wind chimes, a tree or branch, the beautiful quetzal bird
Element: Air

Notes, Reflections, and Synchronicities:

_____

_____

_____

_____

_____

_____

_____

_____

Thoughts About this Past Trecena

_____

_____

_____

_____

_____

_____

_____

_____

_____

_____

_____

_____

_____

_____

_____

_____

_____

_____

_____

_____

_____

_____

_____

_____

_____

_____

_____

_____

_____

What to Expect With Ak'bal

Focus: What would you like to have come to light over the next 13 days?

Ak'bal is not just the night. It is the darkest night, the time when all is still and quiet and the sun is waiting just beneath the horizon. It is hope that the light will return and it's finding things and revealing things. The night is also the lover's time because it is when the energy is right for revealing hidden love! So, declare your love to all those who are important to you during this trecena. Declare your love and expect someone unexpected to declare their love for you!

During the next 13 days, you can expect things to be revealed. Watch for secrets to come to light and lost things to be found. Pay attention because you may find keys you have needed to unlock doors in your life. You may even discover that unsolved mysteries get solved!

Ak'bal is related to water, so expect emotions to surface. Stay in tune with what you are feeling. Listen to your intuition. Your subconscious self has things to say! Listen to your heart and follow its lead. Your sixth sense will be heightened too. So, keep your spirit eye open and expect to receive!

Astronomer from the Madrid Codex

Bat from a carved vase

Ak'bal the Blue Night

Trecena Planner

Astronomer from the Madrid Codex

1 Ak'bal the Blue Night - Day/Date:

_____
_____
_____
_____
_____
_____
_____

2 K'an the Yellow Seed – Day/Date:

_____
_____
_____
_____
_____
_____
_____

3 Chikchan the Red Serpent – Day/Date:

_____
_____
_____
_____
_____
_____
_____

4 Kimi the White World Bringer – Day/Date:

_____
_____
_____
_____
_____
_____
_____

5 Manik the Blue Deer – Day/Date:

_____
_____
_____
_____
_____
_____
_____

6 Lamat the Yellow Star Flower – Day/Date:

_____

_____

_____

_____

_____

_____

_____

7 Muluk the Red Moon – Day/Date:

_____

_____

_____

_____

_____

_____

_____

8 Ok the White Dog - Day/Date:

_____

_____

_____

_____

_____

_____

_____

9 Chuwen the Blue Monkey - Day/Date:

_____

_____

_____

_____

_____

_____

_____

10 Eb' the Yellow Path - Day/Date:

_____

_____

_____

_____

_____

_____

_____

11 Ben the Red Corn - Day/Date:

_____

_____

_____

_____

_____

_____

12 Ix the White Jaguar - Day/Date:

_____

_____

_____

_____

_____

_____

_____

13 Men the Blue Eagle - Day/Date:

_____

_____

_____

_____

_____

_____

_____

_____

Moon & Stars from
Chilam Balam

1 Ak'bal: Blue Night – Date:

Ak'bal is the night house, the underworld, and the realm of the eternal jaguar sun (the night sun). It is the darkness before the dawn. It is a day of good luck, especially in love! Ak'bal, the night, is generally, this is a tranquil and happy day.

Call in the 4 Directions

The Magical Wave Energy of Jun (1) brings unity and attraction.

Intention: I am a revelation magnet!

🦋 Today's energy is good for:

- Declaring your love: This is a lucky day for love!
- Looking within to find answers.
- Seeking anything: jobs, lovers, friends, answers, knowledge
- Discovering the underlying causes of problems
- Face personal challenges with intuition rather than strength
- Ask for light to reach all things
- Acknowledge feelings from the heart
- Getting a fresh start or new beginning

Color & Direction: Chik'in, the Blue West
Ritual: Make a fire at dusk or dawn and ask for renewal. The Day Ceremony for today is Chik'in the West. Chik'in brings the energies or cooperation, duality, adjusting, and change. During your Day Ceremony, you can ask the energy of Chik'in to help you find the answers you are looking for.
Energetic Power Places: Caves, pyramids, mountains, and valleys especially at dusk and dawn.
Amulet/Totem: Jaguar, pyramid, the color black
Element: Water

Notes, Reflections, and Synchronicities:

_____

_____

_____

_____

_____

_____

_____

_____

2 K'an: Yellow Seed – Date:

A day of gathering, collecting, harvest, and abundance. An abundant harvest is indicated here. The meaning is also linked to the net that is traditionally used to gather the corn and can represent tangling or untangling.

Magical Wave Energy of Ka'a (2) is dual and polarizing.

Intention: I am gathering in all sorts of things today!

🦋 Today is good for:

- Paying off debts
- Collecting things (even collecting your thoughts)
- Reaping the rewards of your work
- Piecing things together
- Do something associated with the interNET
- Witchy stuff (casting spells like one might cast a net)
- Disentangling things

Color & Direction: Nohol, the Yellow South
Element: Earth
Ritual: The Day Ceremony is Nohol, the south. Place seeds or yellow flowers around your candle. Nohol brings the energy of harvest, increase, and abundance! As you burn your candle, let it send prayers to the Heart of Sky and ask to be freed (untangled) from anything that prevents you from receiving the harvest you have worked for.
Energetic Power Places: The sea, farmer's fields, gardens
Amulet: Seeded jewelry or accessories, dream catcher (net).
Element: Earth

Notes, Reflections, and Synchronicities:

_____

_____

_____

_____

_____

_____

_____

3 Chikchan: Red Feathered Serpent – Date:

The sky serpent, the cosmological snake, also known as Kukulkan. Chikchan is Framer and shaper of the Universe. This is an extremely powerful sign. It is the fire at the base of the spine, the Kundalini. It is associated with sexual magic and the rain gods. Key elements for this day are truth and justice.

The Magical Wave energy of Oox (3) is action oriented!

Intention: I am taking action in harmony with truth.

🦋 Today is a good day to:

- Pursue or deliver truth and knowledge
- Deliver and receive justice
- Find or bring balance
- Pursue inner peace
- Enjoy great sex
- Take fast and direction action
- Beware of fast and direct action
- Stay on guard against anger in both yourself and others

Color & Direction: Lak'in, the Red East
Ritual: The Day Ceremony is Lak'in: unity, beginnings, and creation. This is a powerful day. It is a day to go to the mountains and commune with them. Light a fire and speak directly to the earth and ask for protection. You can also ask for justice, truth, peace, and balance.
Power Places: Mountains, volcanoes, pyramids, starry night
Amulet: Jade, snake, or pyramid—especially the one at Chichen Itza (where the temple of Kukulkan is). An especially powerful totem for today is a jade pyramid.
Element: Fire

Notes, Reflections, and Synchronicities:

_____

_____

_____

_____

_____

_____

_____

_____

4 Kimi: White World Bringer – Date:

The god of death and the lords of the underworld. Kimi is all about transformation and change. This usually applies to things like a job, relationship, living location, or some other part of your life that is in flux. Energies end and others begin. Change is an integral part of life and, if we harness it correctly, can keep moving us toward becoming more enlightened beings.

The Magical Wave of Kan (4) is about finding stability.

Intention: I am finding stability in the midst of transformation.

🦋 Today is a good day to:

- A great day to make or think about changes
- End relationships (business, friendships, or romantic)
- Work towards tranquility among friends and colleagues, both living and dead
- Both give and ask for forgiveness
- Remember the dead
- Do up-keep on and take care of equipment
- A tranquil day to be patient and conservative in your energy

Color & Direction: Xaman, the White North
Ritual: The Day Ceremony today is for Xaman, the North who brings Transparency, clarity and truth. During your day ceremony you can give thanks to the ancestors who continue to give you guidance and ask for peace, love, money, health, and forgiveness.
Energetic Power Places: Pyramids, sacred sites, ceremonial sites, the fireplace, temples
Amulet: Skull, butterfly (transformation), corn seed, skeleton
Element: Air

Notes, Reflections, and Synchronicities:

_____

_____

_____

_____

_____

_____

_____

_____

5 Manik: Blue Deer ~ Date:

Balance, support, and the game of life. Manik is a very important day to focus on balance. Without balance, support cannot function properly. Think of the four legs of a table. If all the legs are different heights (unbalanced) how good is the table? Manik is the deer and the Lord of the hunt. It is a day to get into the game of life. You can think of hunting in our modern world as doing any activities that involve the pursuit of sustenance and strength. That makes Manik a good day for business. It is also a good day for long range travel. (Deer travel vast distances.)

The Magical Wave energy of Jo'o (5) focuses on your core purpose and takes joy in it!

Intention: I am finding joy in my core purpose in the game of life!

🦋 Today is good for:

- Teamwork & meetings
- Business pursuits, getting out "in the field" and talking to customers
- Long range travel
- Staying alert for traps in business and the game of life
- An excellent day for diviners

Color & Direction: Chik'in, the Blue West
Ritual: The Day Ceremony is for Chik'in, the West. Chik'in brings you duality, cooperation, and change. As you perform your Day Ceremony, consider asking Chik'in to bless your finances and business.
Energetic Power Places are forests, and fields (places where you might find deer)
Amulet: Anything to do with the deer, anything with the number 4 or four parts to it.
Element: Water

Notes, Reflections, and Synchronicities:

_____

_____

_____

_____

_____

_____

_____

_____

6 Lamat: Yellow Star Flower – Date:

Today is all about planting, abundance, and growing! It's a wonderful day to plant something, be it friendships, project ideas, or actual flowers. Lamat is also about fertility and is represented by the planet (star) Venus and the color gold.

The Magical Wave energy of Wak (6) is the ability to let go of control and be in the flow of forward movement. Trust the river and let it take you where it wants to go!

Intention: **I am in the flow with growing things.**

🦋 **Today is good for:**

- Planting new things: flowers, friendships, projects
- Honoring past works
- Tending to your crops (in our modern times, that also means tending to business or whatever it is that sustains you)
- Star gazing (Lamat is also associated with Venus)
- Thinking about the Universe
- Feeding the world
- Fertility

Color: Yellow
Direction: Today the wind is blowing from the south. It brings harvest, abundance, and endings.
Ritual: The Day Ceremony today is Nohol, the South. Try placing some wildflowers, especially yellow ones, or seeds around your candle today.
Energetic Power Places today are forests, places where wildflowers grow, rivers and lakes
Amulet: Flowers (especially yellow ones), stars, or Venus
Element: Earth

Notes, Reflections, and Synchronicities:

_____

_____

_____

_____

_____

_____

_____

_____

7 Muluk: Red Moon – Date:

A day to make payments, give offerings, and ask for dark things to come to light. Muluk is also about emotions and using your intuition. This is a day of cycles, rhythms and water since water is intrinsically connected to the moon.

The Magical Wave energy of Uk (7) is about being attuned to the practical application of your mystical powers and includes the ability to channel!

Intention: I am channeling intuition and balancing karma!

🦋 Today is good for:

- Paying off debts (financial, relational, societal, spiritual)
- Asking people to pay you back for their debts to you
- Working to end suffering
- Giving offerings to the earth
- Asking for rain
- Asking for dark things to come to light
- Pay attention to your dreams
- Use your intuition

Color & Direction: Lak'in the Red East
Ritual: The day ceremony for today is Lak'in the East. You can also cleanse your candles and other alter items under the moon today.
Energetic Power Places today are the beach, big rocks, oceans, rivers, and lakes
Amulets: Shark or whale or other large aquatic creature, jade, the moon
Element: Fire

Notes, Reflections, and Synchronicities:

_____

_____

_____

_____

_____

_____

_____

_____

_____

8 Ok: White Dog - Date:

The one who guides the night sun through the underworld. Ok is about guidance and protection. Your guides are with you today in a powerful way to guide you through the underworld. This is also a day about justice and truth. On the lighter side, Ok is the most sexually charged day of the Nawales.

The Magical Wave energy of Waxak is about being in harmony with yourself. It is strong and balanced energy and is a good day for rituals and ceremonies!

Intention: I am in harmony with my guides.

Call in the 4 Directions

🦋 Today is good for:

- Asking for guidance
- Giving guidance
- Short distance travel (like around your town)
- Being alert for dangers/update home security
- Having great sex
- Looking for hidden truth

Color & Direction: Xaman, the White North.
Element: Air
Ritual: The Day Ceremony for today is for Xaman, the North. Consider asking the energy of Xaman to guide you today. Xaman brings transparency, clarity and truth.
Energetic Power Places today are mountains and beaches. If you don't live near these places, try a watching a video with beautiful scenery to add a little nature energy to your day.
Amulets: Anything related to dogs
Element: Air

Notes, Reflections, and Synchronicities:

_____

_____

_____

_____

_____

_____

_____

_____

9 Chuwen: Blue Monkey – Date:

The great craftsman, patron of the arts, the thread of that symbolizes destiny and maintains the continuity the past, the present, and the future. Monkey is all about being creative and having fun! It is a highly positive day that is full of energy that is friendly and happy!

The Magical Wave energy of Bolon (9) is the divine feminine. It's about finding mastery!

Intention: I am mastering creativity and the art of having fun!

🦋 Today is good for:

- Partying and celebrating
- Dancing, singing, writing, painting
- Getting married
- Studying the sacred calendar
- Taking time to look for patterns in life
- Starting projects
- Watch for synchronicities today!

Color & Direction: Chik'in the Blue/Black West
Ritual: This is a great day for burning incense, especially copal or frankincense. The Day Ceremony for today is Chik'in, the West.
Element: Water
Energetic Power Places where the energy is strong today are lakes and forests.
Amulet: Try wearing something woven today, especially a cloth wrist band or bracelet or something made from woven threads. Something that reminds you of monkeys.
Element: Water

Notes, Reflections, and Synchronicities:

_____

_____

_____

_____

_____

_____

_____

_____

10 Eb: Yellow Path – Date:

Travel and destiny...your path in life. This day can also be about following the path of the sacred calendar. It is a day when the ancestors are ready to listen.

The Magical Wave energy of Lajun, (10) is perfect. It is the highest point on the wave, just before it breaks. This is the point where the immaterial becomes material. It is the point of manifestation!

Intention: I am manifesting my path in life!

🦋 Today is good for:

- Travel or making plans to travel
- Spending time considering your path in life
- Making changes in your path in life
- Starting a new business or making a business plan
- Asking for good luck in both spiritual and material pursuits
- Being careful of dangers along the way

Color & Direction: Nohol, the Yellow South
Ritual: The Day Ceremony for today is Nohol, the south. Nohol bring abundance, increase, and harvest!
Energetic Power Places: Mountains and Woods and paths, especially ancient ones.
Amulets: Good amulets for today are pyramid, ladder, tooth (there is a tooth in the glyph to remind you to be careful of dangers along the road), compass or globe. Anything else that you associate with travel or your path in life.
Element: Earth

Notes, Reflections, and Synchronicities:

_____

_____

_____

_____

_____

_____

_____

_____

11 Ben: Red Corn Stalk – Date:

Ben is the rod of virtues of divine power! It is the corn stalk and is associated with harvest and success! The energy is both growing & surging upward like corn stalks after a heavy rain. It is a very meaningful day, associated with triumph! ALSO, the staff (stalk) symbolizes the spine and the internal fire which moves upward and activates the secret powers. (I love this stuff!)

The Magical Wave is the energy of Buluk (11) is the point where the wave breaks. Its time to let go! The power is too strong and now you can stand back and watch what takes place!

Intention: I am letting go and watching harvest and success come!

🦋 Today is a good day to:

- Plant a seed or start a project
- Spend time with family or friends
- Follow your intuition and listen to your dreams
- Ask the ancestors for help in teaching and caretaking
- Study and investigate things
- Ask for rain and growth

Color & Direction: Lak'in the Red East
Ritual: The day ceremony for today is Lak'in the East. Consider requesting help from the ancestors in caring for your home and family or ask for help in starting a new business or project or help with your finances.
Amulet: Carry with you or wear small seeds (especially corn seeds), a small stone (used for grinding corn) ... hahaha....you will like the next one....whisky, bourbon, or rum. . .also sugar, and yellow clothes or jewelry.
Energetic Power Places: fields, meadows, forests, beaches
Element: Fire

Notes, Reflections, and Synchronicities:

_____
_____
_____
_____
_____
_____
_____
_____

12 Ix: White Jaguar – Date:

Ix (pronounced *Ish*) is feminine energy and all things related to the earth, strength, and vitality. Think of the qualities of a jaguar. They are stealthy, strong, and hunt at night. This energy is powerful and wise and is related to the goddess Ixchel.

The Magical Wave energy of Lajka'a (12) is where things crystalize. They are formed and beautiful and now you can see what they have become and understand them.

Intention: I understand the Divine Feminine.

Today is a good day to:

- Meditate on the Earth as our home and how to live in harmony with Her.
- Use magic powers
- Take care of your home, especially by getting rid of things that no longer serve you.
- Use feminine energy
- Get pregnant
- Hunt for things such as knowledge, truth, wisdom
- Any ecological projects

Color & Direction: Xaman, the White North.
Ritual: The Day Ceremony is for Xaman, the North. Xaman brings transparency, clarity, and truth. After asking this energy to work with you today, give thanks to the ancestors for all things related to the earth. Consider placing some treasures from the earth around your candle today.
Energetic Power Places: Ceremonial places (especially the pyramids), forests, and mountains (high places)
Amulet: Jaguar, pyramid, or something with a jaguar or spotted design.
Element: Air

Notes, Reflections, and Synchronicities:

_____

_____

_____

_____

_____

_____

_____

_____

13 Men: Blue Eagle – Date:

Men the eagle is all about flying high, ambition, and vision. This is a day of good fortune, a day of freedom and of spiritual advancement! It is also about financial advancement. Men is the day of business, merchants, and money. So, this is also the day to dream big and reach for the sky in regard to your business ideas and dreams.

The Magical Wave energy of Ooxlajun (13) is chaos. It is the rushing power of the gods, synchronicities, the wild card. Be amazed because today is the day when magic happens!

Intention: I am amazed at the magic in my vision!

🦋 This is a good day to:

- Communicate with Heart of Sky, the creator god
- Ask for money for buying things
- Consider the big picture
- Focus on goals and consider how to best meet them
- Pursue goals that have already been set
- Spiritual elevation
- Work on self-improvement

Color & Direction: Chik'in, the Blue West
Ritual: The Day Ceremony is Chik'in the West. Chik'in brings cooperation, duality, and change. This is a very important day for a sacrificial ritual to give thanks for money. The required offering is CHOCOLATE! Simply thank the gods and your ancestors for providing material goods and money, offer them some chocolate. When you finish, then eat it!
Energetic Power Places: Mountains, lakes, misty places, upland forests
Amulet: Bird feathers, dream catchers, anything with a bird, eagle, or quetzal on it
Element: Water

Notes, Reflections, and Synchronicities:

_____

_____

_____

_____

_____

_____

_____

_____

Thoughts About this Past Trecena

Trecena: Kib the Yellow Owl

Focus: How do you want to practice waiting for the perfect timing over the next 13 days?

Kib is the warrior owl, the vulture, the night birds. It is a time to wait. A time to be patient, a time to choose your moment carefully. It is also a time to relax and a time to connect with the things of the night like your intuition or communing with your ancestors.

So, take your time this trecena. Be patient and give yourself lots of opportunity to chill out and relax. This is not a time for rapid movement, but for careful consideration when it comes to making choices. The warrior owl is poised to move with force in the right moment. He sits and waits, controlled and careful. However, when he does act, it is with intensity. Even though this is a time of careful reflection, understand that when you KNOW the time is right, you can make your move with confidence.

Also, be on the lookout for communication from the beyond during these next 13 days. This is the time of darkness and the death birds. It is a time of communicating with those who have gone on before you and, if you listen carefully and pay close attention, you can expect your ancestors to take this time to communicate with you.

Kib is also a good time to focus on your intuition. So, as you move through this trecena, allow your intuitive powers to guide you. Listen to your dreams. Watch for signs. Pay attention to your inner guide and feelings. For now, they are coming to the forefront and they have much to show you!

Owl god, Grolier Codex

Owl Headdress: Stela at Piedras Negras

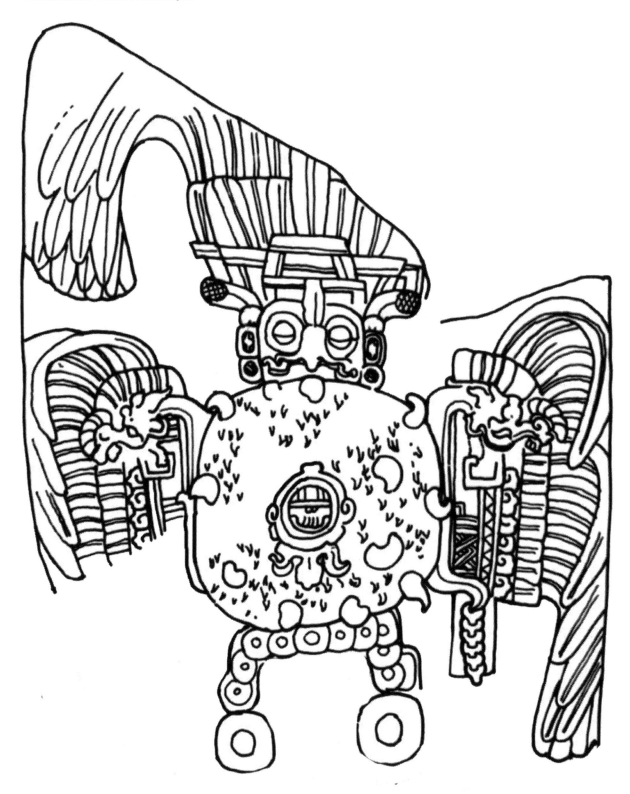

Kib the Yellow Owl

Trecena Planner

Owl god, codex style vase

1 Kib the Yellow Owl - Day/Date:

_____
_____
_____
_____
_____
_____
_____

2 Kaban the Red Earth – Day/Date:

_____
_____
_____
_____
_____
_____
_____

3 Etz'nab the White Knife – Day/Date:

_____
_____
_____
_____
_____
_____
_____

4 Kawak the Blue Storm – Day/Date:

_____
_____
_____
_____
_____
_____
_____

5 Ahaw the Yellow Sun – Day/Date:

_____
_____
_____
_____
_____
_____
_____

6 Imix the Red Crocodile – Day/Date:

_____

_____

_____

_____

_____

_____

_____

7 Ik the White Wind – Day/Date:

_____

_____

_____

_____

_____

_____

_____

8 Ak'bal the Blue Night - Day/Date:

_____

_____

_____

_____

_____

_____

_____

9 K'an the Yellow Seed - Day/Date:

_____

_____

_____

_____

_____

_____

_____

10 Chikchan the Red Serpent - Day/Date:

_____

_____

_____

_____

_____

_____

_____

11 Kimi the World Bringer - Day/Date:

_____

_____

_____

_____

_____

_____

_____

12 Manik the Blue Deer - Day/Date:

_____

_____

_____

_____

_____

_____

_____

13 Lamat the Yellow Star Flower - Day/Date:

_____

_____

_____

_____

_____

_____

_____

Horned Owl Lintel,
Palenque

1 Kib: Yellow Owl – Date:

Kib, the warrior owl, is all about taking it easy, relaxation, patience, and timing. The warrior is careful in his timing. He is patient, not rushed. Like the warrior, today is about choosing your timing carefully. This day is also about the illusion of the material world. The night birds Today is a very spiritual day, indeed!

The Magical Wave energy of Jun (1) rules this day. It is strong and balanced and all about attracting!

Intention: I am attracting perfect timing!

Call in the 4 Directions

🦋 This is a good day to:

- Go with the flow
- Relax
- Commune with the ancestors
- Wash your clothes, especially your good clothes
- Be a spiritual guide
- Ask for forgiveness for ignoring moral teachings
- This is a very special day to spend time preventing mistakes
- Kib is not a good day to start a new project because the energy is low.

Color & Direction: Nohol, the Yellow South
Ritual: The day ceremony is for Nohol which brings increase, abundance, and harvest. Consider taking time to commune with your ancestors during your Day Ceremony today.
Energetic Power Places: Mountains, volcanoes, tropical forests, lakes
Amulet: The earth, any rocks or crystals
Element: Earth

Notes, Reflections, and Synchronicities:

_____

_____

_____

_____

_____

_____

_____

_____

2 Kaban: Red Earth – Date:

Kaban, the earth is the energy of thoughts, logic, ideas, and science. It is movement and sweeping change. Kaban is the earthquake: A day of formidable power and wisdom, a day of shaking the foundations and sudden revelations

The Magical Wave energy of Ka'a (2) is the duality of bringing opposite energies into balance.

Intention: I am using logic to balance sweeping changes.

🦋 Today is good for:

- Thinking creativity
- Working with others
- Scientific investigation
- Being connected to the earth
- Coming into agreement with the creator
- Movement, travel
- Travel on the spiritual plane
- Shaking things up/sudden revelation/revelations that shake your foundations

Color & Direction: Lak'in, the Red East
Ritual: The Day Ceremony is for Lak'in. Lak'in bring the energy of beginnings, creation, and unity. As you ask Lak'in to work with you today, consider adding some rocks or crystals to your altar space.
Energetic Power Places: Mountains, volcanoes, tropical forests, lakes
Amulet: The earth, any rocks or crystals
Element: Fire

Notes, Reflections, and Synchronicities:

_____

_____

_____

_____

_____

_____

_____

_____

3 Etz'nab: White Knife – Date:

The obsidian sacrificial blade. A day to cut to the core of things. This is a day to reduce, clean out, and cleanse. Its energy is also about healing because the knife can both cut and heal. The obsidian blade is shined to the point of reflection and so the energy of the mirror also comes into play today.

The Magical Wave energy of Oox (3) brings the gift of taking creative action for the benefit of all.

Intention: I am taking creative action to cleanse my life!

Today is a good day to:

- Clean out your closet
- Do some editing (writing, song writing)
- Sort things out
- End an unproductive relationship
- Have a sale
- Let go of the past
- Diagnose and cure illness (physical, mental, and spiritual)
- Make predictions about the future

NOTE: Today is not a good day for travel or to start something new.

Color & Direction: Xaman, the White North.
Ritual: The Day Ceremony is for Xaman, the North. Xaman brings transparency, clarity, and truth. Today is a good day to make up for things you neglected to do or should not have done and to receive forgiveness. You can also ask for protection from disease and accidents. No other ceremonies are performed on a knife day.
Energetic Power Places: Pyramids, cliffs, waterfalls, lightning storms
Amulet: Obsidian stone, jade, a knife, a pyramid (the glyph has a pyramid on it) or a mirror
Element: Air

Notes, Reflections, and Synchronicities:

_____

_____

_____

_____

_____

_____

_____

_____

4 Kawak: Blue Storm – Date:

Storm is the Nawal of women and strength. It is the lightening flash of inspiration, the warmth and safety of the home, and the cleansing and purification of the rain. Imagine what it feels like to run inside as a storm approaches. That is the energy of Kawak. The rage of the wind and the comfort of home and the care of the woman who wraps loved ones in her arms.

The Magical Wave energy of Kan (4) brings stability.

Intention: I am finding stability in the comfort of home.

🦋 Today is a good day to:

- Tend to your family and home
- Do volunteer work
- Use your authority
- Ask for the actions of your enemies to turn against them
- Be prepared for trouble
- Heal mental illness
- Receive flashes of inspiration

Color & Direction: Chik'in, the Blue West
Ritual: The Day Ceremony is Chik'in the West. Chik'in brings cooperation, duality, and change. As you ask the energy of Chik'in to work with you today, you can also give thanks for the women in your life.
Energetic Power Places: Pine and cypress forests
Amulet: Storm cloud, lightening, Mayan goddess, or pyramid
Element: Water

Notes, Reflections, and Synchronicities:

_____

_____

_____

_____

_____

_____

_____

_____

5 Ahaw: Yellow Sun – Date:

Illumination and growth. The most powerful and positive nawal, radiating energy in all things. Its light not only lights up the day and the night (the moon is a reflection of the sun) but it also brings enlightenment and vision!

The Magical Wave energy Jo'o brings empowerment!

Intention: I am empowered by illumination!

🦋 Today is a good day to:

- Contact the dead
- Be brave against things that scare you
- Ask for illumination
- Build a house
- Start or continue projects
- Have a party
- Reflect on the positive things in life
- Place flowers on the graves of loved ones
- Seek spiritual illumination

Color & Direction: Nohol, the Yellow South
Ritual: The day ceremony is for Nohol which brings increase, abundance, and harvest. Consider doing this at sunrise or sunset today.
Energetic Power Places: Sunrise and sunset, find a beautiful view, especially on the beach or in a field of flowers
Amulet: Anything that shows the sun or flowers (especially yellow)
Element: Earth

Notes, Reflections, and Synchronicities:

_____

_____

_____

_____

_____

_____

_____

6 Imix: Red Crocodile – Date:

Imix is a day of turbulent, stirring waters, of birth, new beginnings, and nurturing. It is a day of raw creative power. Because the crocodile lives in the mangroves, water lilies are associated with this day.

The Magical Wave energy of Wak (6) is flowing today and moving things forward.

Intention: I am flowing in the energy of the new!

🦋 **Today is a good day to:**

- Ask for water/rain
- Start the day with grounding exercises and/or meditation
- Make sweeping changes and lay new foundations
- Stay aware of the tendency to take wild and unpredictable actions.
- Be creative
- Develop your powers of intuition
- Receive messages from beyond
- Cleanse yourself from negative energy
- Ask for the calming of mental issues, spiritual problems, climate change

Color & Direction: Lak'in, the Red East
Ritual: The wind is blowing from the east today, so the Day Ceremony for is Lak'in. Lak'in brings new beginnings, unity, and creation. During your Day Ceremony, you can ask for guidance as you align with this powerful energy of creation!
Power Places: Lakes, lagoons, and other in-land bodies of water
Amulet: Crocodile, lotus blossom, crystals and images associated with the sea.
Element: Fire

Notes, Reflections, and Synchronicities:

_____

_____

_____

_____

_____

_____

_____

_____

7 Ik: White Wind ~ Date:

The breath of life and creativity. It is also a day of air, heavy showers, and hurricanes. The wind can carry news, bring change, and inspire creativity. It is a day to use your voice and is good for communication and letting your "voice" be heard.

The Magical Wave Energy of Uk (7) is the ability to channel mystical powers!

Intention: I am channeling the breath of life and creativity!

Today is a good day to:

- Use your voice, let your voice be heard.
- This is the best day for writing!
- Do something creative
- Cure respiratory illness
- Work on spiritual growth
- Go on a picnic or hike
- Do some gardening

Color & Direction: Xaman, the White North
Ritual: Burn pine or copal incense. This is the sacred day of stone alters. You can place stones around your altar or in a special place at home. Then perform the day ceremony for Xaman the North. Xaman brings transparency, clarity, and truth. During the day ceremony, you can ask for protection for friends and family and ask for protection against the rage of overly strong human emotions.
Energetic Power Places: Canyons, mountains, valleys, forests, and stone alters
Amulet: Hang wind chimes, a tree or branch, the beautiful quetzal bird
Element: Air

Notes, Reflections, and Synchronicities:

_____

_____

_____

_____

_____

_____

_____

_____

8 Ak'bal: Blue Night – Date:

Ak'bal is the night house, the underworld, and the realm of the eternal jaguar sun (the night sun). It is the darkness before the dawn. It is a day of good luck, especially in love! Ak'bal, the night, is generally, this is a tranquil and happy day.

The Magical Wave energy of Waxak (8) is strong and balanced. The most balanced of the energies. Today is about being in harmony!

Intention: I am in harmony with good luck and love!

Call in the 4 Directions

🦋 Today's energy is good for:

- Declaring your love: This is a lucky day for love!
- Looking within to find answers.
- Seeking anything: jobs, lovers, friends, answers, knowledge
- Discovering the underlying causes of problems
- Face personal challenges with intuition rather than strength
- Ask for light to reach all things
- Acknowledge feelings from the heart
- Getting a fresh start or new beginning

Color & Direction: Chik'in, the Blue West
Ritual: Make a fire at dusk or dawn and ask for renewal. The Day Ceremony for today is Chik'in the West. Chik'in brings the energies or cooperation, duality, adjusting, and change. During your Day Ceremony, you can ask the energy of Chik'in to help you find the answers you are looking for.
Energetic Power Places: Caves, pyramids, mountains, and valleys especially at dusk and dawn.
Amulet/Totem: Jaguar, pyramid, the color black
Element: Water

Notes, Reflections, and Synchronicities:

_____

_____

_____

_____

_____

_____

_____

_____

9 K'an: Yellow Seed – Date:

A day of gathering, collecting, harvest, and abundance. An abundant harvest is indicated here. The meaning is also linked to the net that is traditionally used to gather the corn and can represent tangling or untangling.

The Magical Wave energy of Bolon (9) is the power of the divine feminine. It is about expanding and mastering!

Intention: I am a master of bringing in the harvest!

🦋 Today is good for:

- Paying off debts
- Collecting things (even collecting your thoughts)
- Reaping the rewards of your work
- Piecing things together
- Do something associated with the interNET
- Witchy stuff (casting spells like one might cast a net)
- Disentangling things

Color & Direction: Nohol, the Yellow South
Element: Earth
Ritual: The Day Ceremony is Nohol, the south. Place seeds or yellow flowers around your candle. Nohol brings the energy of harvest, increase, and abundance! As you burn your candle, let it send prayers to the Heart of Sky and ask to be freed (untangled) from anything that prevents you from receiving the harvest you have worked for.
Energetic Power Places: The sea, farmer's fields, gardens
Amulet: Seeded jewelry or accessories, dream catcher (net).
Element: Earth

Notes, Reflections, and Synchronicities:

_____

_____

_____

_____

_____

_____

_____

_____

10 Chikchan: Red Feathered Serpent – Date:

The sky serpent, the cosmological snake, also known as Kukulkan. Chikchan is Framer and shaper of the Universe. This is an extremely powerful sign. It is the fire at the base of the spine, the Kundalini. It is associated with sexual magic and the rain gods. Key elements for this day are truth and justice.

The Magical Wave energy of Lajun (10) brings the perfect power of manifesting today! It is where dreams become reality!

Intention: I am manifesting the power of truth and justice.

Today is a good day to:

- Pursue or deliver truth and knowledge
- Deliver and receive justice
- Find or bring balance
- Pursue inner peace
- Enjoy great sex
- Take fast and direction action
- Beware of fast and direct action
- Stay on guard against anger in both yourself and others

Color & Direction: Lak'in, the Red East
Ritual: The Day Ceremony is Lak'in: unity, beginnings, and creation. This is a powerful day. It is a day to go to the mountains and commune with them. Light a fire and speak directly to the earth and ask for protection. You can also ask for justice, truth, peace, and balance.
Power Places: Mountains, volcanoes, pyramids, starry night
Amulet: Jade, snake, or pyramid—especially the one at Chichen Itza (where the temple of Kukulkan is). An especially powerful totem for today is a jade pyramid.
Element: Fire

Notes, Reflections, and Synchronicities:

_____

_____

_____

_____

_____

_____

_____

_____

_____

11 Kimi: White World Bringer – Date:

The god of death and the lords of the underworld. Kimi is all about transformation and change. This usually applies to things like a job, relationship, living location, or some other part of your life that is in flux. Energies end and others begin. Change is an integral part of life and, if we harness it correctly, can keep moving us toward becoming more enlightened beings.

The Magical Wave energy of Buluk (11) asks you to let go. The energy is too strong today!

Intention: I am letting go and embracing transformation!

Today is a good day to:

- A great day to make or think about changes
- End relationships (business, friendships, or romantic)
- Work towards tranquility among friends and colleagues, both living and dead
- Both give and ask for forgiveness
- Remember the dead
- Do up-keep on and take care of equipment
- A tranquil day to be patient and conservative in your energy

Color & Direction: Xaman, the White North
Ritual: The Day Ceremony today is for Xaman, the North who brings Transparency, clarity and truth. During your day ceremony you can give thanks to the ancestors who continue to give you guidance and ask for peace, love, money, health, and forgiveness.
Energetic Power Places: Pyramids, sacred sites, ceremonial sites, the fireplace, temples
Amulet: Skull, butterfly (transformation), corn seed, skeleton
Element: Air

Notes, Reflections, and Synchronicities:

_____

_____

_____

_____

_____

_____

_____

_____

12 Manik: Blue Deer – Date:

Balance, support, and the game of life. Manik is a very important day to focus on balance. Without balance, support cannot function properly. Think of the four legs of a table. If all the legs are different heights (unbalanced) how good is the table? Manik is the deer and the Lord of the hunt. It is a day to get into the game of life. You can think of hunting in our modern world as doing any activities that involve the pursuit of sustenance and strength. That makes Manik a good day for business. It is also a good day for long range travel. (Deer travel vast distances.)

The Magical Wave energy of Lajka'a bring clarity!

Intention: Being in balance is bringing clarity to me today!

Today is good for:

- Teamwork & meetings
- Business pursuits, getting out "in the field" and talking to customers
- Long range travel
- Staying alert for traps in business and the game of life
- An excellent day for diviners

Color & Direction: Chik'in, the Blue West
Ritual: The Day Ceremony is for Chik'in, the West. Chik'in brings you duality, cooperation, and change. As you perform your Day Ceremony, consider asking Chik'in to bless your finances and business.
Energetic Power Places are forests, and fields (places where you might find deer)
Amulet: Anything to do with the deer, anything with the number 4 or four parts to it.
Element: Water

Notes, Reflections, and Synchronicities:

_____

_____

_____

_____

_____

_____

_____

_____

13 Lamat: Yellow Star Flower – Date:

Today is all about abundance and growing! It's a wonderful day to plant something, be it friendships, project ideas, or actual flowers. Lamat is also about fertility and is represented by the planet (star) Venus and the color gold.

The Magical Wave energy of Ooxlajun (13) is asking you to be prepared for the cosmic wild card. Today is about magic. Anything can happen!

Intention: I am prepared for magic as I plant new things today!

🦋 Today is good for:

- Planting new things: flowers, friendships, projects
- Honoring past works
- Tending to your crops (in our modern times, that also means tending to business or whatever it is that sustains you)
- Star gazing (Lamat is also associated with Venus)
- Thinking about the Universe
- Feeding the world
- Fertility

Color: Yellow
Direction: Today the wind is blowing from the south. It brings harvest, abundance, and endings.
Ritual: The Day Ceremony today is Nohol, the South. Try placing some wildflowers, especially yellow ones, or seeds around your candle today.
Energetic Power Places today are forests, places where wildflowers grow, rivers and lakes
Amulet: Flowers (especially yellow ones), stars, or Venus
Element: Earth

Notes, Reflections, and Synchronicities:

_____

_____

_____

_____

_____

_____

_____

_____

Thoughts About this Past Trecena

_____

_____

_____

_____

_____

_____

_____

_____

_____

_____

_____

_____

_____

_____

_____

_____

_____

_____

_____

_____

_____

_____

_____

_____

_____

_____

_____

_____

_____

What Muluk Brings

Focus: What responsibilities do you want to take care of during the next 13 days?

Muluk, the moon, brings you the energies of intuition and of payment this trecena. "Payment?" you ask. Well, the moon is tied to the woman's cycle and, in the Popul Vuh, Blood Woman had to prove she was the mother of the hero twins by bringing payment of an

offering of her blood found in the corn. This trecena brings the energy of balancing the books of life. It is a great time to make sure you have honored your commitments, whatever they may be. If you have bills to catch up on, this is a great time to do it. If you have relationships you want to work on, this is also a great time to do that.

Moon Goddess, Ixchel, codex style vase

All that being said, Muluk is also about using your intuitive powers. You can expect your intuition to be strong during the next thirteen days. Pay attention to it. As things come to you, flow with them. Muluk is also related to the water. The deep ocean is profound and holds many secrets. This is a time to allow things hidden in your subconscious to come to the surface. The energy of Muluk supports revelation and understanding at an intuitive level.

I know these two things, payment and intuition, may not seem like they flow together, but you will be surprised this trecena at how connections are made. Watch for opportunities to dive deep into the waters of your psyche under the power of the moon and expect to find yourself balancing the book of karma in your life!

Moon goddess, Ixchel, carved stone panel at Bonampak

Muluk the Red Moon

Trecena Planner

Moon Goddess on a carved conch shell

1 Muluk the Red Moon - Day/Date:

_____

_____

_____

_____

_____

_____

_____

2 Ok the White Dog – Day/Date:

_____

_____

_____

_____

_____

_____

_____

3 Chuwen the Blue Monkey – Day/Date:

_____

_____

_____

_____

_____

_____

_____

4 Eb' the Yellow Path – Day/Date:

_____

_____

_____

_____

_____

_____

_____

5 Ben the Red Corn Stalk – Day/Date:

_____

_____

_____

_____

_____

_____

_____

6 Ix the White Jaguar – Day/Date:

_____
_____
_____
_____
_____
_____
_____

7 Men the Blue Eagle – Day/Date:

_____
_____
_____
_____
_____
_____
_____

8 Kib the Yellow Eagle - Day/Date:

_____
_____
_____
_____
_____
_____
_____

9 Kaban the Red Earth - Day/Date:

_____
_____
_____
_____
_____
_____
_____

10 Etz'nab the White Knife - Day/Date:

_____
_____
_____
_____
_____
_____
_____

11 Kawak the Blue Storm - Day/Date:

_____
_____
_____
_____
_____
_____

12 Ahaw the Yellow Sun - Day/Date:

_____

_____

_____

_____

_____

_____

_____

13 Imix the Red Crocodile - Day/Date:

_____

_____

_____

_____

_____

_____

_____

_____

Ixchel's rabbit blowing a conch shell
Codex style vase

1 Muluk: Red Moon ~ Date:

A day to make payments, give offerings, and ask for dark things to come to light. Muluk is also about emotions and using your intuition. This is a day of cycles, rhythms and water since water is intrinsically connected to the moon.

The Magical Wave energy of Jun, the power of ONE rules this day. Its gift is attraction!

Intention: I am attracting balanced karma.

🦋 Today is good for:

- Paying off debts (financial, relational, societal, spiritual)
- Asking people to pay you back for their debts to you
- Working to end suffering
- Giving offerings to the earth
- Asking for rain
- Asking for dark things to come to light
- Pay attention to your dreams
- Use your intuition

Call in the 4 Directions

Color & Direction: Lak'in the Red East
Ritual: The day ceremony for today is Lak'in the East. You can also cleanse your candles and other alter items under the moon today.
Energetic Power Places today are the beach, big rocks, oceans, rivers, and lakes
Amulets: Shark or whale or other large aquatic creature, jade, the moon
Element: Fire

Notes, Reflections, and Synchronicities:

_____

_____

_____

_____

_____

_____

_____

_____

_____

2 Ok: White Dog – Date:

The one who guides the night sun through the underworld. Ok is about guidance and protection. Your guides are with you today in a powerful way to guide you through the underworld. This is also a day about justice and truth. On the lighter side, Ok is the most sexually charged day of the Nawales.

The Magical Wave energy of Ka'a, the duality of 2, brings the ability to balance polar opposites!

Intention: **I am being guided into balance.**

🦋 Today is good for:

- Asking for guidance
- Giving guidance
- Short distance travel (like around your town)
- Being alert for dangers/update home security
- Having great sex
- Looking for hidden truth

Color & Direction: Xaman, the White North.
Element: Air
Ritual: The Day Ceremony for today is for Xaman, the North. Consider asking the energy of Xaman to guide you today. Xaman brings transparency, clarity, and truth.
Energetic Power Places today are mountains and beaches. If you don't live near these places, try a watching a video with beautiful scenery to add a little nature energy to your day.
Amulets: Anything related to dogs
Element: Air

Notes, Reflections, and Synchronicities:

_____

_____

_____

_____

_____

_____

_____

_____

3 Chuwen: Blue Monkey – Date:

The great craftsman, patron of the arts, the thread of that symbolizes destiny and maintains the continuity the past, the present, and the future. Monkey is all about being creative and having fun! It is a highly positive day that is full of energy that is friendly and happy!

The Magical Wave energy of Oox, the power of three, bring the gift of taking creative action for the benefit of all.

Intention: I am taking action to be creative and have more fun!

🦋 Today is good for:

- Partying and celebrating
- Dancing, singing, writing, painting
- Getting married
- Studying the sacred calendar
- Taking time to look for patterns in life
- Starting projects
- Watch for synchronicities today!

Color & Direction: Chik'in the Blue/Black West
Ritual: This is a great day for burning incense, especially copal or frankincense. The Day Ceremony for today is Chik'in, the West.
Element: Water
Energetic Power Places where the energy is strong today are lakes and forests.
Amulet: Try wearing something woven today, especially a cloth wrist band or bracelet or something made from woven threads. Something that reminds you of monkeys.
Element: Water

Notes, Reflections, and Synchronicities:

_____

_____

_____

_____

_____

_____

_____

_____

4 Eb: Yellow Path ~ Date:

Travel and destiny...your path in life. The Maya question< "Bix a bel?" asks, "How is your path?" it is central to the Maya life and following the calendar is called, Following the path! It is a day when the ancestors are ready to listen.

The Magical Wave energy of Kan is the power of four to bring stability as things take form in your life.

Intention: My path is taking form and becoming stable.

🦋 Today is good for:

- Travel or making plans to travel
- Spending time considering your path in life
- Making changes in your path in life
- Starting a new business or making a business plan
- Asking for good luck in both spiritual and material pursuits
- Being careful of dangers along the way

Color & Direction: Nohol, the Yellow South
Ritual: The Day Ceremony for today is Nohol, the south. Nohol bring abundance, increase, and harvest!
Energetic Power Places: Mountains and Woods and paths, especially ancient ones.
Amulets: Good amulets for today are pyramid, ladder, tooth (there is a tooth in the glyph to remind you to be careful of dangers along the road), compass or globe. Anything else that you associate with travel or your path in life.
Element: Earth

Notes, Reflections, and Synchronicities:

_____

_____

_____

_____

_____

_____

_____

_____

_____

5 Ben: Red Corn Stalk – Date:

Ben is the rod of virtues of divine power! It is the corn stalk and is associated with harvest and success! The energy is both growing & surging upward like corn stalks after a heavy rain. It is a very meaningful day, associated with triumph! ALSO, the staff (stalk) symbolizes the spine and the internal fire which moves upward and activates the secret powers. (I love this stuff!)

The Magical Wave energy of Jo'o (5) is the gift of empowerment!

Intention: I am empowered with stunning growth!

🦋 Today is a good day to:

- Plant a seed or start a project
- Spend time with family or friends
- Follow your intuition and listen to your dreams
- Ask the ancestors for help in teaching and caretaking
- Study and investigate things
- Ask for rain and growth

Color & Direction: Lak'in the Red East
Ritual: The day ceremony for today is Lak'in the East. Consider requesting help from the ancestors in caring for your home and family or ask for help in starting a new business or project or help with your finances.
Amulet: Carry with you or wear small seeds (especially corn seeds), a small stone (used for grinding corn), whisky, bourbon, or rum. . .also sugar, and yellow clothes or jewelry.
Energetic Power Places: fields, meadows, forests, beaches
Element: Fire

Notes, Reflections, and Synchronicities:

_____

_____

_____

_____

_____

_____

_____

_____

6 Ix: White Jaguar – Date:

Ix (pronounced *Ish*) is feminine energy and all things related to the earth, strength, and vitality. Think of the qualities of a jaguar. They are stealthy, strong, and hunt at night. This energy is powerful and wise and is related to the goddess Ixchel.

The Magical Wave energy of Wak (6) is the ability to go with the flow and allow the universe to move you forward!

Intention: I am flowing into all the vitality of the Divine Feminine!

🦋 Today is a good day to:

- Meditate on the Earth as our home and how to live in harmony with Her.
- Use magic powers
- Take care of your home, especially by getting rid of things that no longer serve you.
- Use feminine energy
- Get pregnant
- Hunt for things such as knowledge, truth, wisdom
- Any ecological projects

Color & Direction: Xaman, the White North.
Ritual: The Day Ceremony is for Xaman, the North. Xaman brings transparency, clarity, and truth. After asking this energy to work with you today, give thanks to the ancestors for all things related to the earth. Consider placing some treasures from the earth around your candle today.
Energetic Power Places: Ceremonial places (especially the pyramids), forests, and mountains (high places)
Amulet: Jaguar, pyramid, or something with a jaguar or spotted design.
Element: Air

Notes, Reflections, and Synchronicities:

_____

_____

_____

_____

_____

_____

_____

_____

7 Men: Blue Eagle ~ Date:

Men the eagle is all about flying high, ambition, and vision. This is a day of good fortune, a day of freedom and of spiritual advancement! It is also about financial advancement. Men is the day of business, merchants, and money. So, this is also the day to dream big and reach for the sky in regard to your business ideas and dreams.

The Magical Wave energy of Uk, the power of seven, is the ability to channel your magic powers!

Intention: I am channeling high vision!

This is a good day to:

- Communicate with Heart of Sky, the creator god
- Ask for money for buying things
- Consider the big picture
- Focus on goals and consider how to best meet them
- Pursue goals that have already been set
- Spiritual elevation
- Work on self-improvement

Color & Direction: Chik'in, the Blue West
Ritual: The Day Ceremony is Chik'in the West. Chik'in brings cooperation, duality, and change. This is a very important day for a sacrificial ritual to give thanks for money. The required offering is CHOCOLATE! Simply thank the gods and your ancestors for providing material goods and money, offer them some chocolate. When you finish, then eat it!
Energetic Power Places: Mountains, lakes, misty places, upland forests
Amulet: Bird feathers, dream catchers, anything with a bird, eagle, or quetzal on it
Element: Water

Notes, Reflections, and Synchronicities:

_____

_____

_____

_____

_____

_____

_____

_____

8 Kib: Yellow Owl – Date:

Kib, the warrior owl, is all about taking it easy, relaxation, patience, and timing. The warrior is careful in his timing. He is patient, not rushed. Like the warrior, today is about choosing your timing carefully. This day is also about the illusion of the material world. The night birds Today is a very spiritual day, indeed!

The Magical Wave energy of Waxak (8) is the most balanced of the energies. Its gift is the ability to come into harmony with your truest self!

Intention: I am in harmony with choosing perfect timing!

Call in the 4 Directions

🦋 **This is a good day to:**

- Go with the flow
- Relax
- Commune with the ancestors
- Wash your clothes, especially your good clothes
- Be a spiritual guide
- Ask for forgiveness for ignoring moral teachings
- This is a very special day to spend time preventing mistakes
- Kib is not a good day to start a new project because the energy is low.

Color & Direction: Nohol, the Yellow South
Ritual: The day ceremony is for Nohol which brings increase, abundance, and harvest. Consider taking time to commune with your ancestors during your Day Ceremony today.
Energetic Power Places: Mountains, volcanoes, tropical forests, lakes
Amulet: The earth, any rocks or crystals
Element: Earth

Notes, Reflections, and Synchronicities:

_____

_____

_____

_____

_____

_____

_____

_____

9 Kaban: Red Earth ~ Date:

Kaban, the earth is the energy of thoughts, logic, ideas, and science. It is movement and sweeping change. Kaban is the earthquake: A day of formidable power and wisdom, a day of shaking the foundations and sudden revelations

The Magical Wave energy of Bolon (9) is the ability to find mastery in the divine feminine.

Intention: The divine feminine is bringing sudden revelation to me!

🦋 Today is good for:

- Thinking creativity
- Working with others
- Scientific investigation
- Being connected to the earth
- Coming into agreement with the creator
- Movement, travel
- Travel on the spiritual plane
- Shaking things up/sudden revelation/revelations that shake your foundations

Color & Direction: Lak'in, the Red East
Ritual: The Day Ceremony is for Lak'in. Lak'in bring the energy of beginnings, creation, and unity. As you ask Lak'in to work with you today, consider adding some rocks or crystals to your altar space.
Energetic Power Places: Mountains, volcanoes, tropical forests, lakes
Amulet: The earth, any rocks or crystals
Element: Fire

Notes, Reflections, and Synchronicities:

_____

_____

_____

_____

_____

_____

_____

_____

10 Etz'nab: White Knife – Date:

The obsidian sacrificial blade. A day to cut to the core of things. This is a day to reduce, clean out, and cleanse. Its energy is also about healing because the knife can both cut and heal. The obsidian blade is shined to the point of reflection and so the energy of the mirror also comes into play today.

The Magical Wave energy of Lajun (10) is the gift of powerful manifestation!

Intention: I am manifesting cleansing!

Today is a good day to:

- Clean out your closet
- Do some editing (writing, song writing)
- Sort things out
- End an unproductive relationship
- Have a sale
- Let go of the past
- Diagnose and cure illness (physical, mental, and spiritual)
- Make predictions about the future

NOTE: Today is not a good day for travel or to start something new.

Color & Direction: Xaman, the White North.
Ritual: The Day Ceremony is for Xaman, the North. Xaman brings transparency, clarity and truth. Today is a good day to make up for things you neglected to do or should not have done and to receive forgiveness. You can also ask for protection from disease and accidents. No other ceremonies are performed on a knife day.
Energetic Power Places: Pyramids, cliffs, waterfalls, lightning storms
Amulet: Obsidian stone, jade, a knife, a pyramid (the glyph has a pyramid on it) or a mirror
Element: Air

Notes, Reflections, and Synchronicities:

_____

_____

_____

_____

_____

_____

_____

_____

11 Kawak: Blue Storm – Date:

Storm is the Nawal of women and strength. It is the lightening flash of inspiration, the warmth and safety of the home, and the cleansing and purification of the rain. Imagine what it feels like to run inside as a storm approaches. That is the energy of Kawak. The rage of the wind and the comfort of home and the care of the woman who wraps loved ones in her arms.

The Magical Wave energy of Buluk (11) is too powerful to handle. So, it's time to just let go!

Intention: I am letting go as the storm flashes about me and brings revelation in its thunderings!

🦋 Today is a good day to:

- Tend to your family and home
- Do volunteer work
- Use your authority
- Ask for the actions of your enemies to turn against them
- Be prepared for trouble
- Heal mental illness
- Receive flashes of inspiration

Color & Direction: Chik'in, the Blue West
Ritual: The Day Ceremony is Chik'in the West. Chik'in brings cooperation, duality and change. As you ask the energy of Chik'in to work with you today, you can also give thanks for the women in your life.
Energetic Power Places: Pine and cypress forests
Amulet: Storm cloud, lightening, Mayan goddess, or pyramid
Element: Water

Notes, Reflections, and Synchronicities:

_____

_____

_____

_____

_____

_____

_____

_____

12 Ahaw: Yellow Sun – Date:

Illumination and growth. The most powerful and positive nawal, radiating energy in all things. Its light not only lights up the day and the night (the moon is a reflection of the sun) but it also brings enlightenment and vision!

The Magical Wave energy of Lajka'a is the power of 12. It is the ability to understand what has happened, what you have created, and what is crystalizing!

Intention: I understand the sun!

Today is a good day to:

- Contact the dead
- Be brave against things that scare you
- Ask for illumination
- Build a house
- Start or continue projects
- Have a party
- Reflect on the positive things in life
- Place flowers on the graves of loved ones
- Seek spiritual illumination

Color & Direction: Nohol, the Yellow South
Ritual: The day ceremony is for Nohol which brings increase, abundance, and harvest. Consider doing this at sunrise or sunset today.
Energetic Power Places: Sunrise and sunset, find a beautiful view, especially on the beach or in a field of flowers
Amulet: Anything that shows the sun or flowers (especially yellow)
Element: Earth

Notes, Reflections, and Synchronicities:

_____

_____

_____

_____

_____

_____

_____

_____

13 Imix: Red Crocodile – Date:

Imix is a day of turbulent, stirring waters, of birth, new beginnings, and nurturing. It is a day of raw creative power. Because the crocodile lives in the mangroves, water lilies are associated with this day.

The Magical Wave energy of Ooxlajun is the power of 13! It is magic, chaos, the cosmic wild card, synchronicities, the impossible becoming possible. This is a day when anything can happen!

Intention: I am attracting wonderful energy for new beginnings.

🦋 Today is a good day to:

- Ask for water/rain
- Start the day with grounding exercises and/or meditation
- Make sweeping changes and lay new foundations
- Stay aware of the tendency to take wild and unpredictable actions.
- Be creative
- Develop your powers of intuition
- Receive messages from beyond
- Cleanse yourself from negative energy
- Ask for the calming of mental issues, spiritual problems, climate change

Color & Direction: Lak'in, the Red East
Ritual: The wind is blowing from the east today, so the Day Ceremony for is Lak'in. Lak'in brings new beginnings, unity, and creation. During your Day Ceremony, you can ask for guidance as you align with this powerful energy of creation!
Power Places: Lakes, lagoons, and other in-land bodies of water
Amulet: Crocodile, lotus blossom, crystals and images associated with the sea.
Element: Fire

Notes, Reflections, and Synchronicities:

_____

_____

_____

_____

_____

_____

_____

_____

_____

Thoughts About this Past Trecena

_____
_____
_____
_____
_____
_____
_____
_____
_____
_____
_____
_____
_____
_____
_____
_____
_____
_____
_____
_____
_____
_____
_____
_____
_____
_____
_____
_____
_____

What Ik has in Store For YOU!

Focus: What do you want the power of the wind to bring as it blows through your life over the next 13 days?

Ik is the wind, the hurricane, the breath of life, and your voice! It's also a time of creativity. During this trecena you may find the wind bringing messages to you. You may also find that the winds of change are blowing through. Be open to change and listen carefully for the messages that are coming through!

This is also a time to speak your truth, use your voice, say what's really on your mind. You are empowered by this wind! Because Ik brings creativity into play, this is a great time to write or express your "voice" by painting, dance, and other art forms.

So, listen to the wind during the next thirteen days, hear what it has to say. . . and let your voice rise with it!

Ancestor of the Winds, Carved stela in Tikal

Chac-xib-chah, paddler

Ik the White Wind

Trecena Planner

Huracan, Chilam Balam

1 Ik the White Wind - Day/Date:

_____
_____
_____
_____
_____
_____
_____
_____

2 Ak'bal the Blue Night – Day/Date:

_____
_____
_____
_____
_____
_____
_____
_____

3 K'an the Yellow Seed – Day/Date:

_____

_____

_____

_____

_____

_____

_____

4 Chikchan the Red Serpent – Day/Date:

_____

_____

_____

_____

_____

_____

_____

5 Kimi the White World Bringer – Day/Date:

_____

_____

_____

_____

_____

_____

_____

6 Manik the Blue Deer – Day/Date:

_____

_____

_____

_____

_____

_____

_____

7 Lamat the Yellow Star Flower – Day/Date:

_____

_____

_____

_____

_____

_____

_____

8 Muluk the Red Moon - Day/Date:

_____

_____

_____

_____

_____

_____

_____

9 Ok the White Dog - Day/Date:

_____

_____

_____

_____

_____

_____

_____

10 Chuwen the Blue Monkey - Day/Date:

_____

_____

_____

_____

_____

_____

_____

11 Eb' the Yellow Path - Day/Date:

_____

_____

_____

_____

_____

_____

12 Ben the Red Corn Stalk – Day/Date:

_____

_____

_____

_____

_____

_____

_____

13 Ix the White Jaguar – Day/Date:

_____

_____

_____

_____

_____

_____

_____

The Descending God
Stucco mask, Tikal

1 Ik: White Wind – Date:

The breath of life and creativity. It is also a day of air, heavy showers, and hurricanes. The wind can carry news, bring change, and inspire creativity. It is a day to use your voice and is good for communication and letting your "voice" be heard.

The Magical Wave energy of the number one, Jun, is the power of attracting!

Intention: I am attracting great communication!

Call in the 4 Directions

🦋 **Today is a good day to:**

- Use your voice, let your voice be heard.
- This is the best day for writing!
- Do something creative
- Cure respiratory illness
- Work on spiritual growth
- Go on a picnic or hike
- Do some gardening

Color & Direction: Xaman, the White North
Ritual: Burn pine or copal incense. This is the sacred day of stone alters. You can place stones around your altar or in a special place at home. Then perform the day ceremony for Xaman the North. Xaman brings transparency, clarity, and truth. During the day ceremony, you can ask for protection for friends and family and ask for protection against the rage of overly strong human emotions.
Energetic Power Places: Canyons, mountains, valleys, forests, and stone alters
Amulet: Hang wind chimes, a tree or branch, the beautiful quetzal bird
Element: Air

Notes, Reflections, and Synchronicities:

_____

_____

_____

_____

_____

_____

_____

_____

2 Ak'bal: Blue Night ~ Date:

Ak'bal is the night house, the underworld, and the realm of the eternal jaguar sun (the night sun). It is the darkness before the dawn. It is a day of good luck, especially in love! Ak'bal, the night, is generally, this is a tranquil and happy day.

The Magical Wave energy of Ka'a is the dual energy of balance. It's two things balancing each other, even though they are different!

Intention: I am balancing things that come to light!

🦋 **Today's energy is good for:**

- Declaring your love: This is a lucky day for love!
- Looking within to find answers.
- Seeking anything: jobs, lovers, friends, answers, knowledge
- Discovering the underlying causes of problems
- Face personal challenges with intuition rather than strength
- Ask for light to reach all things
- Acknowledge feelings from the heart
- Getting a fresh start or new beginning

Color & Direction: Chik'in, the Blue West
Ritual: Make a fire at dusk or dawn and ask for renewal. The Day Ceremony for today is Chik'in the West. Chik'in brings the energies or cooperation, duality, adjusting, and change. During your Day Ceremony, you can ask the energy of Chik'in to help you find the answers you are looking for.
Energetic Power Places: Caves, pyramids, mountains, and valleys especially at dusk and dawn.
Amulet/Totem: Jaguar, pyramid, the color black
Element: Water

Notes, Reflections, and Synchronicities:

_____

_____

_____

_____

_____

_____

_____

_____

3 K'an: Yellow Seed – Date:

A day of gathering, collecting, harvest, and abundance. An abundant harvest is indicated here. The meaning is also linked to the net that is traditionally used to gather the corn and can represent tangling or untangling.

Magical Wave Energy of Oox, the power of three, brings the power of taking creative action. It is a lifting, rising energy.

Intention: I am taking creative action to bring in an abundant harvest.

🦋 Today is good for:

- Paying off debts
- Collecting things (even collecting your thoughts)
- Reaping the rewards of your work
- Piecing things together
- Do something associated with the interNET
- Witchy stuff (casting spells like one might cast a net)
- Disentangling things

Color & Direction: Nohol, the Yellow South
Element: Earth
Ritual: The Day Ceremony is Nohol, the south. Place seeds or yellow flowers around your candle. Nohol brings the energy of harvest, increase, and abundance! As you burn your candle, let it send prayers to the Heart of Sky and ask to be freed (untangled) from anything that prevents you from receiving the harvest you have worked for.
Energetic Power Places: The sea, farmer's fields, gardens
Amulet: Seeded jewelry or accessories, dream catcher (net).
Element: Earth

Notes, Reflections, and Synchronicities:

_____

_____

_____

_____

_____

_____

_____

_____

4 Chikchan: Red Feathered Serpent – Date:

The sky serpent, the cosmological snake, also known as Kukulkan. Chikchan is Framer and shaper of the Universe. This is an extremely powerful sign. It is the fire at the base of the spine, the Kundalini. It is associated with sexual magic and the rain gods. Key elements for this day are truth and justice.

The Magical Wave energy of Kan (4) is the power of energy taking form and becoming stable.

Intention: Truth and justice and taking form and becoming stable in my life!

Today is a good day to:

- Pursue or deliver truth and knowledge
- Deliver and receive justice
- Find or bring balance
- Pursue inner peace
- Enjoy great sex
- Take fast and direction action
- Beware of fast and direct action
- Stay on guard against anger in both yourself and others

Color & Direction: Lak'in, the Red East
Ritual: The Day Ceremony is Lak'in: unity, beginnings, and creation. This is a powerful day. It is a day to go to the mountains and commune with them. Light a fire and speak directly to the earth and ask for protection. You can also ask for justice, truth, peace, and balance.
Power Places: Mountains, volcanoes, pyramids, starry night
Amulet: Jade, snake, or pyramid—especially the one at Chichen Itza (where the temple of Kukulkan is). An especially powerful totem for today is a jade pyramid.
Element: Fire

Notes, Reflections, and Synchronicities:

_____
_____
_____
_____
_____
_____
_____
_____

5 Kimi: White World Bringer – Date:

The god of death and the lords of the underworld. Kimi is all about transformation and change. This usually applies to things like a job, relationship, living location, or some other part of your life that is in flux. Energies end and others begin. Change is an integral part of life and, if we harness it correctly, can keep moving us toward becoming more enlightened beings.

The Magical Wave energy of Jo'o is the power of five. It is radiant and linked to your core purpose. It brings the gift of empowerment!

Intention: I am in the empowered by transformation.

🦋 Today is a good day to:

- A great day to make or think about changes
- End relationships (business, friendships, or romantic)
- Work towards tranquility among friends and colleagues, both living and dead
- Both give and ask for forgiveness
- Remember the dead
- Do up-keep on and take care of equipment
- A tranquil day to be patient and conservative in your energy

Color & Direction: Xaman, the White North
Ritual: The Day Ceremony today is for Xaman, the North who brings Transparency, clarity and truth. During your day ceremony you can give thanks to the ancestors who continue to give you guidance and ask for peace, love, money, health, and forgiveness.
Energetic Power Places: Pyramids, sacred sites, ceremonial sites, the fireplace, temples
Amulet: Skull, butterfly (transformation), corn seed, skeleton
Element: Air

Notes, Reflections, and Synchronicities:

_____

_____

_____

_____

_____

_____

_____

_____

6 Manik: Blue Deer – Date:

Balance, support, and the game of life. Manik is a very important day to focus on balance. Without balance, support cannot function properly. Think of the four legs of a table. If all the legs are different heights (unbalanced) how good is the table? Manik is the deer and the Lord of the hunt. It is a day to get into the game of life. You can think of hunting in our modern world as doing any activities that involve the pursuit of sustenance and strength. That makes Manik a good day for business. It is also a good day for long range travel. (Deer travel vast distances.)

The Magical Wave energy of Wak (6) is the gift of getting in the flow!

Intention: I am flowing with and moving forward in the game of life.

🦋 Today is good for:

- Teamwork & meetings
- Business pursuits, getting out "in the field" and talking to customers
- Long range travel
- Staying alert for traps in business and the game of life
- An excellent day for diviners

Color & Direction: Chik'in, the Blue West
Ritual: The Day Ceremony is for Chik'in, the West. Chik'in brings you duality, cooperation, and change. As you perform your Day Ceremony, consider asking Chik'in to bless your finances and business.
Energetic Power Places are forests, and fields (places where you might find deer)
Amulet: Anything to do with the deer, anything with the number 4 or four parts to it.
Element: Water

Notes, Reflections, and Synchronicities:

_____

_____

_____

_____

_____

_____

_____

_____

7 Lamat: Yellow Star Flower – Date:

Today is all about abundance and growing! It's a wonderful day to plant something, be it friendships, project ideas, or actual flowers. Lamat is also about fertility and is represented by the planet (star) Venus and the color gold.

The Magical Wave energy of Uk (7) is inspiring. It is the ability to come into alignment, to be in tune.

Intention: I am in tune with growing things.

🦋 Today is good for:

- Planting new things: flowers, friendships, projects
- Honoring past works
- Tending to your crops (in our modern times, that also means tending to business or whatever it is that sustains you)
- Star gazing (Lamat is also associated with Venus)
- Thinking about the Universe
- Feeding the world
- Fertility

Color: Yellow
Direction: Today the wind is blowing from the south. It brings harvest, abundance, and endings.
Ritual: The Day Ceremony today is Nohol, the South. Try placing some wildflowers, especially yellow ones, or seeds around your candle today.
Energetic Power Places today are forests, places where wildflowers grow, rivers and lakes
Amulet: Flowers (especially yellow ones), stars, or Venus
Element: Earth

Notes, Reflections, and Synchronicities:

_____

_____

_____

_____

_____

_____

_____

_____

8 Muluk: Red Moon ~ Date:

A day to make payments, give offerings, and ask for dark things to come to light. Muluk is also about emotions and using your intuition. This is a day of cycles, rhythms and water since water is intrinsically connected to the moon.

The Magical Wave energy of Waxak, the power of eight, is about being in harmony.

Intention: I am in harmony with the cycles and rhythms of nature.

🦋 Today is good for:

Call in the 4 Directions

- Paying off debts (financial, relational, societal, spiritual)
- Asking people to pay you back for their debts to you
- Working to end suffering
- Giving offerings to the earth
- Asking for rain
- Asking for dark things to come to light
- Pay attention to your dreams
- Use your intuition

Color & Direction: Lak'in the Red East
Ritual: The day ceremony for today is Lak'in the East. You can also cleanse your candles and other alter items under the moon today.
Energetic Power Places today are the beach, big rocks, oceans, rivers, and lakes
Amulets: Shark or whale or other large aquatic creature, jade, the moon
Element: Fire

Notes, Reflections, and Synchronicities:

_____

_____

_____

_____

_____

_____

_____

_____

_____

9 Ok: White Dog – Date:

The one who guides the night sun through the underworld. Ok is about guidance and protection. Your guides are with you today in a powerful way to guide you through the underworld. This is also a day about justice and truth. On the lighter side, Ok is the most sexually charged day of the Nawales.

The **Magical Wave** energy of Bolon is the power of expansion and mastery.

Intention: I am moving into mastery with guidance.

Today is good for:

- Asking for guidance
- Giving guidance
- Short distance travel (like around your town)
- Being alert for dangers/update home security
- Having great sex
- Looking for hidden truth

Color & Direction: Xaman, the White North.
Element: Air
Ritual: The Day Ceremony for today is for Xaman, the North. Consider asking the energy of Xaman to guide you today. Xaman brings transparency, clarity, and truth.
Energetic Power Places today are mountains and beaches. If you don't live near these places, try a watching a video with beautiful scenery to add a little nature energy to your day.
Amulets: Anything related to dogs
Element: Air

Notes, Reflections, and Synchronicities:

_____

_____

_____

_____

_____

_____

_____

_____

10 Chuwen: Blue Monkey – Date:

The great craftsman, patron of the arts, the thread of that symbolizes destiny and maintains the continuity the past, the present, and the future. Monkey is all about being creative and having fun! It is a highly positive day that is full of energy that is friendly and happy!

The Magical Wave energy of Lajun, the power of ten, is the gift of manifesting!

Intention: I am manifesting creativity and fun!

🦋 Today is good for:

- Partying and celebrating
- Dancing, singing, writing, painting
- Getting married
- Studying the sacred calendar
- Taking time to look for patterns in life
- Starting projects
- Watch for synchronicities today!

Color & Direction: Chik'in the Blue/Black West
Ritual: This is a great day for burning incense, especially copal or frankincense. The Day Ceremony for today is Chik'in, the West.
Element: Water
Energetic Power Places where the energy is strong today are lakes and forests.
Amulet: Try wearing something woven today, especially a cloth wrist band or bracelet or something made from woven threads. Something that reminds you of monkeys.
Element: Water

Notes, Reflections, and Synchronicities:

_____

_____

_____

_____

_____

_____

_____

_____

11 Eb: Yellow Path – Date:

Travel and destiny...your path in life. This day can also be about following the path of the sacred calendar. It is a day when the ancestors are ready to listen.

The Magical Wave energy of Buluk, the power of eleven, is the force of letting go. The wave has created and broken and now it is powerfully rushing on shore. There is nothing you can do now but stand back and watch!

Intention: I am letting go of control as I move into my destiny.

Today is good for:

- Travel or making plans to travel
- Spending time considering your path in life
- Making changes in your path in life
- Starting a new business or making a business plan
- Asking for good luck in both spiritual and material pursuits
- Being careful of dangers along the way

Color & Direction: Nohol, the Yellow South
Ritual: The Day Ceremony for today is Nohol, the south. Nohol bring abundance, increase, and harvest!
Energetic Power Places: Mountains and Woods and paths, especially ancient ones.
Amulets: Good amulets for today are pyramid, ladder, tooth (there is a tooth in the glyph to remind you to be careful of dangers along the road), compass or globe. Anything else that you associate with travel or your path in life.
Element: Earth

Notes, Reflections, and Synchronicities:

_____

_____

_____

_____

_____

_____

_____

_____

12 Ben: Red Corn Stalk – Date:

Ben is the rod of virtues of divine power! It is the corn stalk and is associated with harvest and success! The energy is both growing & surging upward like corn stalks after a heavy rain. It is a very meaningful day, associated with triumph! ALSO, the staff (stalk) symbolizes the spine and the internal fire which moves upward and activates the secret powers. (I love this stuff!)

The Magical Wave is the energy of Lajka'a is the power of twelve. It is the ability to understand.

Intention: Tremendous growth and my secret powers magic are crystalizing for me!

🦋 Today is a good day to:

- Plant a seed or start a project
- Spend time with family or friends
- Follow your intuition and listen to your dreams
- Ask the ancestors for help in teaching and caretaking
- Study and investigate things
- Ask for rain and growth

Color & Direction: Lak'in the Red East
Ritual: The day ceremony for today is Lak'in the East. Consider requesting help from the ancestors in caring for your home and family or ask for help in starting a new business or project or help with your finances.
Amulet: Carry with you or wear small seeds (especially corn seeds), a small stone (used for grinding corn), whisky, bourbon, or rum. . .also sugar, and yellow clothes or jewelry.
Energetic Power Places: fields, meadows, forests, beaches
Element: Fire

Notes, Reflections, and Synchronicities:

_____

_____

_____

_____

_____

_____

_____

_____

13 Ix: White Jaguar – Date:

Ix (pronounced *Ish*) is feminine energy and all things related to the earth, strength, and vitality. Think of the qualities of a jaguar. They are stealthy, strong, and hunt at night. This energy is powerful and wise and is related to the goddess Ixchel.

The Magical Wave energy of Ooxlajun is the cosmic wild card. This is when the impossible becomes possible!

Intention: I am in awe of how the vital power of the jaguar is unfolding in my life.

🦋 Today is a good day to:

- Meditate on the Earth as our home and how to live in harmony with Her.
- Use magic powers
- Take care of your home, especially by getting rid of things that no longer serve you.
- Use feminine energy
- Get pregnant
- Hunt for things such as knowledge, truth, wisdom
- Any ecological projects

Color & Direction: Xaman, the White North.
Ritual: The Day Ceremony is for Xaman, the North. Xaman brings transparency, clarity, and truth. After asking this energy to work with you today, give thanks to the ancestors for all things related to the earth. Consider placing some treasures from the earth around your candle today.
Energetic Power Places: Ceremonial places (especially the pyramids), forests, and mountains (high places)
Amulet: Jaguar, pyramid, or something with a jaguar or spotted design.
Element: Air

Notes, Reflections, and Synchronicities:

_____

_____

_____

_____

_____

_____

_____

_____

Thoughts About this Past Trecena

Eagle from the Temple of The Warriors, Chichen Itza

What to Expect with Men the Blue Eagle

Focus: What vision work do you want to do over the next 13 days?

The eagle soars high overhead. His vision is vast. He can see the tiniest things from afar. This is a trecena to dream, to raise your vision higher, to let your vision soar! The energy of this trecena brings the capacity to see. This plays out in several ways. Believe it or not, Men is the nawal of merchants. It is the energy for doing business. So, you can expect to have some great vision for business and marketing ideas over the next thirteen days. The eagle is also about ambition. Expect to feel motivated to succeed and then work with that energy and during this trecena, you will find yourself making headway in your business plans!

The eagle is also about having vision in the other-worldly planes. You will find the veil is thinner during Men. So, you may want to take some time to really focus on meditation, communing with your ancestors, and improving your intuitive abilities.

Wow! What a powerful time! Cast your vision higher. Reach for the stars. Break out of the box. And do it on both the material and the meta-physical planes! The energy of Men the Eagle will help you soar!

Celestial Bird, Carvings at Chichen Itza

Men the Blue Eagle

Trecena Planner

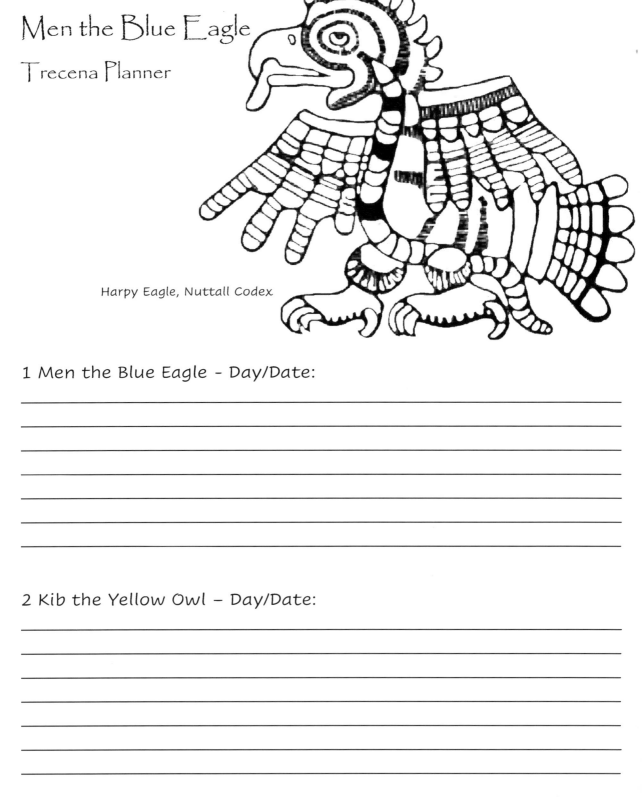

Harpy Eagle, Nuttall Codex

1 Men the Blue Eagle - Day/Date:

_____

_____

_____

_____

_____

_____

_____

2 Kib the Yellow Owl – Day/Date:

_____

_____

_____

_____

_____

_____

_____

3 Kaban, the Red Earth – Day/Date:

_____

_____

_____

_____

_____

_____

_____

4 Etz'nab the White Knife – Day/Date:

_____

_____

_____

_____

_____

_____

_____

5 Kawak the Blue Storm – Day/Date:

_____

_____

_____

_____

_____

_____

_____

6 Ahaw the Yellow Sun – Day/Date:

_____

_____

_____

_____

_____

_____

_____

7 Imix the Red Crocodile – Day/Date:

_____

_____

_____

_____

_____

_____

_____

8 Ik the White Wind - Day/Date:

_____

_____

_____

_____

_____

_____

_____

9 Ak'bal the Blue Night - Day/Date:

_____

_____

_____

_____

_____

_____

_____

10 K'an the Yellow Seed - Day/Date:

_____

_____

_____

_____

_____

_____

_____

11 Chikchan the Red Serpent - Day/Date:

_____

_____

_____

_____

_____

_____

_____

12 Kimi the White World Bringer - Day/Date:

_____

_____

_____

_____

_____

_____

_____

13 Manik the Blue Deer - Day/Date:

_____

_____

_____

_____

_____

_____

_____

Eagle and cactus

1 Men: Blue Eagle – Date:

Men the eagle is all about flying high, ambition, and vision. This is a day of good fortune, a day of freedom and of spiritual advancement! It is also about financial advancement. Men is the day of business, merchants, and money. So, this is also the day to dream big and reach for the sky in regard to your business ideas and dreams.

The Magical Wave energy of Jun, the power of one, rules this day. Jun is strong and stable. It is the energy of unity and is magnetic and attracting.

Intention: I am attracting higher vision!

Call in the 4 Directions

🦋 This is a good day to:

- Communicate with Heart of Sky, the creator god
- Ask for money for buying things
- Consider the big picture
- Focus on goals and consider how to best meet them
- Pursue goals that have already been set
- Spiritual elevation
- Work on self-improvement

Color & Direction: Chik'in, the Blue West
Ritual: The Day Ceremony is Chik'in the West. Chik'in brings cooperation, duality, and change. This is a very important day for a sacrificial ritual to give thanks for money. The required offering is CHOCOLATE! Simply thank the gods and your ancestors for providing material goods and money, offer them some chocolate. When you finish, then eat it!
Energetic Power Places: Mountains, lakes, misty places, upland forests
Amulet: Bird feathers, dream catchers, anything with a bird, eagle, or quetzal on it
Element: Water

Notes, Reflections, and Synchronicities:

_____

_____

_____

_____

_____

_____

_____

_____

_____

2 Kib: Yellow Owl – Date:

Kib, the warrior owl, is all about taking it easy, relaxation, patience, and timing. The warrior is careful in his timing. He is patient, not rushed. Like the warrior, today is about choosing your timing carefully. This day is also about the illusion of the material world and the night birds. Today is a very spiritual day, indeed!

The Magical Wave energy of Ka'a, the power of two is a dual energy. It is opposites finding balance.

Intention: I am balancing patience and perfect timing.

This is a good day to:

- Go with the flow
- Relax
- Commune with the ancestors
- Wash your clothes, especially your good clothes
- Be a spiritual guide
- Ask for forgiveness for ignoring moral teachings
- This is a very special day to spend time preventing mistakes
- Kib is not a good day to start a new project because the energy is low.

Color & Direction: Nohol, the Yellow South
Ritual: The day ceremony is for Nohol which brings increase, abundance, and harvest. Consider taking time to commune with your ancestors during your Day Ceremony today.
Energetic Power Places: Mountains, volcanoes, tropical forests, lakes
Amulet: The earth, any rocks or crystals
Element: Earth

Notes, Reflections, and Synchronicities:

_____

_____

_____

_____

_____

_____

_____

_____

3 Kaban: Red Earth – Date:

Kaban, the earth is the energy of thoughts, logic, ideas, and science. It is movement and sweeping change. Kaban is the earthquake: A day of formidable power and wisdom, a day of shaking the foundations and sudden revelations

The Magical Wave energy of Oox (3) is the gift of taking creative action.

Intention: I am finding great wisdom as I step out and take creative action

🦋 Today is good for:

- Thinking creativity
- Working with others
- Scientific investigation
- Being connected to the earth
- Coming into agreement with the creator
- Movement, travel
- Travel on the spiritual plane
- Shaking things up/sudden revelation/revelations that shake your foundations

Color & Direction: Lak'in, the Red East
Ritual: The Day Ceremony is for Lak'in. Lak'in bring the energy of beginnings, creation, and unity. As you ask Lak'in to work with you today, consider adding some rocks or crystals to your altar space.
Energetic Power Places: Mountains, volcanoes, tropical forests, lakes
Amulet: The earth, any rocks or crystals
Element: Fire

Notes, Reflections, and Synchronicities:

_____

_____

_____

_____

_____

_____

_____

_____

4 Etz'nab: White Knife – Date:

The obsidian sacrificial blade. A day to cut to the core of things. This is a day to reduce, clean out, and cleanse. Its energy is also about healing because the knife can both cut and heal. The obsidian blade is shined to the point of reflection and so the energy of the mirror also comes into play today.

The Magical Wave energy of Kan (4) rules this day. It is energy taking form and becoming stable. It is a balanced energy and good for planning.

Intention: I am finding stability in letting go of things that do not serve my highest good.

🦋 Today is a good day to:

- Clean out your closet
- Do some editing (writing, song writing)
- Sort things out
- End an unproductive relationship
- Have a sale
- Let go of the past
- Diagnose and cure illness (physical, mental, and spiritual)
- Make predictions about the future

NOTE: Today is not a good day for travel or to start something new.

Color & Direction: Xaman, the White North.
Ritual: The Day Ceremony is for Xaman, the North. Xaman brings transparency, clarity and truth. Today is a good day to make up for things you neglected to do or should not have done and to receive forgiveness. You can also ask for protection from disease and accidents. No other ceremonies are performed on a knife day.
Energetic Power Places: Pyramids, cliffs, waterfalls, lightning storms
Amulet: Obsidian stone, jade, a knife, a pyramid (the glyph has a pyramid on it) or a mirror
Element: Air

Notes, Reflections, and Synchronicities:

_____

_____

_____

_____

_____

_____

_____

5 Kawak: Blue Storm ~ Date:

Storm is the Nawal of women and strength. It is the lightening flash of inspiration, the warmth and safety of the home, and the cleansing and purification of the rain. Imagine what it feels like to run inside as a storm approaches. That is the energy of Kawak. The rage of the wind and the comfort of home and the care of the woman who wraps loved ones in her arms.

The Magical Wave energy of Jo'o (5) brings empowerment!

Intention: I am empowered to make my home a haven

🦋 Today is a good day to:

- Tend to your family and home
- Do volunteer work
- Use your authority
- Ask for the actions of your enemies to turn against them
- Be prepared for trouble
- Heal mental illness
- Receive flashes of inspiration

Color & Direction: Chik'in, the Blue West
Ritual: The Day Ceremony is Chik'in the West. Chik'in brings cooperation, duality and change. As you ask the energy of Chik'in to work with you today, you can also give thanks for the women in your life.
Energetic Power Places: Pine and cypress forests
Amulet: Storm cloud, lightening, Mayan goddess, or pyramid
Element: Water

Notes, Reflections, and Synchronicities:

_____
_____
_____
_____
_____
_____
_____
_____

6 Ahaw: Yellow Sun – Date:

Illumination and growth. The most powerful and positive nawal, radiating energy in all things. Its light not only lights up the day and the night (the moon is a reflection of the sun) but it also brings enlightenment and vision!

The Magical Wave energy of Wak (6) is about going with the flow!

Intention: I am going with the flow of illumination!

Today is a good day to:

- Contact the dead
- Be brave against things that scare you
- Ask for illumination
- Build a house
- Start or continue projects
- Have a party
- Reflect on the positive things in life
- Place flowers on the graves of loved ones
- Seek spiritual illumination

Color & Direction: Nohol, the Yellow South
Ritual: The day ceremony is for Nohol which brings increase, abundance, and harvest. Consider doing this at sunrise or sunset today.
Energetic Power Places: Sunrise and sunset, find a beautiful view, especially on the beach or in a field of flowers
Amulet: Anything that shows the sun or flowers (especially yellow)
Element: Earth

Notes, Reflections, and Synchronicities:

_____

_____

_____

_____

_____

_____

_____

7 Imix: Red Crocodile ~ Date:

Imix is a day of turbulent, stirring waters, of birth, new beginnings, and nurturing. It is a day of raw creative power. Because the crocodile lives in the mangroves, water lilies are associated with this day.

The Magical Wave Uk (7) carries the energy of aligning. It is the ability to apply your mystical powers in a practical manner. You are the channel!

Intention: I am channeling wonderful energy for new beginnings.

Today is a good day to:

- Ask for water/rain
- Start the day with grounding exercises and/or meditation
- Make sweeping changes and lay new foundations
- Stay aware of the tendency to take wild and unpredictable actions.
- Be creative
- Develop your powers of intuition
- Receive messages from beyond
- Cleanse yourself from negative energy
- Ask for the calming of mental issues, spiritual problems, climate change

Color & Direction: Lak'in, the Red East
Ritual: The wind is blowing from the east today, so the Day Ceremony for is Lak'in. Lak'in brings new beginnings, unity, and creation. During your Day Ceremony, you can ask for guidance as you align with this powerful energy of creation!
Power Places: Lakes, lagoons, and other in-land bodies of water
Amulet: Crocodile, lotus blossom, crystals and images associated with the sea.
Element: Fire

Notes, Reflections, and Synchronicities:

_____

_____

_____

_____

_____

_____

_____

_____

8 Ik: White Wind – Date:

The breath of life and creativity. It is also a day of air, heavy showers, and hurricanes. The wind can carry news, bring change, and inspire creativity. It is a day to use your voice and is good for communication and letting your "voice" be heard.

The Magical Wave Energy of Waxak (8) is you coming into harmony with your true self.

Intention: I have found my voice. My true self is expressing itself creatively!

🦋 **Today is a good day to:**

Call in the 4 Directions

- Use your voice, let your voice be heard.
- This is the best day for writing!
- Do something creative
- Cure respiratory illness
- Work on spiritual growth
- Go on a picnic or hike
- Do some gardening

Color & Direction: Xaman, the White North
Ritual: Burn pine or copal incense. This is the sacred day of stone alters. You can place stones around your altar or in a special place at home. Then perform the day ceremony for Xaman the North. Xaman brings transparency, clarity, and truth. During the day ceremony, you can ask for protection for friends and family and ask for protection against the rage of overly strong human emotions.
Energetic Power Places: Canyons, mountains, valleys, forests, and stone alters
Amulet: Hang wind chimes, a tree or branch, the beautiful quetzal bird
Element: Air

Notes, Reflections, and Synchronicities:

_____

_____

_____

_____

_____

_____

_____

_____

9 Ak'bal: Blue Night – Date:

Ak'bal is the night house, the underworld, and the realm of the eternal jaguar sun (the night sun). It is the darkness before the dawn. It is a day of good luck, especially in love! Ak'bal, the night, is generally, this is a tranquil and happy day.

The Magical Wave Energy of Bolon (9) expresses itself as mastery! It is the expanding power of the divine feminine.

Intention: I am mastering the power of bringing things into the light.

Today's energy is good for:

- Declaring your love: This is a lucky day for love!
- Looking within to find answers.
- Seeking anything: jobs, lovers, friends, answers, knowledge
- Discovering the underlying causes of problems
- Face personal challenges with intuition rather than strength
- Ask for light to reach all things
- Acknowledge feelings from the heart
- Getting a fresh start or new beginning

Color & Direction: Chik'in, the Blue West
Ritual: Make a fire at dusk or dawn and ask for renewal. The Day Ceremony for today is Chik'in the West. Chik'in brings the energies or cooperation, duality, adjusting, and change. During your Day Ceremony, you can ask the energy of Chik'in to help you find the answers you are looking for.
Energetic Power Places: Caves, pyramids, mountains, and valleys especially at dusk and dawn.
Amulet/Totem: Jaguar, pyramid, the color black
Element: Water

Notes, Reflections, and Synchronicities:

_____

_____

_____

_____

_____

_____

_____

_____

10 K'an: Yellow Seed – Date:

A day of gathering, collecting, harvest, and abundance. An abundant harvest is indicated here. The meaning is also linked to the net that is traditionally used to gather the corn and can represent tangling or untangling.

Magical Wave Energy today Lajun (10) is the ability to manifest.

Intention: I am manifesting an abundant harvest!

🦋 Today is good for:

- Paying off debts
- Collecting things (even collecting your thoughts)
- Reaping the rewards of your work
- Piecing things together
- Do something associated with the interNET
- Witchy stuff (casting spells like one might cast a net)
- Disentangling things

Color & Direction: Nohol, the Yellow South
Element: Earth
Ritual: The Day Ceremony is Nohol, the south. Place seeds or yellow flowers around your candle. Nohol brings the energy of harvest, increase, and abundance! As you burn your candle, let it send prayers to the Heart of Sky and ask to be freed (untangled) from anything that prevents you from receiving the harvest you have worked for.
Energetic Power Places: The sea, farmer's fields, gardens
Amulet: Seeded jewelry or accessories, dream catcher (net).
Element: Earth

Notes, Reflections, and Synchronicities:

_____

_____

_____

_____

_____

_____

_____

_____

11 Chikchan: Red Feathered Serpent – Date:

The sky serpent, the cosmological snake, also known as Kukulkan. Chikchan is Framer and shaper of the Universe. This is an extremely powerful sign. It is the fire at the base of the spine, the Kundalini. It is associated with sexual magic and the rain gods. Key elements for this day are truth and justice.

The Magical Wave energy of Buluk (11) is roaring through, so stand back and let go!

Intention: I am standing back in awe as the Wisdom of the Universe appears to me!

🦋 Today is a good day to:

- Pursue or deliver truth and knowledge
- Deliver and receive justice
- Find or bring balance
- Pursue inner peace
- Enjoy great sex
- Take fast and direction action
- Beware of fast and direct action
- Stay on guard against anger in both yourself and others

Color & Direction: Lak'in, the Red East
Ritual: The Day Ceremony is Lak'in: unity, beginnings, and creation. This is a powerful day. It is a day to go to the mountains and commune with them. Light a fire and speak directly to the earth and ask for protection. You can also ask for justice, truth, peace, and balance.
Power Places: Mountains, volcanoes, pyramids, starry night
Amulet: Jade, snake, or pyramid—especially the one at Chichen Itza (where the temple of Kukulkan is). An especially powerful totem for today is a jade pyramid.
Element: Fire

Notes, Reflections, and Synchronicities:

_____

_____

_____

_____

_____

_____

_____

_____

12 Kimi: White World Bringer – Date:

The god of death and the lords of the underworld. Kimi is all about transformation and change. This usually applies to things like a job, relationship, living location, or some other part of your life that is in flux. Energies end and others begin. Change is an integral part of life and, if we harness it correctly, can keep moving us toward becoming more enlightened beings.

The Magical Wave energy of Lajka'a (12) comes with the power of causing things to crystalize. This brings understanding.

Intention: Transformation is crystalizing.

Today is a good day to:

- A great day to make or think about changes
- End relationships (business, friendships, or romantic)
- Work towards tranquility among friends and colleagues, both living and dead
- Both give and ask for forgiveness
- Remember the dead
- Do up-keep on and take care of equipment
- A tranquil day to be patient and conservative in your energy

Color & Direction: Xaman, the White North
Ritual: The Day Ceremony today is for Xaman, the North who brings Transparency, clarity, and truth. During your day ceremony you can give thanks to the ancestors who continue to give you guidance and ask for peace, love, money, health, and forgiveness.
Energetic Power Places: Pyramids, sacred sites, ceremonial sites, the fireplace, temples
Amulet: Skull, butterfly (transformation), corn seed, skeleton
Element: Air

Notes, Reflections, and Synchronicities:

_____

_____

_____

_____

_____

_____

_____

_____

13 Manik: Blue Deer – Date:

Balance, support, and the game of life. Manik is a very important day to focus on balance. Without balance, support cannot function properly. Think of the four legs of a table. If all the legs are different heights (unbalanced) how good is the table? Manik is the deer and the Lord of the hunt. It is a day to get into the game of life. You can think of hunting in our modern world as doing any activities that involve the pursuit of sustenance and strength. That makes Manik a good day for business. It is also a good day for long range travel. (Deer travel vast distances.)

The Magical Wave energy of Ooxlajun (13) rules this day. It is the power of transcendence. It is the cosmic wild card. This is a day when anything is at play!

Intention: The Universe is creating everything I need!

🦋 Today is good for:

- Teamwork & meetings
- Business pursuits, getting out "in the field" and talking to customers
- Long range travel
- Staying alert for traps in business and the game of life
- An excellent day for diviners

Color & Direction: Chik'in, the Blue West
Ritual: The Day Ceremony is for Chik'in, the West. Chik'in brings you duality, cooperation, and change. As you perform your Day Ceremony, consider asking Chik'in to bless your finances and business.
Energetic Power Places are forests, and fields (places where you might find deer)
Amulet: Anything to do with the deer, anything with the number 4 or four parts to it.
Element: Water

Notes, Reflections, and Synchronicities:

_____

_____

_____

_____

_____

_____

_____

_____

Thoughts About this Past Trecena

The Energy Lamat Brings to You

Focus: What do you want to harvest?

Lamat is the both the star and the flower. Lamat is also the net. What does that all mean? Well, the star is Venus, who is all about fertility. So, this is a time to plant! What would you like to plant during the next thirteen days? The energy is ripe for new projects, new flowers, veggies or even trees, new friendships, new job opportunities. You name it! Anything new!

Lamat also holds the energy of growth and harvest. Things you plant during this trecena will grow quite successfully. Soon you will reap a harvest. The flower is growth. Lamat is also the net. The net is used to gather in the seeds. It is about harvest and abundance and gathering in. So, this is a time for not just planting, but also a time that promises a good harvest! Maybe there is a project you have been wanting to get started, but you just didn't feel the timing was right. Well, now the timing is perfect. Do you have a house project you have been wanting to work on? Or maybe you have been wanting to learn how to dance. This is the perfect time to start taking lessons, begin learning a new language, or take a master gardening class and start growing some fabulous plants!

Flower shield art

Things WILL grow that you plant over the next thirteen days, so be careful about your thoughts, words, and actions. You want to plant things that you WANT to grow! So, in addition to thinking about planting material things, think about what immaterial things you want to plant in your life. Plant more joy. Plant peace, Plant compassion and happiness! The time to plant is here and you will reap a harvest, so plant things that you will love to see come to fruition!

Tree of Life Personified, codex style vase

Lamat the Yellow Star Flower

Trecena Planner

Waterlily god

1 Lamat the Yellow Star Flower - Day/Date:

_____
_____
_____
_____
_____
_____
_____

2 Muluk the Red Moon – Day/Date:

_____
_____
_____
_____
_____
_____
_____

3 Ok the White Dog – Day/Date:

_____
_____
_____
_____
_____
_____
_____

4 Chuwen the Blue Monkey – Day/Date:

_____
_____
_____
_____
_____
_____
_____

5 Eb the Yellow Path – Day/Date:

_____
_____
_____
_____
_____
_____
_____

6 Ben the Red Corn Stalk – Day/Date:

_____

_____

_____

_____

_____

_____

_____

7 Ix the White Jaguar – Day/Date:

_____

_____

_____

_____

_____

_____

_____

8 Men the Blue Eagle - Day/Date:

_____

_____

_____

_____

_____

_____

_____

9 Kib the Yellow Owl - Day/Date:

_____
_____
_____
_____
_____
_____
_____

10 Kaban the Red Earth - Day/Date:

_____
_____
_____
_____
_____
_____
_____

11 Etz'nab the White Knife - Day/Date:

_____
_____
_____
_____
_____
_____

12 Kawak the Blue Storm - Day/Date:

_____
_____
_____
_____
_____
_____
_____

13 Ahaw the Yellow Sun - Day/Date:

_____
_____
_____
_____
_____
_____
_____

Flower from a vase

1 Lamat: Yellow Star Flower – Date:

Today is all about abundance and growing and harvest! It's a wonderful day to plant something, be it friendships, project ideas, or actual flowers. Lamat is also about fertility and is represented by the planet (star) Venus and the color gold.

The Magical Wave energy today is Jun (1). Jun is the energy of attraction!

Intention: I am in attracting a fantastic harvest!

Call in the 4 Directions

🦋 Today is good for:

- Planting new things: flowers, friendships, projects
- Honoring past works
- Tending to your crops (in our modern times that also means tending to business or whatever it is that sustains you)
- Star gazing (Lamat is also associated with Venus)
- Thinking about the Universe
- Feeding the world
- Fertility

Color: Yellow
Direction: Today the wind is blowing from the south. It brings harvest, abundance, and endings.
Ritual: The Day Ceremony today is Nohol, the South. Try placing some wildflowers, especially yellow ones, or seeds around your candle today.
Energetic Power Places today are forests, places where wildflowers grow, rivers and lakes
Amulet: Flowers (especially yellow ones), stars, or Venus
Element: Earth

Notes, Reflections, and Synchronicities:

_____

_____

_____

_____

_____

_____

_____

 ## 2 Muluk: Red Moon – Date:

A day to make payments, give offerings, and ask for dark things to come to light. Muluk is also about emotions and using your intuition. This is a day of cycles, rhythms and water since water is intrinsically connected to the moon.

The Magical Wave energy of Ka'a (2) rules this day. Duality is found in Ka'a and it brings the power of opposing things coming into balance.

Intention: I am balancing the books!

🦋 Today is good for:

- Paying off debts (financial, relational, societal, spiritual)
- Asking people to pay you back for their debts to you
- Working to end suffering
- Giving offerings to the earth
- Asking for rain
- Asking for dark things to come to light
- Pay attention to your dreams
- Use your intuition

Color & Direction: Lak'in the Red East
Ritual: The day ceremony for today is Lak'in the East. You can also cleanse your candles and other alter items under the moon today.
Energetic Power Places today are the beach, big rocks, oceans, rivers, and lakes
Amulets: Shark or whale or other large aquatic creature, jade, the moon
Element: Fire

Notes, Reflections, and Synchronicities:

_____

_____

_____

_____

_____

_____

_____

_____

3 Ok: White Dog – Date:

The one who guides the night sun through the underworld. Ok is about guidance and protection. Your guides are with you today in a powerful way to guide you through the underworld. This is also a day about justice and truth. On the lighter side, Ok is the most sexually charged day of the Nawales.

The Magical Wave energy that wants to work with you today is Oox (3). Oox is all about taking creative action.

Intention: I am taking creative action to work with my guides today.

 Today is good for:

- Asking for guidance
- Giving guidance
- Short distance travel (like around your town)
- Being alert for dangers/update home security
- Having great sex
- Looking for hidden truth

Color & Direction: Xaman, the White North.
Element: Air
Ritual: The Day Ceremony for today is for Xaman, the North. Consider asking the energy of Xaman to guide you today. Xaman brings transparency, clarity and truth.
Energetic Power Places today are mountains and beaches. If you don't live near these places, try a watching a video with beautiful scenery to add a little nature energy to your day.
Amulets: Anything related to dogs
Element: Air

Notes, Reflections, and Synchronicities:

_____

_____

_____

_____

_____

_____

_____

_____

4 Chuwen: Blue Monkey – Date:

The great craftsman, patron of the arts, the thread of that symbolizes destiny and maintains the continuity the past, the present, and the future. Monkey is all about being creative and having fun! It is a highly positive day that is full of energy that is friendly and happy!

The Magical Wave energy of Kan (4) is here to work with you today. Kan is the energy of things taking form and stabilizing. Things that are being created can now be measured.

Intention: Creativity and fun are taking form and stabilizing in my life today!

🦋 Today is good for:

- Partying and celebrating
- Dancing, singing, writing, painting
- Getting married
- Studying the sacred calendar
- Taking time to look for patterns in life
- Starting projects
- Watch for synchronicities today!

Color & Direction: Chik'in the Blue/Black West
Ritual: This is a great day for burning incense, especially copal or frankincense. The Day Ceremony for today is Chik'in, the West.
Element: Water
Energetic Power Places where the energy is strong today are lakes and forests.
Amulet: Try wearing something woven today, especially a cloth wrist band or bracelet or something made from woven threads. Something that reminds you of monkeys.
Element: Water

Notes, Reflections, and Synchronicities:

_____
_____
_____
_____
_____
_____
_____
_____

5 Eb: Yellow Path – Date:

Travel and destiny...your path in life. You may be going on an actual trip, or you may be considering the direction your life is going. This day can also be about following the path of the sacred calendar. It is a day when the ancestors are ready to listen.

The Magical Wave energy today that is here today is Jo.o (5). Jo'o is empowering. It is the time when you observe your creation and take delight in it!

Intention: I take delight in the direction of my path

🦋 Today is good for:

- Travel or making plans to travel
- Spending time considering your path in life
- Making changes in your path in life
- Starting a new business or making a business plan
- Asking for good luck in both spiritual and material pursuits
- Being careful of dangers along the way

Color & Direction: Nohol, the Yellow South
Ritual: The Day Ceremony for today is Nohol, the south. Nohol bring abundance, increase and harvest!
Energetic Power Places: Mountains and Woods and paths, especially ancient ones.
Amulets: Good amulets for today are pyramid, ladder, tooth (there is a tooth in the glyph to remind you to be careful of dangers along the road), compass or globe. Anything else that you associate with travel or your path in life.
Element: Earth

Notes, Reflections, and Synchronicities:

_____

_____

_____

_____

_____

_____

_____

_____

6 Ben: Red Corn Stalk – Date:

Ben is the rod of virtues of divine power! It is the corn stalk and is associated with harvest and success! The energy is both growing & surging upward like corn stalks after a heavy rain. It is a very meaningful day, associated with triumph! ALSO, the staff (stalk) symbolizes the spine and the internal fire which moves upward and activates the secret powers. (I love this stuff!)

The Magical Wave is the energy of Wak (6) is here today, flowing and moving you forward. Trust it!

Intention: I am moving forward in triumph!

🦋 Today is a good day to:

- Plant a seed or start a project
- Spend time with family or friends
- Follow your intuition and listen to your dreams
- Ask the ancestors for help in teaching and caretaking
- Study and investigate things
- Ask for rain and growth

Color & Direction: Lak'in the Red East
Ritual: The day ceremony for today is Lak'in the East. Consider requesting help from the ancestors in caring for your home and family or ask for help in starting a new business or project or help with your finances.
Amulet: Carry with you or wear small seeds (especially corn seeds), a small stone (used for grinding corn), whisky, bourbon, or rum. . .also sugar, and yellow clothes or jewelry.
Energetic Power Places: fields, meadows, forests, beaches
Element: Fire

Notes, Reflections, and Synchronicities:

_____

_____

_____

_____

_____

_____

_____

_____

7 Ix: White Jaguar ~ Date:

Ix (pronounced *Ish*) is feminine energy and all things related to the earth, strength, and vitality. Think of the qualities of a jaguar. They are stealthy, strong, and hunt at night. This energy is powerful and wise and is related to the goddess Ixchel.

The Magical Wave energy of Uk (7) rules this day. Uk is when you become attuned, aligned, with the practical application of your mystic powers!

Intention: My mystical powers are in alignment with sleek strength and vitality!

Today is a good day to:

- Meditate on the Earth as our home and how to live in harmony with Her.
- Use magic powers
- Take care of your home, especially by getting rid of things that no longer serve you.
- Use feminine energy
- Get pregnant
- Hunt for things such as knowledge, truth, wisdom
- Any ecological projects

Color & Direction: Xaman, the White North.
Ritual: The Day Ceremony is for Xaman, the North. Xaman brings transparency, clarity, and truth. After asking this energy to work with you today, give thanks to the ancestors for all things related to the earth. Consider placing some treasures from the earth around your candle today.
Energetic Power Places: Ceremonial places (especially the pyramids), forests, and mountains (high places)
Amulet: Jaguar, pyramid, or something with a jaguar or spotted design.
Element: Air

Notes, Reflections, and Synchronicities:

_____

_____

_____

_____

_____

_____

_____

_____

8 Men: Blue Eagle - Date:

Men the eagle is all about flying high, ambition, and vision. This is a day of good fortune, a day of freedom and of spiritual advancement! It is also about financial advancement. Men is the day of business, merchants, and money. So, this is also the day to dream big and reach for the sky in regard to your business ideas and dreams.

The **Magical Wave** energy of Waxak (8) brings you into perfect balance. You are in harmony with your authentic self.

Intention: My vision is perfectly aligned with my authentic self.

🦋 This is a good day to:

Call in the 4 Directions

- Communicate with Heart of Sky, the creator god
- Ask for money for buying things
- Consider the big picture
- Focus on goals and consider how to best meet them
- Pursue goals that have already been set
- Spiritual elevation
- Work on self-improvement

Color & Direction: Chik'in, the Blue West
Ritual: The Day Ceremony is Chik'in the West. Chik'in brings cooperation, duality, and change. This is a very important day for a sacrificial ritual to give thanks for money. The required offering is CHOCOLATE! Simply thank the gods and your ancestors for providing material goods and money, offer them some chocolate. When you finish, then eat it!
Energetic Power Places: Mountains, lakes, misty places, upland forests
Amulet: Bird feathers, dream catchers, anything with a bird, eagle, or quetzal on it
Element: Water

Notes, Reflections, and Synchronicities:

_____

_____

_____

_____

_____

_____

_____

_____

9 Kib: Yellow Warrior Owl – Date:

Kib, the warrior owl, is all about taking it easy, relaxation, patience, and timing. The warrior is careful in his timing. He is patient, not rushed. Like the warrior, today is about choosing your timing carefully. This day is also about the illusion of the material world. The night birds Today is a very spiritual day, indeed!

The Magical Wave energy of Bolon (9) comes to you today. It brings mastery and expansion in the power of the divine feminine.

Intention: I have mastered the art of perfect timing.

This is a good day to:

- Go with the flow
- Relax
- Commune with the ancestors
- Wash your clothes, especially your good clothes
- Be a spiritual guide
- Ask for forgiveness for ignoring moral teachings
- This is a very special day to spend time preventing mistakes
- Kib is not a good day to start a new project because the energy is low.

Color & Direction: Nohol, the Yellow South
Ritual: The day ceremony is for Nohol which brings increase, abundance, and harvest. Consider taking time to commune with your ancestors during your Day Ceremony today.
Energetic Power Places: Mountains, volcanoes, tropical forests, lakes
Amulet: The earth, any rocks or crystals
Element: Earth

Notes, Reflections, and Synchronicities:

_____

_____

_____

_____

_____

_____

_____

_____

10 Kaban: Red Earth – Date:

Kaban, the earth is the energy of thoughts, logic, ideas, and science. It is movement and sweeping change. Kaban is the earthquake: A day of formidable power and wisdom, a day of shaking the foundations and sudden revelations

The Magical Wave energy of Lajun (10) brings the power of manifestation. It is perfect in form.

Intention: I am manifesting sweeping change with wisdom.

Today is good for:

- Thinking creativity
- Working with others
- Scientific investigation
- Being connected to the earth
- Coming into agreement with the creator
- Movement, travel
- Travel on the spiritual plane
- Shaking things up/sudden revelation/revelations that shake your foundations

Color & Direction: Lak'in, the Red East
Ritual: The Day Ceremony is for Lak'in. Lak'in bring the energy of beginnings, creation, and unity. As you ask Lak'in to work with you today, consider adding some rocks or crystals to your altar space.
Energetic Power Places: Mountains, volcanoes, tropical forests, lakes
Amulet: The earth, any rocks or crystals
Element: Fire

Notes, Reflections, and Synchronicities:

_____

_____

_____

_____

_____

_____

_____

_____

11 Etz'nab: White Knife ~ Date:

The obsidian sacrificial blade. A day to cut to the core of things. This is a day to reduce, clean out, and cleanse. Its energy is also about healing because the knife can both cut and heal. The obsidian blade is shined to the point of reflection and so the energy of the mirror also comes into play today.

The Magical Wave energy of Buluk (11) rules this day. It brings the power to let go. Stand back and watch now what your work has produced!

Intention: I am letting go of things in my life that do not serve me.

🦋 Today is a good day to:

- Clean out your closet
- Do some editing (writing, song writing)
- Sort things out
- End an unproductive relationship
- Have a sale
- Let go of the past
- Diagnose and cure illness (physical, mental, and spiritual)
- Make predictions about the future

NOTE: Today is not a good day for travel or to start something new.

Color & Direction: Xaman, the White North.
Ritual: The Day Ceremony is for Xaman, the North. Xaman brings transparency, clarity and truth. Today is a good day to make up for things you neglected to do or should not have done and to receive forgiveness. You can also ask for protection from disease and accidents. No other ceremonies are performed on a knife day.
Energetic Power Places: Pyramids, cliffs, waterfalls, lightning storms
Amulet: Obsidian stone, jade, a knife, a pyramid (the glyph has a pyramid on it) or a mirror
Element: Air

Notes, Reflections, and Synchronicities:

_____

_____

_____

_____

_____

_____

_____

_____

12 Kawak: Blue Storm – Date:

Storm is the Nawal of women and strength. It is the lightening flash of inspiration, the warmth and safety of the home, and the cleansing and purification of the rain. Imagine what it feels like to run inside as a storm approaches. That is the energy of Kawak. The rage of the wind and the comfort of home and the care of the woman who wraps loved ones in her arms.

The Magical Wave energy is Lajka'a (12) the gift of things crystalizing so you can use, appreciate, and understand them.

Intention: The comforts of home have crystalized in my life.

🦋 Today is a good day to:

- Tend to your family and home
- Do volunteer work
- Use your authority
- Ask for the actions of your enemies to turn against them
- Be prepared for trouble
- Heal mental illness
- Receive flashes of inspiration

Color & Direction: Chik'in, the Blue West
Ritual: The Day Ceremony is Chik'in the West. Chik'in brings cooperation, duality, and change. As you ask the energy of Chik'in to work with you today, you can also give thanks for the women in your life.
Energetic Power Places: Pine and cypress forests
Amulet: Storm cloud, lightening, Mayan goddess, or pyramid
Element: Water

Notes, Reflections, and Synchronicities:

_____

_____

_____

_____

_____

_____

_____

_____

13 Ahaw: Yellow Sun ~ Date:

Illumination and growth. The most powerful and positive nawal, radiating energy in all things. Its light not only lights up the day and the night (the moon is a reflection of the sun) but it also brings enlightenment and vision!

The Magical Wave energy of Ooxlajun (13) is the gift of chaos which transcends what we know and works with the unknowable force of the universe to re-arrange everything, cleanse, re-order, build, and bring us into a new reality. The wild card!

Intention: I trust the transcendent power of illumination as it has its way!

🦋 Today is a good day to:

- Contact the dead
- Be brave against things that scare you
- Ask for illumination
- Build a house
- Start or continue projects
- Have a party
- Reflect on the positive things in life
- Place flowers on the graves of loved ones
- Seek spiritual illumination

Color & Direction: Nohol, the Yellow South
Ritual: The day ceremony is for Nohol which brings increase, abundance, and harvest. Consider doing this at sunrise or sunset today.
Energetic Power Places: Sunrise and sunset, find a beautiful view, especially on the beach or in a field of flowers
Amulet: Anything that shows the sun or flowers (especially yellow)
Element: Earth

Notes, Reflections, and Synchronicities:

_____

_____

_____

_____

_____

_____

_____

_____

Thoughts About this Past Trecena

_____
_____
_____
_____
_____
_____
_____
_____
_____
_____
_____
_____
_____
_____
_____
_____
_____
_____
_____
_____
_____
_____
_____
_____
_____
_____
_____
_____

About the Author

Laura LaBrie has been living in Mexico and Central America for more than ten years, learning from the lovely people there, and studying the ways of the modern Maya people. This is her ninth book and she hopes to continue writing about her passions of living in Mexico and the wonders she finds there!

You can find Laura online at www.lauralabrie.com

Made in the USA
Columbia, SC
30 December 2020